Learning After College

Nevitt Sanford

edited by
Craig Comstock

Montaigne, Inc.

99 El Toyonal, Orinda, California 94563

Manufactured in the United States of America
First edition

Since this page cannot legibly accommodate all permissions, please see the acknowledgements on pages 263–264.

This book was designed by Craig Comstock and was composed, printed and bound by Dharma Press of Emeryville, California. The paperback cover art is a photographic detail of "97 Fix," a sculpture by Barbara Comstock.

Library of Congress Catalogue Card Number 79-92581.
International Standard Book Number:
ISBN 0-917430-04-2 (hardcover),
0-917430-03-4 (paperback).

Contents

Editor's Preface

"Imagine that you could arrange a meeting between any two of the savants and men of affairs we have studied." So began an exam question in cultural history. "Whom would you invite, and what do you think they would say to one another?" If Nevitt Sanford were ever to arrange such an evening, it would probably begin with the words, "Mr. Jefferson, may I introduce Dr. Freud." In *Learning After College*, Sanford continues his project of placing psychoanalytic insight in the service of the country's most enlightened educational values.

His general approach will be familiar to the many readers who know *The American College* (1962), *Where Colleges Fail* (1967), or almost any of his papers on the personality development of undergraduates. In this book, however, his subject shifts from the college experience to various kinds of learning that may occur later. In particular, the author examines higher education as it is experienced by faculty and graduate students; outlines some alternatives to the current system; and shows how "action research" could reinvigorate psychology as it exists in and around the university.

Drawn from work over the past dozen years, these papers were originally written for symposia or other professional occasions, and many are published here for the first time.

After a brief introductory chapter on how Sanford came to study adults, Part One sets the stage by bringing up to date the author's approach to human development (chapter 2), his view of undergraduate education (chapter 3), and his critique of forces that tend to diminish personality (chapter 4). Basic principles of adult development are summarized in chapter 5, which deals directly with "learning after college."

Part Two offers a comparison among leading graduate schools in the 1930's and 40's, the corresponding milieu in the 1970's, and a new kind of institution such as Sanford himself has founded. In chapters 6 and 9, the author draws general lessons from his own graduate education at the Harvard Psychological Clinic and his early years of teaching at the University of California in Berkeley. In chapters 7 and 8, he reflects upon the formation of The Wright Institute, an independent center for research and graduate education in socio-clinical psychology.

Attention turns in Part Three to the working conditions of professors within the academic culture. Using ideas from Kurt Lewin, the Tavistock Institute, and the author's own experience of studying undergraduates, chapter 10 introduces a method for studying (and even for improving) the professional world of faculty. This approach, it subsequently appears, is based upon the well-developed educational values reflected in chapter 11, and upon a shrewd sense of what is possible, expressed in chapter 12 in the form of advice to a recent Ph.D.

Following the general critique of conditions now available for learning after college, Part Four turns to consequences for the author's own field, psychology. Several themes predominate here: the need to train clinicians to society, to create new professional settings for them, and to organize much of their work according to a model of action research. Again, the ideas are developed in several forms: a commencement address to psychology graduates (chapter 13), journal columns to colleagues who share the author's concern for social issues (chapters 14 and 15), and a formal case for value-explicit research conducted through, and itself constituting, social action (chapter 16).

Moral character is the subject of Part Five. Apparently the least demanding material in the book, these chapters might have come first, except that the very mention of moral character arouses resistance, even in the aftermath of the national scandals characterized by its absence. We may fear that, when it comes to morality, any statement is likely to be platitudinous, parochial, or just too harsh to act upon. In the author's view, however, moral character depends less on prohibitions than on the growth of capabilities; its purpose, beyond social order, is the enjoyment of life (chapter 17); and its development can be aided not only by early social experience but by formal education (chapter 18). It becomes clear that the author's stress on moral character is motivated, in part, by a careful study of how people behave after becoming fixated at some early stage of personality development (chapters 19 and 20).

In this book, as elsewhere, Sanford repeatedly addresses the question of how to encourage individual development in the context of face-to-face relationships. As a psychologist, he favors concepts that become sharpest when they focus upon the individual and, concurrently, the small group. In *The Authoritarian Personality* (1950), the main group under discussion was the family; in *The American College* (1962) it was of course teachers and their students; and in *Self and Society* (1966) it was a variety of educational, mental health, and human service organizations.

Sanford's vision of adult development has been enriched by the multiplicity in his own career, and by his courage in marching to his own drummer. At Harvard he was identified not with its mainline psychology department but with the unorthodox clinic which, in the words of its director, Henry Murray, was devoted to "the vast and intricate architecture" of personality. As an academic psychologist Sanford has always been a clinician and social activist in a discipline dominated by value-free experimentalism.[1] He became a lay psychoanalyst in a movement nearly monopolized, in America, by graduates of medical schools. As a so-called WASP, he became one of the leading researchers on anti-semitism; and as a professor at Berkeley he lost his job for a principled refusal to sign a "loyalty oath" during the hysteria of Joseph McCarthy's era.[2] At Vassar College he directed a project engaged in the nearly unheard-of practice of studying the actual development of undergraduates. When he moved to Stanford University, the author started an institute that employed known anthropologists, public health people, political scientists, therapists, public policy experts, and even sociologists.[3] Around the age of sixty, he left his job to found The Wright Institute, but even in his own free-standing organization he attained a kind of creative marginality. The Institute quickly attracted able students who, as young adults of the late 1960's, sometimes seemed either too disruptive or else too intent on a lucrative clinical practice at the expense of social action. In all of these settings, Sanford was richly provided with what Kenneth Burke once called "perspective by incongruity."

In spite of becoming a dignitary, he has remained critical, open to challenge, and sometimes even playful. As a devotee of general systems theory he is latitudinarian in his tendency to keep theoretical systems open lest they end up smaller than the job they are meant to do. As a scholar, he has shown unusual tolerance and imagination in helping researchers from many fields to collaborate.

The other side of Sanford's inclusiveness is his persistence at trying to integrate. As this book again makes clear, he is always trying to show how the hip bone's connected to the thigh bone and the thigh bone to the knee bone. He uses personality itself as an integrating concept, somewhat in the way the prior generation had used "soul." His holism goes back at least to Murray's clinic and its studies of how personality fits together. A stress on the whole person certainly underlies Sanford's broadly-conceived research on authoritarian personality and on development in the college years and later. The author is never so delighted as when discovering (and explaining) a syndrome, or how one part of a complex system affects another and is affected by it, whether on the level of the person or of a small group.

I should add a final word about the style in which this book is written, or rather, the variety of styles. Some of the chapters could appear (and in fact, did appear) in professional journals, but in general the prose reminds us less of the *Journal of Abnormal and Social Psychology* than of an essayist who, like Montaigne, tries to combine close observation, humane learning, personal experience, formal arguments, vivid examples, social criticism, stories, and even a dialogue with the self. I hope the reader will enjoy, as I have, comparing a theoretical piece on psychoanalytic theory with a memoir of university life in the 1930's, or a research paper on various adaptations made by professors to recent change in the academic world, with an artful account of advice given to a recent graduate of that system. Perhaps more than any of his other books, *Learning After College* incorporates the distinctive blend of personal qualities that has made Nevitt Sanford such a notable teacher and colleague.

I would also like to thank David Soskice of University College, Oxford, for making possible a season in that "towery city and branchy between towers," where I had the pleasure, among others, of editing this book.

CRAIG COMSTOCK

Berkeley, January 1980

1. "Will psychologists study human problems?" *American Psychologist*, 1965, *20*, 192–202.
2. "Individual and social change in a community under pressure," in Nevitt Sanford, *Self and Society*. New York: Atherton Press, 1966.
3. "The human problems institute and general education," *Daedalus*, 1965, *94*:3, 642–662.

Studying Adults in Higher Education

1

In an era of "lifelong learning" with its stress on "human potential," ideas about adult development are at last finding an eager audience. Gail Sheehy's *Passages*, a journalistic account of "predictable crises of adult life," became a best-seller in 1976; and partly as a result, the media gave extraordinary coverage the next year to George Vaillant's *Adaptation to Life*, a study of changes in a group of Harvard men between the ages of 20 and 50. In 1978 Daniel Levinson and his associates at Yale published *The Seasons of a Man's Life*, a scholarly yet accessible report on major research that had already been popularized by Sheehy.

Until recently, detailed attention to adult development has been rare among psychologists (if not among biographers and novelists). To mention some leading exceptions is to underline how few there have been. As early as 1915 C. G. Jung was writing about "individuation" in the second half of life. In the 1930's Charlotte Bühler directed empirical studies on the course of life (Bühler, 1935), and at the Harvard Psychological Clinic Henry Murray described life as a series of temporal gestalts (Murray, 1938). Among former associates of the Clinic, Erik Erikson was shaping his ideas about life-cycle development in the late 1940's, and not long after, Robert White published his remarkable book, *The Study of Lifes* (1952).

When my colleagues and I began research on Vassar College students in 1952 we were no doubt helped by this early work on adult development as well as by some studies of attitude change in college (Katz and Stotland, 1959, and Newcomb, 1958). If attitudes changed, we thought, why not personality? And within personality, why not authoritarianism? I had been much struck by Jane Loevinger's suggestion to me that authoritarianism could be regarded as an early stage of development in which some people got stuck while others outgrew it. With

Mervin Freedman and Harold Webster, I sought to find or construct psychological instruments to measure "variables that on one theory or another showed some likelihood of changing as the student went through college." Through these instruments and likewise through comparative case studies, we found development of many kinds, and in *The American College* (Sanford, 1962) I presented a theory to account for the complex data we reported there.

Since then the general theory has been tested both in further studies of undergraduates (Katz, 1968) and, since about 1967, in research with graduate students and college and university professors. Although derived primarily from observations of people in higher education, the theory is not inconsistent with data appearing in psychological studies of adults in other occupations (White, 1952; Vaillant, 1977; Levinson, 1978).

What the book does

In this book I summarize the most recent form of the theory, explore its relation to educational values and practices, look closely not only at graduate students but at the micro-culture in which professors live, discuss a method already used to improve conditions for adult development in colleges and universities, and recapitulate the core values of development under the heading of "moral character." I examine such questions as these: Regardless of whether or not stages of adult development are invariant or tightly linked to specific ages, as recent theories contend, what is it that actually brings about the changes? What forms of readiness, of challenge, and of local culture are necessary to sustain the process? In particular, what kinds of academic settings best favor not only professional but emotional, intellectual and moral development? And what can social scientists and educational leaders do to help build such environments? In this brief introductory chapter I illustrate some of the themes through the story of how I came to study adults.

My previous books on higher education focused almost wholly on undergraduates, in part because I was then stressing a distinction between education and training (Sanford, 1962, 1967). I saw the former as liberating and individuating, the latter as a form of socialization that made people more alike and should be postponed until after education had been given a fair chance. I still find the distinction useful, but upon returning from Vassar to Berkeley and teaching graduate students again I began to see that personality development, which we had shown did not stop at age 17, did not stop at age 21 either, or even at 25. Indeed, this experience enabled me to recall, and see in a new light, my own years in graduate school when I moved through a series of dramatic challenges and responses from adolescence to—well, to late adolescence. (Any time now, I expect to begin to feel grown-up.)

Although it proved difficult to arouse the interest of funding agencies in the development of graduate students, in 1967 I discovered something already well-known but rarely commented upon, that to do many kinds of serious research one does not need a grant: all it takes is some ideas and some students. During my year as a visiting professor at the Graduate Theological Union, one of my classes carried out the first comprehensive study of graduate students as persons, interviewing one another and 50 of their fellows. During this exciting project, one of the students broached the idea of also interviewing faculty, and this was done the following year (Brown and Shukraft, 1971).

Eager to be interviewed

I was a little surprised by the high degree of cooperation faculty members gave us. We composed a letter that went out over my signature to a sample of around a hundred professors living in the San Francisco Bay Area, and shortly afterwards students telephoned to ask for appointments. Hardly anyone turned us down. My surprise came from the fact that at Vassar College it had not occurred to the research group that we might interview faculty about their lives and concerns. They would see this, we assumed, as an unwelcome intrusion. It was hard enough to persuade them to tolerate our study of undergraduates. Even after the publication of *The American College*, when I lectured on higher education at various colleges and universities around the country, I was impressed by the lack of receptivity to the idea of viewing students in the perspective of developmental theory.

This is in sharp contrast to the state of affairs today. In the spring of 1979 I assisted John Noonan in a workshop for faculty at St. Louis University. He interviewed me in front of the whole group, which consisted of 40 faculty members from various departments, and then asked them to pair off and interview each other. Later in the day they all came back together and took turns bringing up for discussion some of the problems in teaching that had been encountered in the interviews. Everybody was relaxed and good-humoured; the discussion was lively and very much to the point.

What has happened between the early 1950's and now? For one thing, people such as myself who would like to assist institutions in bringing about desirable change are not so nervous about talking with faculty as we once were. We *could* have interviewed faculty at Vassar had we gone about it in the right way. We simply did not see what now seems obvious: that the way to interest faculty in the development of students is to talk with them about their own lives.

Helping professors to develop

In the years since 1968 my colleagues and I at the Wright Institute have talked with a great many faculty members, probably as many as 600, about their development. We have never been able to get any funding for straightforward *studies* of personality development in faculty members, but we have been employed as consultants by various academic institutions and have been able to make comprehensive interviews with professors a part of our work. We have given a lot of thought to what we observed, and have set forth numerous specific suggestions as to what institutions might do to enhance the development of their faculty (Sanford, 1971; Brown and Shukraft, 1971; Freedman, 1973; Freedman and Sanford, 1973; Comstock, 1974; Bergquist and Phillips, 1975; Freedman and others, 1980).

The receptivity to this sort of thing, to what we should have done in the 1950's, has certainly increased during the last decade. This has been due most largely to the fact that beginning around 1970, some of the large foundations, influenced to some extent by our work, began making substantial grants to colleges and universities for programs designed to help their faculty to become more effective. Since that time the idea of faculty development has spread rapidly, helped along by the growing recognition that continuing retrenchment in higher education will require institutions to make do for a long time with the faculty they have now (Comstock, 1974). Today it appears that most colleges and universities have shown some measure of interest in "faculty development."

In their content the programs in this area range all the way from specific procedures for improving teaching to patterns of activities aimed at enhancing the well-being and personal development of faculty members. Some first-rate work is being done, but nearly all of the programs suffer, as they have since the beginning, from the lack of an adequate basis in theory. Recently, academic "career development" has been examined in the light of the developmental stages proposed by Erikson (Super and Hall, 1978) and by Levinson (Baldwin, 1979), but arguing that faculty members, like other people, go through more or less predictable stages in the course of their careers does not in itself tell us what helps developmental change to occur. We need a theory that makes a clear distinction between career or professional development and personality development and is capable of coming to grips with the ways in which the two interact. What happens in the course of an individual's professional life can have profound effects upon personality, while personality is a major determinant not only of professional behavior but of all behavior, inside or outside the academic world. The central question, then, is how a college or university environment affects personality development and how it might be changed in ways favorable to development.

Culture as well as personality

The most important feature of that environment is its culture, the patterns of beliefs, values, and practices shared by all who teach or study there. Specialists in the psychology of personality, including me, have been talking about the impact of culture on personality ever since the early 1930's, but without fully appreciating that impact. As Archibald MacLeish once said, "We know these things but we do not know them with enthusiasm." Such psychologists could hardly know academic culture with enthusiasm as long as they believed that culture had done its work for the developing person by the time that person was 17 or 18 years old. I, at any rate, had to become involved with adult development before I could begin to understand the ways in which the adult personality is sustained and shaped by culture. Even now most of us academics are at least partially blind to aspects of the cultures in which we spend our days. To paraphrase an ancient Chinese philosopher, one cannot talk with a fish about water, or with a professor about academic culture.

Just to use the words "academic culture" is to say that "culture" can refer not only to whole societies such as the United States or the Navajo, but to reference groups, such as academic men and women or professional psychologists, and to face-to-face groups such as colleges and universities, academic departments, and students at a particular institution. I first encountered this use of the concept in Elliot Jacques' book *The Changing Culture of a Factory* (Jacques, 1951), and when my colleagues and I started our studies at Vassar, we had the concept very much in mind (Bushnell, 1962).

Focusing on the culture of particular groups and organizations enables one to think, with some hope, about how they might be changed. It is stultifying to think of the culture of the United States as *the* source of, let us say, sex-role stereotypes and then to bemoan the fact that it takes so long for the culture of an entire nation to change. On the other hand, it is exciting to examine at close range the culture of a particular academic department, and to see how it might be altered; to see, indeed, that it might be less difficult to change a decisive element of that culture than it would be to change the personality of any one of its members. The approach to change advocated in this book stresses the interaction of culture and personality. In general, a new member of a department will conform, in behavior, with the culture that was there when she arrived and in time will probably incorporate, in her own way, some of that culture within her personality. But if one asks how the culture was generated in the first place and sees that it came in part out of the needs, conflicts, and anxieties of individuals, there will be no alternative to a dynamic theory of personality as a basis of explanation.

To understand it try to change it

A serious effort to bring about change in an academic institution will, of necessity as I see it, involve "action-research." Kurt Lewin, who gave us this term, wisely said that the way to understand the working of an institution was to try to change it, rather in the way a therapist learns about a person by trying to help him. In Freud's psychoanalytic method, analyst and patient cooperate in an inquiry that has the capability of changing them both in desirable ways. The full potential of this model for social action will be realized when it is widely applied to organizations and groups as well as to individuals. As I show in Chapter 10, interviewing students or faculty for research purposes amounts to a major intervention in their lives, while the entrance of a research team into an organization like a college or a university department can send shock waves throughout the whole structure. Thus, a researcher must be prepared to take responsibility for the effects of his work.

Woke up one morning

The reader may note that the last chapter on "the loss and rediscovery of moral character" was written comparatively recently, although the first paper I ever wrote about education for a professional journal (Sanford, 1956) and all my writings on that subject have been infused with some degree of moral passion. Any educational activity, it has seemed to me, must be guided by some commitment to value. One morning about seven years ago, however, I woke up with the idea of making my own values more explicit. This was shortly after Watergate. In the academic community as in the rest of the nation there was a wave of interest in morality, ethics, and moral development. Special courses were installed, programs were funded, centers were set up. What was needed, it seemed to me, was a theory of moral development, such as the one embodied in my general theory of personality. But educators had greeted this general theory with something less than a warm embrace; so why not take advantage of their new-found interest, putting moral development up front and allowing it to draw along the general theory? In the event, I found it much easier and more rewarding to talk to academic audiences about moral development, which no one could put down at the time, than to talk about the whole personality.

As a matter of style I should alert the reader to my reluctance to raise a red flag when introducing theoretical ideas that are new. Nor do I always pause in these chapters to explain the source of ideas or compare them with the contributions of other theorists. In evaluating the theory I hope the reader will not be further distracted by questions about where I am coming from, as some of my students would do, but will give first attention to the ability of the theory to explain the facts that are presented. Nonetheless I want to note here that writers on adult development before (say) 1950 were ahead of their time and are now in danger of being neglected. Personality research in recent years often brings to mind the Victorian explorers who were out to discover the source of the Nile. After years of heroics and frustration, someone had a bright idea: "Why not ask the Arabs?" Today there appears to be ample readiness for adult development, and a splendid opportunity for researchers to ask those who all along, in this broad sense, have been learning after college.

Personality
Development

A Short Course on Personality

2

During the years 1952–58 I began to study the effects of college education and in particular what happened to students during their four years at Vassar (Sanford, 1962). Early in that period I learned two things of continuing significance, both for undergraduate education and for various forms of learning after college. One lesson concerned the limitations of psychoanalytic reductionism, and the other lesson, if I may risk an apparent contradiction, was the pervasiveness of unconscious processes in academic life.

Our project at Vassar had an advisory committee, constituted of distinguished psychologists, psychoanalysts and sociologists, who visited us on campus several times a year. At one such meeting my colleagues and I sought to convey something of what we were learning, through presentation of a case study. By that time we had interviewed a number of freshmen, members of a sample we intended to see again when they were seniors. The young woman whose case we presented had been interviewed four times, each time by a different investigator. The interviews were comprehensive, covering pretty well, we thought, childhood, classroom education, values, and various aspects of life at the college. In preparing the case study we ordered and summarized a lot of material.

So what was her problem?

We were hardly through presenting the childhood history before a member of the advisory committee asked what was this student's "problem." We asked for and received permission to continue the presentation but there was no denying the eagerness of the committee to get on with the reduction of a college student's behavior to a formula embodying infantile needs, conflicts, and defenses. This was called "the psychodynamic formulation of the case." For example, the student's motivation for achievement, seen as abnormally high, was supposed by various members of the committee to derive from a desire to please her father, or an identification with her father, or hostility toward her mother, or rivalry toward her older brother. And so for other aspects of her behavior.

I won't say those of us on the study were shocked, for we were not very far beyond engaging in such psychodynamic exercises ourselves, and might occasionally revert under stress. In this case, however, we thought we were describing a quite healthy student of unusual interest and promise. Far from needing psychiatric help she sailed through college with ease and pleasure, benefited greatly from it, and like so many college women of that day, disappointed her teachers by getting married instead of going to graduate school.

There was no denying the continuity of some childhood experiences and behavior patterns in her personality; indeed it was highly significant that her father, not a college man himself, was a great admirer of his wife's and his daughter's intellectual interests and achievements. But it was clear enough to me that vast areas of this student's personality were for all practical purposes *not* connected with what remained of unconscious structures built up in childhood; and that these areas were fully open to influence by educational procedures.

If you want them to get it

The other lesson from the early phases of our work at Vassar is symbolized for me in what was a common complaint of the teachers there: "You have to tell these students six times if you want them to get what you are saying." An exaggeration no doubt, but it calls attention to what most college teachers know: that at the beginning of a course they have to be very careful and persistent in order to insure that all students are clear about such matters as assignments, reading lists, quizzes, method of grading, and so on, not to mention anything of substance that might be presented. The trouble, of course, is that the students are not really listening. They have too many other things on their minds. What they are mainly concerned about, very probably, is what the authority relations in that class are going to be; and, next to that, how they are going to get along with the other students, whether they should try to make friends with the students sitting on either side, and how they might cope with various problems outside of that class.

My colleagues and I connected these observations with something we learned from interviews with students, that they did not really observe their teachers. Even after a semester in a classroom they had the greatest difficulty in ascribing any personal traits to the teacher. They could, of course, comment on role performances—how clear the lectures, how tough the grading—but that was about all. When it came to the beginning of face-to-face interactions with teachers (or, for that matter, with members of the opposite sex), students' perceptions and expectations were heavily influenced by stereotypes brought over from the past.

All schools, from elementary to graduate, have a way of bringing out the most primitive in people. When we were starting our graduate school at the Wright Institute we were amazed to discover that students saw the three-man administration and faculty, all of us gentle, permissive liberals, in exactly the same way they saw the distant authorities in the largest universities.

Re-enacting family dramas

Graduate school is a great stage for the re-enactment of family dramas. I have known a graduate student, a 45 year old woman, who had been psychoanalyzed, practiced psychotherapy for some years under excellent supervision, and counseled school teachers, but who still structured her belated graduate school experience according to a pattern established as a child at home: as it turned out she had a talented mother who represented high standards but didn't understand her, and a father who understood her, and was permissive, but not around very much.

Given the crucial importance of graduate school in the lives of students, the power of professors, and the complex, obscure, and emotionally charged relationships among the professors, students are under strong pressure to transfer to their new relationships attitudes and images generated in childhood. If one student, like the woman just mentioned, wants to find both understanding and insistence upon high standards in the same professor, another wants to pick fights with all the authorities around, or play off one professor against another, while still another is thrown into a panic by signs of disagreement among admired professors.

What I wish to argue then is that every individual at every

stage of life plays host to unconscious processes which are ready to be switched into the individual's functioning and under conditions of stress may assume a dominant role. It is impossible to over-estimate the irrationality, the primitiveness, or the power of these processes. As T. W. Adorno once said, "The only thing that is true about psychoanalysis is its exaggerations."

Open to modification

It begins to appear, then, that our advisory committee was not foolish in supposing that we would necessarily be concerned with persistent unconscious structures in Vassar students, structures that would express themselves under sufficent strain. We may also assume differences in the intensity and in the fixity of the unconscious patterns. Of the two women so far mentioned, the graduate student was probably less healthy as a child and up to the time of her analysis, and was undoubtedly under greater strain as she began her studies.

In both cases, however, it was proper for us to concentrate on education rather than on pathogenic tendencies, on the assumption that large areas of personality were little influenced by unconscious processes and thus were relatively open to modification through experience. The primary educational task, then, is to provide the stimuli to expand and develop these conscious parts of the personality. When this is done the unconscious patterns become relatively less important; indeed, I am going to argue that purely educational procedures can actually modify unconscious patterns themselves, which may eventually more or less wither away.

One requirement, however, is that educators not allow their own neurotic tendencies to get mixed up with those of the students. Teachers should avoid accepting their students' transferences. Ideally, schools, colleges, and universities should be "corrective" environments, provided by people with knowledge of what needs to be corrected. We can't very well ask this of the majority of teachers now; but we can at least ask it of educational researchers.

Developing while you learn

At the time my colleagues and I began our studies at Vassar College the idea of starting out with a philosophy of education never occurred to me. Like most psychologists, I had never given any serious thought to education. But it was easy to become interested in what happened to individual students as they went through college. We learned that personality did indeed develop there; and that in some students these changes were significant and, from the point of view of the great ethical systems, highly desirable. Changes in personality were accompanied by wide-ranging changes in behavior. For example, increased stability of ego-identity was expressed in the way academic content was learned as well as in the way teachers and other students were perceived and related to. Change in one process or feature of the person was accompanied by change in various others. For example, learning a skill seemed to favor self-confidence, and vice versa; self-confidence favors self-insight, self-insight favors sensitivity to the needs of others, and so on.

When we turned from the behavior of students to that of professors, it seemed clear that personality was a determinant of their conceptions of knowledge, philosophies of science, ways of relating to their professions, goals they set for themselves and for their students, and styles of teaching.

We came to realize that personality development is central not only as a determinant of numerous values, but as the focus for various other aims of education that are usually listed as if they were categorically separated. Personality development favors and is favored by familiarity with our cultural heritage, the mastery of a subject area, the acquisition of useful skills, finding a vocation, becoming a good citizen, knowing how to tell a good person, surviving as a human being in an increasingly technological world.

Teaching as you would be taught

What we began saying about the aims of education had been said, essentially, many times before: by the ancient Greeks, by various British educators including Cardinal Newman, by the Founding Fathers, and by a line of modern thinkers. Of these last my favorite is A. N. Whitehead: "Students are alive, and the purpose of education is to assist their self-development." Another more recent statement was expressed in the 1947 report of the President's Commission on Higher Education: "To liberate and perfect the intrinsic powers of every citizen is the central purpose of democracy; and its furtherance of individual self-realization is its greatest glory."

With these values in mind and with our data fast accumulating, my colleagues at Vassar and I saw that the study of education ought to focus sharply on what helped developmental changes to occur. In fact I allowed myself to suggest some changes, in educational theory and practice, that colleges might make. But we found that it is difficult to talk with college teachers about personality development through education. The very word "development" often calls up images of fund raisers, or real estate operators, or remote, recently created nations. If they have a conception of personality at all, teachers are likely to say to psychologists, counselors, or campus ministers, "You take care of personality development, my colleagues and I will take care of education."

When we do begin to talk about the qualities of the educated person it may be more agreeable to talk about values than about development, and to begin with intellectual values, before going on to such things as ethical sensitivity and openness to what is human. Personality embraces knowledge, certainly all that knowledge which can be brought into the service of the individual's practical and imaginative functions. From there it is relatively easy to move on to discussion of the interconnectedness of the values, and of what they depend upon.

Faculty can be interested in their own development, and when this happens they more readily become interested in the development of students. In many situations faculty present themselves to students and colleagues as if they believed their own development was complete; and their environment offers confirmation by rewarding them for being as they are. Yet when faculty are asked, in interviews, about their work, how they arrived at their present status, what they were like as students, what are their hopes and plans for the future, they soon understand that they could very well develop further, attain greater breadth and complexity, in personal as well as professional life. This understanding not only opens possibilities for faculty but alerts them to analagous possibilities for their students.

Exploring their interests

The study of students by means of interviews heightens their awareness of themselves as developing individuals. This will usually be beneficial to them, but we may anticipate some inappropriate responses. I remember when I first lectured on Maslow's concept of "self-actualization." Some of the students immediately began acting as if they were self-actualized. I do not like to see students spending a lot of time cogitating about who they are and where they are going, generally using knowledge of development as a defense against it. What they should be doing is exploring their interests, pursuing a line of inquiry or action until something important happens, or until the possibilities of that line have been exhausted. When they discuss development it would be better if the focus were upon the development of other people.

Impossible without Freud

I have been putting forward my ideas about personality theory and education for more than a few years. Particular colleges have been influenced, some quite a lot, but the impact on American higher education in general has been hardly noticeable. The impact of my work on psychoanalysis and educational research seems to have been even less. How to account for this general lack of response?

The work I have done on human development and education has been, in my opinion, in the tradition of Freud himself. In any case it would not have been possible without Freud. The same is true of *The Authoritarian Personality.* Yet official psychoanalysis has not embraced any of this work, the main trouble being, I think, that it does not really fit into their closed system. We say too much about events outside the "conflict sphere." In the case of academic psychology, the trouble has been that work on something as complex as authoritarianism, or the development of the whole personality in educational institutions, can hardly fit into the experimental or survey-research designs that prevail in psychology and sociology or achieve the degree of exactitude those designs are supposed to make possible.

There is a deeper epistemological issue here. I think the humanistic psychologists are right in saying that closed-system psychoanalysis and behaviorism belong together, in that both go overboard in their reliance upon a psychic determinism. When I was invited to join the Association of Humanistic Psychologists, however, what stopped me was the sense that I was being asked to purify myself, by giving up my psychoanalytic leanings.

Sources of an adequate theory

I have thought for some time that the way to go in developing a personality theory that embraced what was valuable in psychoanalysis and was adequate to a general theory of education was to follow those thinkers, psychologists and others, who were advancing organismic theory, field theory and general systems theory.

Theoretical ideas of these kinds have been appearing in the psychological literature since the 1930's, for example, in the writings of Kurt Goldstein, Charlotte Bühler, Heinz Werner and, most particularly, Kurt Lewin. Indeed, Lewin, said very early in his career that he hoped his work would help to put psychoanalysis on a sound theoretical basis. During the 1940's, when psychoanalysis was riding high in academia and in intellectual circles, there was much discussion of the possibility of integrating psychoanalysis and field theory.

Not much has come of this, I am afraid. Psychoanalysts have continued to believe that they already had about all the theory they needed for practice and they have not been much interested in development. Academic psychologists have likewise neglected field theory because the problems it seemed to raise were not researchable, at least not in ways that accorded with the prevailing scientific model.

I say let us get the theory straight and worry about research later. For me the trouble with almost all the psychologists who have thought well about science is that they have not been psychoanalytic enough. I include here, in addition to those mentioned, Gordon Allport, Edward Tolman, and Abraham Maslow. They have been generally helpful about the forms, but short on the contents, of personality. They have not known psychoanalysis with enough enthusiasm; or taken seriously enough what Adorno praised wryly as its "exaggerations." They have made growth and development seem too easy, as if all that were required was enough desire to develop, or enough responsiveness to exhortation.

Open systems

In the remainder of the chapter I want to sketch a general theory of personality, present briefly a general systems theory of development, and look at some ways in which personality develops under the impact of education.

The best way to approach theory-making in personality is to be practical. But if a practitioner focuses on a single problem or pattern of behavior with a view to its removal or prevention and gives no attention to other parts of the person, his actions are bound to produce unanticipated consequences, some of which are likely to be harmful. Or, to take it the other way around, if one is bent on promoting or facilitating development in some area of the person (say a moral, social, affective, or cognitive function) and if in educational activities one proceeds to focus narrowly upon this to the exclusion of other areas, his efforts can result in one-sidedness, curious distortions of functions, or even the effective shutting off of functions that are essential to the quality of life.

It follows from this that our conception of personality must be comprehensive as well as holistic.

Probably few psychologists would disagree with the proposition that personality is a whole embracing parts or elements, which relate to one another and to the whole in various ways, forming a structure that is separated from its environment by some kind of boundary. Differences among theorists arise when we come to consider the nature of the elements, the manner of their interaction, and the definition of the boundaries.

Holistic thought

Another good way to approach theory-making is to start with Freud. When Freud conceived his tripartite scheme (Id, Superego, Ego), he was under the influence of European holistic thought, starting with a conception of the whole personality and then dividing it along lines suggested by a theory of its organization. Jung did the same thing, coming up with a different scheme of subsystems. This is un-American. American personality theorists, typically, have started with a general theory of behavior and then transposed to personality whatever units of analysis had been adopted, whether habits for stimulus-response theories or needs for functionalist theories.

Like Freud I prefer to think of the personality as comprising three major systems, the id, the superego, and the ego; except that to use these terms today may risk a failure in communication, for they seem at once too familiar and too esoteric. In the late 1950's when colleagues and I were working on *The American College*, I did use these terms in drafting a long chapter on personality development in college. My colleagues persuaded me to translate them into plainer English, arguing that some of our readers would either think they knew all about these concepts and would use them as stereotypes, and others would be turned away by their strangeness. So I settled for impulse system (Id), Ego, and primitive conscience (Superego), and will use the revised terminology here, at least in this theoretical chapter.

Demanding, irrational, asocial

An impulse may be defined, independently of its origins and of how conscious it may become, in terms of its modes of operation. What stands out is the striving for immediate reduction of tension, in disregard of consequences. A primitive impulse is demanding, irrational, asocial, uncontrolled. Often the reduction of tension depends upon there being made available some real object, for example, food, breast, mother. With repetition, objects which have been instrumental in reducing tension become associated in the child's mind with tension reduction, so that when tension is next built up there also arises an image of the object that is capable of reducing it. (Freud called this the *primary process.*) Images such as this are the stuff of dreams, fantasies, hallucinations, and delusions.

Although the aggregate of impulses does not change with time in its basic modes of operation, it nevertheless develops as the infant grows into an adult. It is lent increasing power through the maturation of the motor apparatus. With time the developing person uses more and more different kinds of objects in the reduction of tension, and hence through association and memory expands the domain of wish-fulfilling imagery. At the same time, there is an increase in the strength and variety of stimuli that generate tension; fresh internal stimuli come with the bodily changes of puberty, while external stimuli are brought to bear by the training and discipline which are necessary to the child's socialization. More tension, more frustration, more wishes.

Thus the system of impulses comes early in life to have content of considerable breadth and complexity. And this content may vary from one individual to another, depending on the course of their upbringing. Infantile sexuality, various forms of aggression, rejection, dependence, passivity, rebelliousness, lust for power and other tendencies may be ascribed to the primitive impulse system, *provided* that they operate in ways characteristic of it.

In my view this system is directly connected with the external environment, not buried underneath strata of the personality through which it must pass in order to reach the surface. Social stimuli such as propaganda may make their appeal directly to unconscious primitive impulses, and such impulses may be expressed directly in behavior under conditions of stress or social facilitation. Owing to internal connectedness the energy of this system may be readily displaced from one object to another; and, as we shall see in a moment, the whole system may be affected by changes in the ego or primitive conscience.

Just says "no" or "do this"

The personality soon comes to show evidence of an agency that punishes antisocial thoughts and actions, and rewards what the prevailing social code would call virtues. This primitive conscience is usually more or less directly opposed to the system of impulses I have just outlined. Individuals differ with respect to the kinds of needs or drives the primitive conscience seeks most forcibly to suppress, to the kinds of ideals it favors, and to the kinds of punishments and pressures it has at its disposal. The content of this agency resembles the ideals and values of the social group in which the individual is being brought up. This content changes, within limits, when the social situation changes, as when a nation goes to war (or as Fritz Redl has put it, when the superego dons a uniform).

The child's parents have the major role in transmitting the standards of the community. They have the power to reward desirable behavior and to punish undesirable. And given the child's desire for approval and fear of punishment, the assimilation of something of what the parents stand for follows readily enough—through simple conditioning and through the child's ability to imagine what the parents would say or do.

The primitive conscience is a childish construction. Like the system of impulses, it operates automatically, inflexibly, unreasonably. It does not make fine distinctions, or argue points with the impulse system or ego; it simply says, "No" or "Do this." The parents that are internalized in this manner are not the real parents but the idealized or omnipotent parents conceived by the childish mind. Not merely a copy of prevailing ideas and values as represented by parents, the primitive conscience may make stronger demands than parents do, or be more severe than other external authorities are likely to be. This means, I think, that the severity or demandingness of the primitive conscience in action depends not alone upon how much energy has been channeled into it, but upon the strength of the impulses which it undertakes to counter.

Autonomous fear of impulses

I agree with those theorists, chiefly Melanie Klein, who hold that the rudiments of a primitive conscience exist within the personality even before any parental prohibitions and sanctions are incorporated. Infants, who have only begun to distinguish between what is inside and what outside their own bodies, may have occasion to fear their own impulses. When frustrated and in a mood to tear things up, they may suppose that the things they would like to do might very well happen to them. This theory can explain anxiety and irrational fears in children who have been gently handled; it may also explain why misbehaving children (or students) whose impulses have got beyond their control welcome the restraining, even the punishing, hand of the adult. The presence of this internal punishing force is an additional reason why the child may happily internalize the prohibitions and sanctions that society offers.

The primitive conscience may differ from one individual to another not only in its contents but in (1) *strength* (how much force can be set in opposition to strivings of the primitive impulses or the ego), (2) *strictness* (the number of different kinds of impulsive strivings that will arouse inhibiting or punitive actions), and (3) *rigidity* (the tendency to act in an all or nothing manner).

The primitive conscience may be more or less internalized, in the sense that it operates with different degrees of reinforcement by an external authority. And after it has been more or less firmly internalized it may later be got rid of or rendered virtually ineffective. It may be repressed by the combined forces of the ego and the primitive impulses and kept in that state by a succession of delinquent or anti-social actions. Or it may be replaced by external authorities, as when individuals come to regard organizational or professional practices as sufficient guides to conduct.

Actual objects, effective strategies

The ego acts to bring about reduction of tension when the primitive impulse system fails to do so. Unhappily for the latter system, wishing doesn't alter facts. The primary process gives direction to striving but it can reduce tension only a little. What is required is a plan of action by which a real object, with which the individual can interact, is discovered or produced. (Freud called this the *secondary process.*) Since the ego is in close touch with the external world and can take account of reality in governing behavior, it performs for the personality the essential task of attaining maximum satisfaction of needs.

But to reduce tension through accommodation to or mastery of the environment is not the only task of the ego. It must also deal with internal problems. Numerous needs or strivings operate in the personality at the same time. In order that each of these may get its due, the ego undertakes to establish schedules and hierarchies of importance. But despite its best efforts conflicts arise, and the ego has the further task of finding ways to resolve them. The most common type of conflict, and the one that has the greatest implications for the development of personality, is conflict between an impulse and a conscience which are both primitive. When such impulses are permitted direct gratification, even when there is pleasure in fantasies of gratification, the primitive conscience punishes the ego by arousing guilt feelings. The ego then seeks to avoid these powerful feelings by managing impulses in ways that are tolerable to the primitive conscience and by softening its demands, making it more reasonable and tolerant.

Mechanisms of defense

But often things do not go very smoothly. Impulses may increase in intensity and threaten to explode into action; this arouses in the ego extreme anxiety lest it be punished by the primitive conscience. In critical situations of this kind, which are common in childhood, the ego resorts to maneuvers that deny, falisfy, or distort reality. These defensive mechanisms of the ego, like the struggle to which they are a response, typically operate unconsciously, reinforcing patterns of conflict and defense that are not open to modification through experience and tend to become fixed, even while their stirrings tend to ramify throughout the personality.

It is to these patterns that closed-system psychoanalysis tends to reduce everything. The way out of this trap is not to posit inborn processes outside of the "conflict sphere" but to think of the ego as a truly open system that always has connections with the external environment. This means that as the environment changes, the ego (or any subsystem of it) has no alternative but to adapt. Thus the tendency to grow is at least as natural as the tendency to remain fixed.

It often appears that in children, and in neurotic or disturbed adults, the ego is completely taken up with its negotiations around conflicts between primitive conscience and primitive impulses, but if a personality is to survive, some of its parts must be capable of adapting to environmental changes.

The adaptations required of infants and children are numerous and the ego expands rapidly, coming in time to embrace a great variety of particular needs, together with the cognitive schemata and action patterns that have been built up as means for satisfying them. It is the organization of these contents, the ego system, that in Freud's words, "commends itself to the id." The ego commends itself as an agency for the reduction of tension. As it develops and becomes more and more effective, the gains to the personality from its activities become increasingly greater than the gains that can be achieved by what Freud called the id, and hence some of the energy inherent in the id is transferred to the ego. After this development has proceeded for a time, a stage is reached at which the ego, which functions as a unit, commands more energy than is embodied in a typical id impulse.

As noted above, a given need such as aggression, sex, or dominance may appear in the primitive impulse system or in the ego or in both at once. Some needs may appear in the primitive conscience as well. Consider the need for dominance, for example. In the impulse system, dominance appears as a striving for immediate and absolute power, or as fantasies of omnipotence. In a strong, strict primitive conscience, dominance may appear as an all-out attempt to control the behavior of other people, lest they get away with something that one has to inhibit in oneself. In the ego the need for dominance might be expressed as a temperate desire to influence people and an integrated set of techniques for attaining and keeping positions of leadership.

Similar behaviors, different sources

This is saying, in effect, that the same, or at least very similar, patterns of behavior may have different sources within the personality. As the id, the superego, and the ego develop and carry out their functions in interaction with one another, there comes to intervene between the core and the surface of personality a vast aggregate of subsystems and secondary processes. The elucidation of the dynamic sources of surface manifestations is what the study of personality is mainly about.

When my colleagues and I were doing the work which issued in our book *The Authoritarian Personality* (1950), we came to believe that we were dealing with a conflict between the impulse system and the primitive conscience involving particular contents, a conflict so intense as to require most of the ego's attention, leaving it with the appearance of weakness. Thus when it came to developing our scale for measuring authoritarianism, the "F scale," we composed such items as this: "He is indeed contemptible who does not have an undying love, gratitude, and respect for his parents." Such an all-out expression of virtue, we thought, must be a mask for underlying aggression which, however, in alliance with the primitive conscience, would find an outlet in punitiveness toward other people, all this being possible because of weakness in the ego.

Systems within systems

Personality, a system in itself, can always be seen as a unit in various social systems—interpersonal, social structural, cultural. Personality will change, even in its deeper and more central structures, in proportion to changes in the environment.

Commonly, the individual and some part of his social environment constitute a system whose parts are so closely related that drawing lines of demarcation is difficult. Some theorists prefer to make the "person-environment configuration" the unit for study. In a universe of related events it is necessary to be arbitrary to some extent; we do well to study one order of events without studying all the others to which it is related. There are at least sentimental reasons for focusing on the individual rather than on parts, or on the social systems of which the person is a unit. It is not psychical subsystems or social groups but the individual who knows joy and suffering and bears moral responsibility. Probably the individual will always be the object of a certain amount of sympathetic curiosity.

We may separate personality and the environment conceptually and study the relations between them. The necessary boundary, like the one between subsystems of the personality, can be defined in the terms of general systems theory as a locus of resistance to exchange of energy between neighboring systems. The resistance of a boundary can be thought of as the steepness of a gradient—how much energy is required to go up and over.

Certainly at this stage of the game nothing is to be gained by opposing personality factors and the social system and asking which is the more important. What is needed is more knowledge of how personality systems and social systems actually interact. For example, it hardly suffices to say as some social scientists do, that the person assimilates the culture and that personality is essentially a carrier of culture patterns. I would say that any addition to the individual psychological household is always a product of something from the culture and something that was already there in the person. And I would insist that it is highly important to know to what subsystem of the personality the cultural element is assimilated. If it were assimilated to the primitive conscience, the cultural element would come under the sway of that subsystem's characteristic modes of functioning: it would be somewhat non-rational and unpredictable, remain dependent on external reinforcement, be susceptible to replacement by a different element when this was urged by the social group. If on the other hand, the cultural element were assimilated to the ego, it would become meaningfully related to other values, brought into the service of the individual's larger purposes, and would become an integral and durable feature of the personality.

It follows from what has been said that education should be primarily concerned with the development of the ego. The more the ego develops the better able it is to incorporate the primitive impulse system and primitive conscience, and so to move toward the full integration of personality.

Differentiation, integration

According to general system theory the growth of something (whether an organism, an institution, or a city) begins with expansion, the enlargement of parts or the addition of new parts. Growth occurs in children and infants when they are presented with stimulus situations that require new responses. Expansion makes differentiation necessary, except in an extraordinarily benign environment, for there must be efficiency in coping with the diverse environmental strains to which the child becomes increasingly open. This means that responses must become increasingly specialized.

Integration, which we often speak of as a desideratum, is actually as natural and necessary as adaptation. After growth and differentiation have occurred integration is necessary to restore stability. Children change in response to new stimuli, but they do not change altogether, nor even as a rule in large areas of themselves, and the changes that are made are as consistent as possible with what already existed.

What is favorable to the individual's well-being is not so much integration per se, but a capacity for integration. Healthy and well-developed people are always moving toward integration, but since they are also expanding and becoming more complex, they remain (as it were) somewhat open-ended, ready to include more. What is particularly favorable to well-being is enough flexibility, enough communication among subsystems, so that in critical situations resources can be brought to bear as needed.

In childhood and adolescence there are usually challenges in abundance; in fact we have to worry lest they become so numerous or so extreme as to exceed adaptive capacities and cause regression.

Disassembling, rebuilding

Where college students and adults are concerned, however, effective challenges may have to be sought. Students arrive at college, typically, with the expectation that the cognitive-emotional structures they have built up will suffice for what is to come. Their further education, it seems to me, is largely a matter of breaking up cognitive-emotional structures through challenges and new acquisitions and then re-building structures on a higher level of complexity.

A challenge that an educator might wish to bring to bear must be experienced as such to be effective. We have to reckon with the individual's capacity to *have* experience. There is not much point in offering a European experience to adolescents so sunk in ethnocentrism that they can only compare everything they see unfavorably with what they have been offered at home. The tendency of students to project onto new situations psychological contents from the past has already been mentioned. This brings us to the question of the role of self-insight in personality development.

Some psychoanalysts, fully aware of all that has been said here about unconscious processes, have considered that the most important step in the development of the entering student is making these processes conscious, thus permitting the ordinary educational procedures to do their work. Lawrence Kubie, for example, has argued cogently that educators must find some way to lead students to "self-knowledge in depth" such as people sometimes attain in the consulting room.

This recalls my experience with the advisory committee so eager to ask "So what was her problem?", in response to which I argued that education ought to stress the task of expanding the healthy parts of the personality. This is not to deny, however, that sometimes arrests of development due to unconscious defensive reactions are serious enough so that psychotherapy is fully justified.

But psychotherapy has its limits. By itself, psychotherapy

may not be sufficient for the attainment of self-insight. In any case, it is not a substitute for education; at best it is a means for removing blocks so that education can take its course.

The case of the graduate student mentioned earlier, who tended to structure her experience at graduate school in accord with a pattern brought over from childhood, would be seized upon by behaviorists to illustrate the failure of psychoanalysis or other insight therapies: all that analysis, all that immersion in clinical work, and still the unconscious pattern persisted. Would it not have been better if those concerned with her development had set out to change her behavior in the first place?

As I see it, this student's story in no way tends to diminish the importance of insight; what it shows instead is something of the difficulty of attaining insight into deeply based processes. In her case the process seemed to require that she get away from the fall-out area of her parents, escape from the network of relationships at the clinic where she worked, enter a situation that would provide challenges and resist the projection onto it of old patterns, and engage in some new form of behavior while continuing the work of self-analysis. When insight occurred, she valued it highly as a contribution to the integration of her personality.

What I am saying, then, is that a developmental change in personality, at any age beyond childhood, occurs not through either challenge *or* self-insight alone, not even through challenge *and* self-insight considered as separate or successive processes, but through the interaction of the two.

And finally self-awareness

The attainment of self-insight, by making the unconscious accessible to consciousness, is a major integrative activity of the ego. However much I have been stressing behavior change as a requirement for change in personality, the fact remains that no amount of situation changing or behavior changing will lead to personality development in students or adults unless it is accompanied by self-reflection. Indeed, "change strategies" and interventions of professionals will amount to little more than manipulation, with dehumanizing effects, unless the person involved understands what is happening and is encouraged to think about it in relation to the self.

Full consciousness or self-awareness is not, however, an essential feature of the ego's integrative work. As stated earlier, the central aim of the ego is to integrate the primitive impulse system and the primitive conscience with itself; and its efforts in this direction begin very early, when the ego first "commends itself to the id." Such efforts are in full swing during the college years. The more developed the ego, the better able is the individual to admit underlying impulses into the conscious self-concept; and the more the impulses find forms of expression that are personally comfortable and socially acceptable, the less the necessity for the ego to use its energies for maintaining defenses, and hence the greater its freedom to have experiences that can further develop it.

The situation is similar with ego and primitive conscience. The more the ego is relieved of pressures from the latter, the greater becomes its opennesss to experiences that can expand and differentiate it; and as the ego develops it becomes increasingly able to take over from the fierce prohibitions that were developed in early childhood.

All these principles of personality development hold for people in higher education. What I want to accent here is the role of the curriculum, which is the most central and the most distinctive feature of the college. There is no more effective instrumentality for personality development, in young people and in adults, than the curriculum in the hands of people who know how to use it.

Resistance to dogma

When I speak of the integration of the primitive conscience with the ego I mean a state of affairs in which individuals' moral standards and values are supported by their own knowledge, thought, and judgment rather than by remnants of childhood training, authorities, or the immediate social group. It is through their studies that students may best attain to this condition. Knowledge by itself is vitally important in enabling students to resist dogma. Academic work that requires students to exercise their intellects—to make fine discriminations, to be objective, to analyze, to criticize—contributes directly to independence of thought and judgment, enabling the individual to get away from a literal belief in rules, to see a particular value in its relationship with others, and to stand in opposition to pressures from authority figures or from the social group. It is with the use of the curriculum that teachers may best introduce values that compete with old, automatically accepted ones, and so induce new perceptions and new thinking which lead on to a more complex outlook.

What was said above about encouraging self-insight applies

here. The more students understand the sources of their beliefs and values the less will their moral behavior and outlook be determined by simplistic inner imperatives, the more by a differentiated, flexible, and therefore dependable, conscience.

When it comes to the integration of the primitive impulse system with the ego, the great educational resource is likewise culture, as embodied in the curriculum. In learning to appreciate literature, for example, students extend their human sympathies or, in my terms, they both expand the primitive impulse system and satisfy it through imagination. Thus what may have been an unconscious impulse striving for gratification becomes part of a synthesis achieved by the ego through mediating the demands of impulse and reality.

Other subjects—arts, math, music, science, drama, history, skills, sports—may also open the way to full participation in culture, and thus to the boundless satisfaction available from the life of the imagination. This is a fundamental point of pedagogy. Teachers who would raise reading levels, particularly in children who seem to resist the whole undertaking, should realize that their best ally is not the superego but the primitive impulse system. They should, in concert with the child's ego, "commend themselves to the id," by capturing the imagination, by using materials (no matter how primitive) to enable the child to find joy in activity that involves the use of symbols. The more the impulses come to be expressed in this way, the less will the teacher have to be concerned with discipline and, even more important, the less will the child's ego have to be taken up with defensive activities. The teacher who gives this service to children will have little trouble winning their cooperation in those increasingly difficult tasks that educators want them to perform.

This kind of pedagogy leads me to speak not only of education for the enjoyment of life (chapter 17), but also education for morality (chapter 20). The processes involved are those best calculated to develop the ego. When the ego is highly developed the individual not only has the capacity to see the right but, also given the wide range of alternatives now available, the capacity to choose courses of action that are at once satisfying to the self and beneficial to others.

Education for Individual Development

3

In writing elsewhere about education and personality, I have tried to make the points that, in a changing world, we cannot hope to train students for specific future roles; and that the attitudes, ideals, and personality characteristics a student acquires in college or graduate school affect the way he will use his knowledge—whether his life work will be satisfying to himself or beneficial to others, self-frustrating or socially destructive. What is needed, I have argued, is an education that concentrates not so much on the supposedly straightforward process of imparting facts as on developing the student as a person. When these ideas are acted upon, psychiatry and education are seen to have similar or common aims even if their methods may hardly overlap. Personality theory is as applicable to one as to the other.

By education for individual development, I mean a program consciously undertaken to promote an identity based on such qualities as flexibility, creativity, openness to experience, and responsibility. Although these qualities depend in part on early experience, college can develop them further and in new ways, as shown by research at Vassar College (Sanford, 1956) and by subsequent studies at other institutions (Katz, 1967, 1968). A college must use all of its resources for this sort of developmental education. The curriculum, methods of teaching, organization of teacher-student relationships, living arrangements, extracurricular activities, activities of the president and his assistants—all should be studied anew, with attention to how, guided by a theory of personality, they may contribute to individual development. The same holds true for graduate students and for faculty.

An even shorter version

Summarizing the theory outlined in chapter 2, we may regard personality as compromising three major systems: a system of primitive impulses and feelings; a system of inhibiting or punishing forces that have been automatically taken over from the social environment (the primitive conscience); and a system that controls and adapts and integrates in accordance with the demands of reality (the ego). The inner life of a person consists largely of conflicts and alliances among these systems; and observable traits of personality may be attributed largely to patterns of their interaction.

A high level of development in personality requires both complexity and wholeness. A mature person is characterized by a high degree of differentiation (a large number of different parts or features having different and specialized functions) and a high degree of integration, of communication among parts great enough so that different parts may, without losing their essential identity, become organized into larger wholes in order to serve the person's purposes. In the highly developed person there is a rich and varied impulse life, feelings and emotions having become differentiated and civilized. Conscience has been broadened, enlightened and individualized, and operates in accord with the individual's best thought and judgment. The processes by which the person judges events and manages actions are strong, flexible, responsive to the multitudinous aspects of the environment, and at the same time in close enough touch with the deeper sources of emotion and will so that the person enjoys freedom of imagination and an enduring capacity to be fully alive.

This highly developed structure underlies the individual's sense of direction, his freedom of thought and action, and his capacity to carry out commitments to others and to himself. But the structure is not fixed once and for all. The highly developed individual is always open to new experience and capable of further learning; his stability is fundamental in the sense that he can go on developing while remaining essentially himself.

Helping people to attain these ideals is a common aim of both psychiatry and education, though educators need more often to recognize these goals consciously or explicitly. Like everyone else, a student develops when confronted with challenges that require new kinds of adaptive responses and when he is freed from the necessity of maintaining unconscious defensive devices. The fulfillment of these conditions results in the enlargement and further differentiation of the systems of the personality, and sets the stage for integration on higher levels.

But with luck the cycle does not stop at graduation. The same principles apply to learning after college, provided people are open to change and faced by the right sort of challenges.

The maintenance of cycles

According to the prevailing functionalist point of view in psychology, a person strives to reduce tension and, when unbalanced by tension, will change in order to restore equilibrium. This state of equilibrium is not identical with the state that existed before the tension-inducing stimulus arrived. After each successful striving, the organism is changed. The personality now has new ways of coping with the environment, new images of what it needs and new patterns of action. From this formulation it follows that an expanding personality not only fails to regain its earlier stable states, but also opens itself to new kinds of tension. A more complex personality thus has greater possibilities for frustration and conflict, but for growth as well. These possibilities are not always exercised; adolescents and adults do not change as readily as children, precisely because they have a greater repertory of behavior. Unless they are presented with sufficient challenge, they will react as they have in the past. It is only when old patterns of behavior are insufficient to reduce tension that a change will occur—hence the importance of challenge in the right degree.

A student entering college or graduate school has a wide array of adaptive mechanisms and ways of ordering experience that have served him well in the past and maintain his stability in the present. If he is eager for new experiences, he is often eager not so much for change in himself as for the chance to test the powers he already has and prove to himself his competence and strength. When confronted with challenging situations, he naturally calls into play first his well-tried responses. When they are finally replaced, his natural inclination is to try to make the new structure do for all future contingencies—and so on. The teacher ought to keep challenging this structure in the interest of growth—a task made difficult by the "prematurity" of many college students who feel they already know what they want to be and how they want to live.

This view of development contradicts the belief that all we have to do is protect adolescents from sources of tension and let them grow up naturally, a view applied indiscriminately to college students more by parents and some psychiatrists than by educators. No college would think of applying this method in the realm of intellect, but many adopt the *laisser-aller* approach to broader individual development as if the two spheres could be treated separately.

Readiness for challenge

In understanding how challenges mature people, whether in college or after, one ought to keep in mind that people develop in stages. They remain in one stage for a time before passing on to another marked by greater expansion and complexity of personality but bearing some dynamic relationship to the processes of the prior stage. The fact that people develop step by step implies the concept of readiness to move from one step to the next; and the fact that different people show similar changes at different ages leads one to consider the importance of individual rates of development.

The idea of readiness underlies many of our commonsense practices in child training and education. We suppose that a particular experience, such as going to school or going away from home for a time, will be good for a young person because he is ready for it. If some ordinary salutary set of events, such as going abroad or getting married, proves to be disappointing, we are quick to think of explanations in terms of the individual's unreadiness. Actually, our knowledge about readiness leaves much to be desired. What predisposes a personality to rally in response to a challenge and come through it changed for the better?

Erikson's discussion of life crises offers some light on this point. In his outline of the stages of ego development (Erikson, 1950), the attainment characteristic of each stage is thought to be a precondition for progress to a higher stage; a young person can establish a suitable ego identity only after attaining adequate independence from his parents; and only after his identity is established can he lose himself in a relationship of genuine intimacy. Readiness in itself, though, is not a sufficient cause of development; the personality will not automatically proceed from one "life crisis" to the next, according to a plan of nature. What the state of readiness means, essentially, is that the individual is now open to new kinds of stimuli and prepared to deal with them in an adaptive way.

In a simple society, young people will move through these stages of development on a fairly standard timetable, starting a new thing at a prescribed age; a complex, non-tribal society shows greater individual variations in rates of development.

Most college seniors, for example, are concerned primarily with establishing a place in adult society, with vocational and marriage plans; but some will have settled these questions earlier and been marking time, while many others will still be struggling to gain control over impulses, to overcome their dependence upon their parents, to perceive reality accurately, or even to establish basic trust. These individual differences may be understood in terms of varying degrees of readiness and in the timing of challenging stimuli.

At this rate

If, with Erikson, we conceive of a succession of attainments each of which is necessary to later development, we have to deal with the possibility that an individual may be delayed or "fixated" at any one of these stages. What often happens is that the stimulus situation—the "crisis" in Erikson's sense—that might have led to adaptation on a higher developmental level was actually too upsetting, and evoked a defensive reaction involving unconscious mechanisms, a reaction that prevents an adaptive resolution of the crisis.

The question of optimal rate of development is complex. It is not simply a matter of pushing youngsters over a series of hurdles as expeditiously as possible. Our culture, on the contrary, generally favors a long period in which child and youth are encouraged to develop before taking up adult responsibilities. It is commonly assumed that, within vaguely defined limits, the longer the period of preparation the richer and more productive the adult life will be. We place a great value on four years of college because we assume that the readiness for experience built up in the college years will make all future events more meaningful and will increase the likelihood they will be met in ways that expand and develop the personality. We have little solid information about this. It is not hard to find college students whose lives support this assumption, but there are also many cases of college years that were wasted or constituted failures as preparation for life—as well as people who "found themselves" only long after college and attained extraordinary heights of development.

It is well to emphasize the distinction between arrests of development due to unconscious defensive reactions and failure to develop because of lack of challenge. In the first case a referral to a psychotherapist may be needed, but if development is arrested by lack of challenge, the college itself must supply the missing element. Surely we can afford to be deliberate about introducing young people to the major challenges of adult life, but there would be no advantage in this course unless the time gained by postponement were filled with experiences that develop the personality.

Out of adolescence

Now college students are generally considered "young adults" rather than late adolescents, but to grasp some of the challenges they face we must look back at the whole process of adolescence. In our culture, it is not an orderly process accomplished by defined *rites de passage*; it might more accurately be called a time of disorganization of the personality. Challenged by internal chemical changes and external social novelties, the adolescent is virtually lifted out of the culture that has been "ordinary" for him; he is no longer the tractable, pleasant schoolboy he was during latency, and to his parents he may seem unrecognizable or foreign. The remarkable thing is that after adolescence he will generally "re-enter"the culture in some way of life that parents will acknowledge as related to theirs.

What happens during adolescence has a strong effect on the precise way he does re-enter society. Adolescence is a time when great changes can be effected; the young person, in some degree, is given a chance to repair whatever ravages, small or large, childhood may have worked on him. He can escape the image of himself he formed when a child, can find a new way of relating to authority figures, can establish a new competence in his work. These changes are not discontinuous with his past; they will certainly bear some relation to his life history. But our personalities are not determined absolutely and forever from a very early age, as popularized Freudian theory has led so many to believe. Many students come to college and even more to graduate school already "knowing" Freud and never realizing how much they can change. They are usually delighted to be told how much living they have ahead of them, and they often undertake a serious bout of reading to choose the best direction for change.

Though a student's ability to change may be liberated or enhanced simply by informing him that the possibility exists, this practice is hardly sufficient as a college policy. Because young people are at a developmental stage concerned with the problems of identity and self-esteem, they are not yet ready to take full charge of their own development.

The teacher's role is not only to provide external, logical challenges to the opinions a student proffers in class, but also to turn the student's scrutiny inward in search of the sources of his beliefs. He ought to be encouraged to think (for example, in classes on history, politics, anthropology, economics, and sociology) how his character has been shaped by Western culture, by his social class, and by the town he came from. A teacher of literature may insist that his students understand fictional characters before judging them; this requires a student's ego to identify, at least for the purposes of understanding, with personalities quite alien to his—in short, to develop a measure of tolerance. Education is not psychotherapy, of course, and intellectualization is one of the commonest of defenses used by college students; but students can often achieve a measure of self-understanding that will further their development simply through using information brought to their attention in class or in reading.

Barriers to learning

Usually, however, unconscious processes are not so easily modified, and these barriers to learning frustrate many students: the girl unable to learn economics lest she entertain ideas that might threaten her special relationship with her father, the boy who cannot work in any subject because he fears that his achievement would give away his desire to get the better of his father, or the numerous students so taken up with problems of sexual morality or sexual accomplishment that they can hardly devote attention to anything else.

In the face of unconscious blocks such as these, what can the educator do? I do not suggest that all or even most students should have psychotherapy, but I could again draw attention to Lawrence Kubie's cogent argument that educators must find some way to lead students to "self-knowledge in depth" (Kubie, 1954). In his view, the college ought to take the opportunity to reduce the number of graduates who cut off their chances for fulfillment and who injure not only themselves but other people as well. Moreover, the college ought not to be satisfied with a system of higher education that permits its graduates to put skills and knowledge into the service of unconsciously determined and socially destructive ideologies.

But there are other uses of self-knowledge, apart from those concerned with unblocking learning or repairing the damaged personality. In the theory presented here, development occurs "in the presence of" readiness and challenge; the personality is not entirely dominated by unconscious processes, but is open in part to modification through experience. Knowing the potency of unconscious processes, the teacher is completely justified in devoting himself to the expansion of that part of the student's personality that is *not* dominated by them, on the assumption that as the consciously determined parts of the personality develop, the unconsciously determined parts will become relatively less important. We must learn to recognize those students whose unconscious processes can determine the whole course of their educational experience and will yield only to special therapeutic procedures; but in other students unconscious processes may be expected to wither on the vine as the conscious ego expands.

The ego expands in part through the normal processes of maturation. When a young woman has a baby of her own, for example, she can often understand her mother in a way she never did before. Her new role brings a new conception of herself and of her mother, so that the relationship between the two women is changed. The young woman is able to see and respond to her mother more as she really is and less on the basis of imagery acquired in childhood. Changes like this may reduce the need for repression of images or thoughts even as they require a cognitive reorganization of the interpersonal world.

Growth of imagination

Education can sometimes hasten these changes, and can also make available experiences that have the power to change but that would not be offered as part of the normal process of growing up in a given sub-culture. As in the example quoted above, in which a student may be required to understand a fictional character in a deep, personal way, these experiences often come to us by way of literature. In learning to appreciate *Portrait of the Artist as a Young Man*, *The Immoralist*, or *Man's Fate*, a student extends his human sympathies—or, on our terms, he both expands his impulse life and satisfies it through imagination. His unrepressed impulse system has become richer and fuller, and his ego has become more successful at gratifying impulse in acceptable ways. Thus, what may have been an unconscious impulse striving for gratification has become a part of that synthesis of personality achieved by a strong ego mediating the often conflicting demands of impulses and reality.

As we saw briefly in the last chapter, Freud described this relation between impulses and the imagination in his analysis of "the primary process": when an infant does not have a need gratified immediately—as happens most of the time—he quiets the drive-tension he feels by conjuring up an image of the thing he needs for gratification. This generation of images becomes gratifying in itself; and this fantasy is the source of later poetry, art, or other acts of creation. As he grows, the child obtains some mastery of the symbols of his culture and thus becomes able to participate in collective fantasies and to extend his range by learning what others have dreamed of. The power of reading and the process of education make this extension much greater than is possible in the relatively straightforward enculturation that takes place in simpler societies.

Through the imagination, the individual may expand and release his impulse life without jeopardizing the integration of his personality. By making the cultural world available to the child and teaching him how to use symbols, we enable him to perform all kinds of psychological functions that would be impossible if he were restricted to transactions with concrete things. Thus, education maintains and enhances psychological well-being: it gives adults expanded means by which to remain civilized while gratifying the infantile needs that are still very much with them, and which demand satisfaction.

In applying such a theory to formal education, we can proceed in two ways. One approach is to focus on some aspect of the individual, and to ask what conditions and processes favor, or hamper, his development. The other is to examine various features of the environment. In colleges and graduate schools these factors include the curriculum, methods of teaching, evaluation procedures, teacher-student relations, living arrangements, activities of administrative officers. For adults out in the community the sources of challenge are more diverse, and less easily identifiable; in either case, we should ask what each factor contributes, and how it might contribute more, to individual development.

As an example of the first approach, let us consider independence of thinking. No one will deny this is an important educational goal, but it is not immediately obvious how to achieve the necessary subtle interplay of cognitive or intellectual processes on the one hand and emotional or characterological ones on the other.

To ask how might we achieve independence of thinking is to return to a topic already raised in chapter 1: how might we overcome authoritarianism? It means at the very least that students will need the knowledge to resist dogma; they must have practice in criticism; they must have the self-esteem and confidence that will permit them to stand in opposition to pressures of authority and of the immediate social group; and they must have the awareness of themselves that will free them from the deeper sources of their prejudice. Thus, the development of independence is not just a matter of challenging students so that they are required to think or to become more aware of themselves; it depends upon a general climate of freedom in the university, and it depends upon the presence of some models of independent thinking.

Liberation from what?

Exactly what we should do depends on the stage of development the student is in. Most freshmen in most institutions are fairly authoritarian. If we give them the maximum of freedom right away we drive them into the arms of their peer culture, which is not very enlightened, or we force them to depend upon some authority because, by and large, most of our young people are not as yet prepared to make up their own minds about everything. If, with the aim of encouraging independence of thought, we were to put freshmen into a highly cosmopolitan, liberated kind of environment, many would leave in the first year because they needed some sort of regime to keep some of their anxiety at a moderate level.

This of course is somewhat less true today than it was formerly. All during the 1950's my colleagues and I talked mainly in terms of how to liberate students. In the 1960's we learned from studies of activists in the large cosmopolitan universities that this had already happened to many students. When the members of the "Free Speech Movement" in Berkeley were compared with students at large, the FSM students turned out to be different from the others in much the same way that seniors are different from freshmen (Katz, 1967). They could be regarded as having already reached a more advanced level of development than the average student. This means that the educational task for FSM members was rather different than for those who are still caught in authoritarianism. For the liberated students, encouragement of independent thinking depends more on freedom to take responsibility and make decisions than on support for self-esteem and help toward self-awareness.

Using the curriculum

In considering how the educational environment can influence development, let us use as our example the curriculum, which is that environment's central feature. Those of us who have been professionally concerned with personality development (or, more particularly, with trying to overcome the effects of past failures in development) have to be very explicit about the place of academic learning in our scheme of things. Otherwise, perhaps even so, we will be accused of trying to substitute mental health for educational goals, of trying to turn educational institutions into therapeutic communities, or otherwise to subvert their intellectual activities. Paul Braisted (in Rauschenbush, 1964) has stated the issue sharply:

"Recent discussion of the education of college students, in both professional and popular writing, is based on two largely unrelated assumptions. One reflects the concern of scholars and teachers with the acquisition of knowledge, methods of instruction, training and research. The other reflects the psychologist's preoccupation with the emotional aspects of personality. The first largely ignores the tremendous effect individual differences among students have on the way their studies are assimilated and used in their development. The second obscures the intellectual component of growth, largely ignoring the influence of the curriculum, and pays attention principally to personal relationships and activities outside the classroom."

This statement describes very well the polarization of opinion that occurred when a group of educators gathered at Vassar in the winter of 1962, to discuss *The American College* (Sanford, 1962). Although we had tried in that book to give the curriculum its due, we evidently had not gone far enough, or been clear enough, or induced enough people actually to read the book. Something of a climax of resistance to our point of view was reached when the president of a prominent women's college rose to denounce our supposed clinical preoccupations and said, "My husband always said that psychologists' children turn out worse than anybody else's." We had argued that what students studied was crucially important but that in order for a topic of study to contribute to individual development it had to seem meaningful to the student and that the first task of the teacher was to make subject matter "come alive."

"In praise of academic abandon"

In her book *The Student and His Studies*, Esther Raushenbush has performed the invaluable service of detailing how this actually takes place (Raushenbush, 1964). In 1962 and 1963 she visited several campuses in the United States talking to students "who had become involved, or engaged, in their intellectual life, so that it mattered seriously to them." She chose four students in particular and wrote detailed reports on their college years, drawing from conversations with each student, letters he wrote about his academic experiences, and papers he submitted for courses. Scott Hansen, for example, came to Harvard planning to study mathematics. His high-school mathematics teacher had inspired remarkable achievement in all her students, and Scott was put into an advanced placement section. But in his freshman year he also chose to take a freshman seminar in Social Relations, which required that students register concurrently in a humanities course.

"The most important thing about that seminar for Scott," Mrs. Raushenbush writes, "was that students' questions about important issues were treated as serious questions." By his sophomore year, Scott was majoring in Social Relations. An article appearing in the *Harvard Crimson* at the beginning of that year, "In Praise of Academic Abandon," urged the importance of rising above the demands of assignments and grades, and of reading widely, like a free man (Comstock, 1961). Scott felt this statement described "my relation to college, and I was delighted to learn that there were others like me around."

His personal concerns found expression in academic and other work. The issues of personal freedom and authority were raised by readings on Jewish education; papers on Jack Kerouac and on Huckleberry Finn encouraged his thought about alienation and commitment. He read a great deal in politics and history; he studied conscientious objection; joined Tocsin, the campus disarmament group; went on the Washington Peace March; thought about capital punishment and became exercised over the execution of Caryl Chessman. He wrote as follows about his work in his Social Relations tutorial:

"The first appearance of the political angle in my required work was the spring tutorial paper, on Hoover. Compare it to the fall term one on crime. I can see every difference in the world. Mainly, the emotional content permeating the crime paper has been drained from the latter one. It wasn't that I wasn't working on something personally important; rather, I'd shoved my personal conflicts enough to the side that I was concentrating on the objective situation, on Hoover and FDR as presidents."

At another time he commmented:

"The tutor thought the paper on alienation was too beautiful, too religious . . . too mystical . . . . He advised that I read some Hemingway or Dostoyevski. I don't know how much this lecture affected me. I resented it so much that I put away the notes I'd scribbled during it and completely forgot about it. On the other hand, I have very definitely moved in the direction he advised then. This may be due merely to the passage of time."

In his senior year, Scott petitioned to change his thesis topic from Freud to politics. His starting point was "the belief Orwell expressed in 1936, that socialism was the only possible effective enemy of fascism. Since it actually turned out to be a Tory, not a socialist, Great Britain that waged war so well against the Axis, we may presume that believing as Orwell did could engender a good deal of wasted political effort. I would like to know more about this kind of error of judgment." Mrs. Raushenbush summarizes the importance of this sort of education with reference, as it happens, to another student, who had been learning that "the important thing about one's relations to other men's ideas does not rest with knowing what they are, but what difference they make to the individual who discovers them."

Out of his conflict with authority

It seems safe to say that Scott Hansen's concern with the problem of freedom and authority grew out of his own conflict with authority. It appears that he was trying to resolve this conflict by studying and writing about education, crime, alienation, commitment, and conscientious objection, and by testing his ideas and beliefs in action, as in taking a position on the Chessman case. He was out to build a structure of values and beliefs supported by knowledge, consistent with his ideal self, and within which his personal conflict could disappear or become insignificant. Excitement was generated as he made discoveries that favored the success of his undertaking or as his developing scheme was threatened by facts or considerations that he had failed to take into account.

Systems of knowledge, belief, and value may be regarded as extensions of the self and, as such, they have the same kind of role in personality functioning as do other aspects of the self. Scott Hansen was sensitive to criticism of his paper on alienation. It was his paper, with something of himself in it; so he first responded defensively. But note also that in time he assimilated the criticism and began to incorporate it within his scheme of things—a definite developmental advance. His experience also shows us the opposite side of this coin: in a freshman seminar he discovered that his own ideas had value and were appreciated, and this boost to his self-esteem no doubt had some part in his deciding to change his major to the field represented by the appreciative professor—a definite step in his identity-formation. His experience illustrates the fact that when affect is invested in intellectual matters, the result is an advance in individual development.

What Ever Happened to Personality?

4

The man who probably did more than any other single individual to set the psychology of personality going was Gordon Allport. This he did mainly by his famous book called *Personality, A Psychological Interpretation* (Allport, 1937). It was some years after its publication before I realized that this book sets forth an ethical position as well as a theoretical one. When Allport stressed the wholeness and the uniqueness of the person, he meant not only that fragmented methods could never grasp the person, but also that a person's distinctive integration of his or her subsystems was itself a value. Allport embodied what he advocated. There was no separation between what he said and taught and what he was and did. He acted in the tradition of William James: deeply humane, democratic, and committed to the university ideals of trust, concern for students, tolerance, freedom, and truth. He even wrote like James.

A great trouble of the present time is that our society is failing to nurture or sustain people with the values of Gordon Allport. With this in mind, I want to discuss the decline of individualism in our society as a whole, and likewise the decline in attention to the individual person in various kinds of professional work and practice and in various other specific sectors of our national life. Then I want to show that this decline has been accompanied, perhaps even led, by a downgrading of the concept of the person in theoretical or scientific work and in the teaching that corresponds to it.

While this decline in the study of personality is due in part to the same massive social changes that are responsible for the tendency towards the disappearance of the individual, I want to suggest that scientists themselves have a heavy responsibility for some of the changes in society. (At any rate, it is now up to scientists to do something about these adverse trends.) The necessary steps must be based in very large part upon facts about personality development, and I will mention some concrete steps that can be taken immediately to help restore the individual to his rightful place at the center of our national life, and as the proper subject of research and teaching in social science.

All rolled into one

When I say we don't have enough men like Allport and other pioneers of personality study, I mean that in one sense the whole man, the man who acts as a whole rather than according to the demands of particular roles, is disappearing. I read recently a biography of Arthur Morgan, whom many will recall in connection with TVA, which was his idea, and perhaps in connection with Antioch College, which was also his idea. It never occurred to Morgan that one man should devote himself to producing ideas, another man to testing them in the laboratory, and yet another to "implementing" them in the larger society. He just assumed that the same man should do all these things. Like some others of his generation, Morgan was a scientist, politician, writer, all rolled into one. And in him these diverse functions were fully integrated. Nowadays, these functions are almost always separated, by people who define themselves primarily in terms of their roles.

In corporations, and other large organizations, the individual is often practically indistinguishable from his role. One result is that institutions or organizations may easily behave in ways which, in their effects, are immoral and damaging to society without any single individual in that organization feeling guilty about it or accountable for it. Things just happen.

People seem to vanish into roles not only in the middle ranks but in what are still called leadership positions. We see this, for example, in the college or university presidency. It's hard to remember the names of many presidents of such institutions nowadays, or, for that matter, presidents of any other type of large organization. What they are supposed to do is so well defined in advance that one president can be replaced by another without major changes in the functioning of an organization.

A standing ovation

In the matter of academic leadership young people have to be grateful for small favors. This was brought to mind when

President Pitzer at Stanford emerged as a kind of hero during a student protest against some of the activities of the Applied Electronics Laboratory which contributed to techniques used in the Viet Nam war. What Pitzer said was only what many of us would take for granted but it had so rarely been said by a man in a position of leadership that the faculty gave him a standing ovation and even the students felt that at last they had found an adult whom they could admire.

This same student protest, it seemed, led more than a few of the faculty at Stanford to the pleasant discovery that they had consciences. Their complicity in unworthy activities on the part of the university had not really bothered them until it was called to their attention by students. That they could now take a stand in favor of the traditional values of a university showed, I would say, that the "individual" in them was there all the time but had been rather submerged by corporate processes.

The neglect of students in our universities has its counterpart in the neglect of the individual in the practice of the health professions. No one is treated as a whole person anymore. We have all kinds of specialists who have charge of particular part-functions or organ-systems in which some ill can be located or is thought to be located and nobody, with the possible exception of the mother of a child, takes the responsibility for bringing together the contributions of these various specialists. Only the mother remains in a position to integrate, to see the significance for the particular child, of what the various specialists have to say.

Good enough for poor people

These changes in society, which I am calling a decline in individuality, have been accompanied by a downgrading of the concept of the person in science. After noting the social changes we must face the intellectual questions, "Whatever happened to the concept of a person?" or "Whatever happened to psychoanalysis?" When the Moynihan report on what was then called the Negro family pointed out that fatherless families were more common among blacks in America than among other segments of the population, and that being brought up in such a family is especially hard on boys and young men, some behavioristic psychologists objected to the very idea of digging into the past in trying to explain present behavior. They wanted to stress the existing situation and the need to change it, overlooking perhaps that the family structure described by

Moynihan was still part of that situation. Some social scientists seemed to take the position that as far as poor blacks are concerned, personality doesn't really matter, for everything depends on massive economic and social processes. In other words, sociological theories are good enough for poor people whereas personality theories are to be reserved for middle-class people. Some black leaders then seemed to say that if you accept the view that any structures are built into people by virtue of their upbringing, then you suggest that blacks are somehow to blame for any unconventional or deviant behavior they might show.

There is truth in all of these points of view, but the striking thing for me is the tendency to deprive poor people of their humanity by suggesting that, as far as they are concerned, character and personality do not really matter. We have little or no literature comparable to the work of Dickens or to the fiction of John Steinbeck in the 1930's in which poor people are presented in such a way that we can identify with them. Without the knowledge such literature can provide, this identification is difficult or impossible and, as a result, we are afraid of poor people. We suspect the worst, imagining that if we were in a similar situation we would behave very badly. In short, we tend to regard them as problems, out there. This is a serious obstacle in the way of dealing effectively with poverty in our society.

Embarrassed by soul

The scientific counterpart of this decline of individuality in our society is the tendency for the concept of the person to get lost between a psychology which deals more and more with part-functions of the person and a social science which is concerned with collectivities into which individuals naturally disappear. Actually, I think things began to change for the worse, in the way I am suggesting, when the concept of *soul* was abandoned. This is going back quite a way; but the loss of soul, I think, led to the fragmentation and neglect of the person in scientific work and to the professional impersonality that has accompanied it. For a time in the 1930's and 40's it looked as if the secular concept of personality would serve the kind of conceptual function that soul used to serve—it would stand for the wholeness and uniqueness of a person—but if you have been around psychology departments recently you know that graduate students today regard the concept of "personality" as hardly less embarrassing than that of "soul."

Upon receiving a reprint of an article about personality that I had written for the *Encyclopedia of the Social Sciences*, a colleague at the University of Michigan said, "Hey, so you're still writing about personality?" Did not all right-thinking psychologists know that this occupation had been all but abandoned?

Freud was "subjective"

It is unhappily the case that most theory of personality taught today was produced before 1950. A number of the men who produced that theory are still writing but in the main they are tidying up systems developed earlier. Psychological journals print very few studies which relate patterns of observed behavior to an inferred durable structure in the person. Psychoanalysis, of course, is hardly mentioned anymore, which in my view means that generations of students are being subjected to a kind of cultural deprivation. Quite recently a Stanford graduate student was reported to have said that he paid no attention to Freud and thought he could safely be ignored because his methods were "subjective."

Not surprisingly, then, it is rare to find today any big, complicated, exploratory studies of personality on the order of *The Authoritarian Personality*. Why haven't more studies of that sort been done? It used to be possible to start out with some vaguely formed ideas, make observations, and determine what to do tomorrow on the basis of what had been found today, and thus to permit a study to develop organically. Nowadays, you have to say in advance what you are going to do and what you will find out and, if you are proposing a program of extended research, you have to say what you are going to do this year and next year and the year after that. These requirements of the funding agencies are practically guaranteed to insure that nothing new will be found out about personality; yet it is not wholly fair to blame everything on "those fools in Washington," for it is one's own colleagues in psychology who have the power in government agencies that support psychological research.

I may be overstating the case. Some comprehensive studies aimed at discovery are still going on, and in particular, some psychologists are still producing personality theory. In quite recent decades people like George Klein, Jane Loevinger, Peter Madison, and Sylvan Tomkins have made significant contributions in this area.

For a while it seemed that humanistic psychology would

likewise become a major movement of discovery, and so I am disappointed, if not entirely surprised, that much of the work presented under this banner has shown signs of conceptual malnourishment. When I accepted an invitation to join a panel discussion at the 1968 meeting of the Society for Humanistic Psychology, I hoped to encounter Rollo May, Carl Rogers, Abraham Maslow, or some of the other old-timers who really stood for humanism in psychology. No such luck. I found myself in what turned out to be a vast encounter group. We on the panel were given only five minutes each, before discussion was thrown open to the audience of several hundred people. Whoever could get the floor, often more than one person at a time, spoke from the heart, making confessions, offering testimonials for the latest thing in psychotherapy, or just relieving their feelings. Rarely was there reference to what anyone else had said. One can appreciate the need for this sort of self-expression in the impersonal world of today, but I doubt that such all-too-humanistic psychology will do much to alter the trends in academic departments.

Up the social status scale

We may turn now to the neglect of the person in social science as distinct from psychology. The notion that personality does not really matter has been widely encouraged by the campaign of sociologists to establish their discipline as a science in its own right, with a body of laws about group behavior that do not depend in any way on psychology. We see this neglect of the person in the study not only of poverty, as I have suggested, but of organizations. Can all individual behavior be explained by social forces or institutional processes rather than by personality dispositions? Much of the individual's behavior is indeed shaped by the social structures in which he lives. The trouble is, I think, that too many social scientists have seemed to think that the thing to do about sociological laws is to obey them. When Lloyd Warner's studies of social status were on everybody's tongue, I remember asking a Warner enthusiast what would be the consequences for a sociologist or psychologist if he were to gain extensive knowledge about status and its enormous role in the determination of human behavior. "Well," he replied, "it would make him more effective at going up the social status scale." I think he was probably right.

If one says that individual traits don't matter and if one knows these sociological truths about the ways in which organizations work, then what is there to do but adapt oneself to them? If an individual trait such as courage is irrelevant, why should anyone take it upon himself to be courageous? It might be dangerous or costly.

We see this neglect of the individual and of human values in writings about universities by such important sociologists as Parsons, Lipset, and Glazer. The university seems to be conceived as part of nature which, even if not planned from on high, operates according to certain inexorable laws. According to this view anybody who would try to change the university must be either pathological or seriously misled. In other words, students should simply adapt themselves to this aspect of nature, rather than asking the universities to meet the needs of students.

Inhuman to be neutral

From a humanistic point of view, the question is how to prevent organizations from damaging individuals as they do. If organizations do overwhelm and determine individuals to the extent that social science says, then how can we arrange things in organizations so that individuals will nonetheless have a chance to express themselves and to develop themselves? There are important research questions here. When some colleagues and I were planning a study of the loss of idealism in social welfare systems, we focused initially on the question of whether social welfare workers become increasingly less individualized during their years of adaptation to life in agencies and, as this happens, take an increasingly negative view of their clients. But since it was already a commonplace that work in such organizations tends to be dehumanizing, we shifted to the question of how to arrange things in welfare agencies so that workers and clients are *not* dehumanized.

One of the most seriously dehumanizing tendencies in social science is to be found in the sort of writing which assumes that the course of history has already been determined and can be predicted accurately by an assiduous and neutral social science, and that anyone who opposes or fails to adapt himself to this course must be ignorant, counter-revolutionary or hopelessly idealistic. I am thinking, for example, of writings about the inevitable domination of our lives by technology, or how to survive after atomic war, and so on. My answer is that it is inhuman to be neutral about such matters and that those who pretend to be neutral have already adapted themselves to (or in some cases actually come to desire) the future they envision. To think about the future in that way is to help to bring it about. What we should do is think about futures that are desirable and ask ourselves how we can use our science in order to help ensure those futures.

My main argument is that the changes in psychological and social scientific work, changes in the realm of ideas, have had great impact upon actual practice, particularly in the helping professions and in education. If the person is fragmented conceptually in the psychology taught to future practitioners of the health professions, or to teachers, then naturally these professionals are more prepared to deal with particular functions or processes than with the person as a whole. And if, in theory, the person disappears into collective processes or social structures, then practice is naturally directed to those processes and structures without any particular attention to the person.

I would like now to mention briefly some apparent consequences, in other areas of our national life, of these changes in science and in ideas, starting with the devaluation of privacy, changes in sexual mores and in behavior respecting drugs, and some of the wilder phenomena to be found in recent "encounter groups."

Privacy is violated not only in all kinds of official record-keeping but in the practice of what is called the new honesty or openness. Everybody will agree, of course, that the individual is fundamentally a social being but it seems quite clear that some privacy or solitude is essential to personality development. It is basic to the establishing of boundaries between the self and the rest of the world, and it sustains the individual against society.

Quick solutions

When I say the new sexuality, I have in mind "the adult fun culture," the *Playboy* magazine "philosophy," the phenomenon of meaningless sexuality unrelated to any other processes or structures in the person. When people become alienated from their practices, whether by repression or by a disappearance of meaning, the practices are less enjoyable than in integrated relationships. The phenomenon is well exemplified in *Couples*, a John Updike novel with so little character development that it is hard to keep track of who belongs to which couple. The women, particularly, are distinguished from one another almost entirely on the basis of their explicitly sexual characteristics and behavior. Not related to the inward processes of a person, the sexual patterns cannot be understood as in any way expressive of character; instead they seem to accord with external definitions of what is the going thing in suburbia. Accordingly, it turns out that the characters are in no position to distinguish, for example, between heterosexual behavior that is homosexually determined and other kinds of heterosexual activity. This failure to deal in meaning robs the novel of realism and thus reduces it toward the level of pornography. Even if a type of suburban experience can be described only in this way, one expects something more than dehumanized sex from so gifted a writer, especially one able to portray so clearly the consequences when sex no longer expresses a variety of deep and complicated motives and feelings.

When it comes to drugs and some of the new group phenomena, we find overwhelming belief in quick solutions. We find practices which suggest the belief that people can be liberated right now, with appropriate stimuli, without any attention to what is there to be liberated. And we find the belief in instant friendship, apparently because there is no developed conception of the self, no conception of the complexity of the other person, or of what a durable relationship between persons actually means. Among the leaders of some religious groups are men who seem to conceive of personality as made up of two structures: an impulse system and a primitive conscience. Since the latter no longer recommends itself as the best guide to behavior, the alternative is to release the former as fully as possible and thereby attain to spirituality. These devaluations of our humanity would not be possible if the people involved had an adequate psychology of personality. In the same connection our population seems to have become less shrewd, even if more cynical, in its ability to judge people. You may recall William James' statement that the chief aim of education was to enable people to tell a good man. I have the impression that recent public judgments of people, particularly of political leaders, are often terribly wide of the mark; many people are unable to distinguish between the genuine and the phony. I put this down to a lack of education about people, the kind of education obtained through reading good literature or studying an adequate psychology of personality.

If not us, who?

Now, I have argued that the decline of individuality, neglect of the person in the helping professions and in education, loss of the value for privacy, and dehumanization in sexual mores and in the new drug and encounter group cultures, have all been encouraged or rationalized by the downgrading of the concept of the person in the social sciences; but even if the causal link were slight, I would say that within academic life it is up to those in the sciences to advocate actions that will build our humanity. They dominate the university, and there is really no one else to whom we can turn. Literary men tell us from time to time what we ought to do but they almost never tell us how to proceed. For knowledge of what we might do in order to further our humanity we must turn to the scientists of human development and of society. Who else will systematically explore the aspects of man which develop in interaction with the environment, the nature and normal causes of development, or practices in education that will further the kinds of development we desire?

In all of our work with persons we must deliberately regard the subjects of our research from the start as real, live persons who deserve to have a say about what is being done and need to understand how they can use what is being found out. Subjects of research are both influenced directly by what we do in the interests of our inquiry, and capable of further developing themselves through knowledge of what we find out about them. Research on students, for example, ought to be done largely by students themselves. They should participate in formulating the problems, in recruiting subjects, in collecting the data, and in helping with its analysis. We could, as a matter of fact, teach them best this way; and we could thus bring together what the university has too long separated, teaching and research. In social research, as I said earlier, the major direction for inquiry should be toward arranging social structures that favor the high goal of individual development.

If not here, where?

When it comes to practice, I suggest that we in the university begin at home instead of devoting ourselves solely to developing professionals who some day may be useful. Many of the great problems of social reconstruction are right in front of us. We could begin, for example, by making our departments into livable communities. If we know so much about how societies work, let us use this knowledge to make a good society of the university, which can then become a model. We would in this way advance our ultimate objectives and at the same time do what is best for the students who are with us now.

It is we ourselves who have to do these things. Perhaps some agency will offer us funds, perhaps some leadership will arise in Washington, but we must proceed regardless of what is supported or officially encouraged. Our NIMH study committees that sometimes seem so far off and powerful are in fact faithful reflections of the values that exist in the psychology department next door. Foundations, for their part, have the same ills, but not the moral and intellectual resources of the universities; they are looking for someone else, preferably some consensus, to tell them what to do. If you sent an application proposing to integrate teaching and research, or training and action, to one of the large foundations, they would be hard put to know what department to send it to, and would probably return it to you with the suggestion that you clear up your confusion. Foundations are out to make a name for themselves by exploiting other people's ideas and talents, not in general by having ideas of their own. The place to look is the university.

Our great advantage is that we have students with whom we can work as colleagues, as research subjects, and with whom we can carry on the business of research and teaching at the same time. With students present we are forced to think about what is good for people, to make proposals for action in their interest, and to mean what we say. Researchers without students might as well be some place else, where their ignorance about students would no longer act as a barrier in the way of the university's humanistic goals.

I have gone on rather grimly about the world in which we live today, about seemingly irreversible social trends, galloping technology and so on. I take all this very seriously, yet I cannot altogether suppress my optimism. This, I think, has much to do with the fact that as I try to uphold the values of personality development, I constantly find allies among the youth, and increasingly among older people who have come to regard adulthood not as a fixative but as a license for further stages of development.

Learning After College in Spite of It All

5 So far I have introduced the process of development mainly with examples from childhood (as in chapter 2) or college students (as in chapter 3), but now I want to move toward a practical theory of personality development over the course of the life cycle. Having sketched some of the obstacles (in chapter 4), I hope nonetheless to offer a general theory capable of assisting people of all ages in their self-development, and especially of sustaining the process throughout adult life.

I became keenly aware of the need for such theory in the 1950's when I was trying to understand what happened to the Vassar students as they went through college (Sanford, 1962). I relied not only on Murray and the older organismic theorists and on psychoanalytically oriented theorists such as Lawrence Kubie (1954), Robert White (1952), and Erik Erikson (1950), but on other orgasmic theorists such as Kurt Goldstein (1939) and Charlotte Bühler (1951), on gestalt psychologists such as Heinz Werner (1948) and Kurt Lewin (1935) and on general systems theorists, chiefly Bertalanffy (1943) and Boulding (1956).

During the Vassar study I began to envision college education largely as a matter of breaking up cognitive-emotional structures through challenges and new acquisitions, and then re-building, on a higher level of complexity, structures which embody both form and content. For example, in authoritarianism, a change in psychodynamic processes brings changes in cognitive functioning, and vice versa. And, since personality functions as a whole the fate of any given structure depends upon, and at the same time influences, what is happening in the rest of the personality. We observed that each Vassar student at any given time, was involved mainly in maintaining a structure, dismantling it, or building a new structure. As soon as this cycle was completed a new one began.

A great deal of research on human development has been carried out since then. I am thinking most particularly of work by Norma Haan (1969), Lawrence Kohlberg (1964, 1969), Jane Loevinger (1970), William Perry (1970), Daniel Levinson (1978), and others. My problem as I study this excellent work is, I suppose, a common one for adults who would further develop themselves: how can I keep abreast of the times and incorporate all the new and interesting things without really changing? How can I become more elaborated without any radical change in structure? Perhaps it is my inability to resolve this dilemma that has led me to conclude that the quantitative work of Kohlberg and of Loevinger has to be seen in a larger context.

Enthronement of the cognitive

Kohlberg's theory of cognitive development offers us a fine example of a holistic view, a total structure that changes as the individual passes from one stage of cognitive development to a higher one. With the changes in structure go changes in various specific intellectual functions. Why, then, does Kohlberg insist, contrary to the holistic view, that cognitive development is theoretically independent of the total organismic state, and that "cognitive development is a dialogue between the child's cognitive structures and the environment" (Kohlberg and Mayer, 1972)? Why not go on and say that changes in total organismic state may help induce changes in cognitive functioning, and that cognitive development is, in part, a dialogue between cognitive structures and other structures of the personality?

There are two tendencies at work here. One is the enthronement of the cognitive, the treatment of this part of the personality as if it were the whole or, at least, all that matters; and the other tendency, an expression of the most common style of psychological research, is the search for general laws (of perception, of learning, of violent behavior, of cognitive development) through abstracting a particular function from its personal context.

The belief that cognition is primary contradicts the traditional functionalist point of view in psychology (which holds that the cognitive processes of the person are in the service of his adaptive needs); theorists such as Kohlberg see cognition as a function in its own right which not only acts independently of motive but can determine what motives a person will have. This stress on cognition reflects a reaction over the past 25 years to the brief academic influence of psychodynamic, especially psychoanalytic, theory. This reaction has been successful: virtually all personality theorists today conceptualize cognitive variables of personality and, in their research, study the relations of these variables to other processes in the person. There are enthusiasts, however, like Kohlberg, who attach to cognition the kind of over-arching importance that psychodynamic theorists used to give to the Freudian wish, sometimes acting as if the cognitive part were the whole.

The enthronement of the cognitive, however, does not by itself account for the kind of anti-organismic stance that we see in Kohlberg. Like some others, he appears to believe that general laws are more likely to be found in the structural or formal aspects of the person, than in the content of needs, attitudes, values, and so forth. Similarly Milton Rokeach sought to reduce the complex phenomenon of authoritarianism—a pattern of deep-going needs, conflicts, defenses, and cognitive functions—to a relatively simple matter of cognitive style—"closed versus open-mindedness" (Rokeach, 1960). The same tendency appears in studies of violence which, apparently, seek to discover something basic while leaving out of account virtually everything that could give meaning to the behavior, such as the nature of the victim, how he is conceived, how violence is sanctioned and by whom. Questions such as these are considered not in mainline psychology but only in a few studies such as *Sanctions for Evil: Sources of Social Destructiveness* (Sanford and Comstock, 1970).

Vast and intricate architecture

However alluring the search for general laws in psychology, findings from the search are often worse than useless in practice. Moreover, the search is probably hopeless, at least if we accept, as I do, the organismic view of the person which Henry Murray has done so much to define and further. How can we isolate a single fragment for study if "personality is a vast and intricate architecture" (Kluckhorn and Murray, 1948)? Likewise, how can we hope to grasp, by dividing, what is "at all times an integral whole . . . whose constituent processes are functionally inseparable"; to rely on snapshots if "the life cycle must be taken as a unit" because the organism is its history (Murray, 1938)? In personality we have systems within systems, each expanding, becoming differentiated, becoming integrated with the others as it interacts with an environment which shapes and sustains it.

Over the years since 1938 this point of view has gained wide support, including that of such academic tigers as Raymond Cattell (1950) and David Krech (1951). In the words of Cattell,

"We do not deal with a 'perception' or an 'emotion' or a 'conditioned reflex,' but with an organism perceiving or acquiring a conditioned reflex as part of some large pattern or purpose.... it is a mistake to suppose that laws of learning, or of perception and emotion, can be found that do not take into account the total personality." Or as Krech once explained: "The kind of theory we are advocating is one which views all behavior within the context of the total organism. This is another way of saying that all the processes within the organism are 'adaptive'; each function or behavior serves an organismic purpose."

In what larger structure?

In the 1940's and 1950's, it was safe to say that all theories of personality were holistic theories, in the sense that they sought to relate consistent behavior to larger structures in the person. And the typical research project on personality was designed to test some hypothesis derived from such theory. It is no criticism of the theory to say that this kind of research has more or less gone out of fashion. Current styles are dictated mainly by practical considerations, such as funding and promotion, not to mention a persistent tendency of academic psychology to trivialize everything it touches. Although I see no hope for any immediate change in research styles, we may nonetheless be rescued by the demands of practice.

Practical theory must take account of the "intricate architecture" as well as the "vastness" of personality; it must in other words be holistic as well as comprehensive. If we are to help a person change some particular feature of his personality we have to know within what larger structures that feature is embedded. A person's aggressive behavior, for example, may flow from a diminished concept of himself. And if we set our sights on some larger or more deeply-based structure we have to find a point of leverage, some manageable part-function that has some determining effect upon the whole, as when the acquisition of a particular skill might improve ego functioning generally.

Acquisition of cognitive skills may have highly significant implications for the rest of the personality; but if I were seeking to improve cognitive functioning in an individual I would most certainly ask if his present style might not in some part be determined by anxiety, impulsivity, inner conflict, and so on. When my colleagues and I at the Wright Institute began to study graduate students, what do you suppose was the major characteristic of each new group of entering students—something which they pretty well got over by the time they earned their Ph.D.'s? You guessed it: authoritarianism or, more generally, a kind of "unfreedom" with respect to authority relations.

We must of course reckon with the fact that authoritarian behavior is in part at least a way of coping with a new situation, and that it tends to disappear as people become oriented and gain some sense of competence to deal with their present circumstances. But it stands to reason, and observation confirms, that the authoritarianism of the graduate student is not the same as that of the 13 year old; and neither is the status of qualities in opposition to authoritarianism: more openness to one's inner needs, more differentiated perceptions of other people, a more stable basis for self-esteem. One may hope that such features of the personality are on a firmer basis at 30 than at 13.

The same kind of issue is raised by Norbert Ralph's finding that some seniors at a private high school were higher on ego development—as measured by Loevinger's Sentence Completion Test (Loevinger and Wessler, 1970)—than some university professors (Ralph, 1971). The crisis in academia being what it is, perhaps the egos of these professors were wrestling with a wider range of importunate needs or more deeply-based conflicts demanding immediate resolution; for as psychoanalytic theory says, the strength of the ego at any given time is relative to the burdens placed upon it.

And what, we may ask, will be the fate of those 17-year-olds in one of Kohlberg's samples who had already zipped through all the stages of cognitive development (Kohlberg, 1969), or those college students in Hann, Smith, and Block's study who had already reached the highest stage of moral development (Hann, 1968)? Will they just sustain it? Will there be periods of regression, after which much of the developing will have to be done over again? And one may ask, too, whether indeed the attainment of the stages the next time round will have to be precisely in the invariant order Kohlberg has laid out.

To be sure, one can observe in adults something like the "mileposts" that Loevinger describes, the attainment of a structure that prepares the way for movement onto a higher level of development. Brown and Shukraft (1971), on the basis of our interviews with several hundred college and university professors, suggested that these adults must attain a sense of competence in their discipline before they can move on to self-discovery, and then to the discovery of others. This is reminiscent of what C. G. Jung (1933) has had to say about how people accent some of their functions, or some one side of their natures, while making their careers in the world and, having reached a place where there is no more to be done on that front, are finally able to allow other functions or aspects of themselves to come forward.

From one stage to another

Alongside the debate about holism runs the question about how people change from one state of personality development to the next, if we may speak of something as definite as stages at all. It is a bit difficult to think of adults as continuing to unfold according to a ground-plan of life, as in the embryological model, but there do seem to be stages of life, broadly defined, marked by events which are significant for development and which have some association with age (Neugarten, 1968; Peck, 1968; Lidz, 1968; Levinson, 1978).

Getting married, becoming fully committed to a career, having children, are generally linked to age; so are various events we ordinarily associate with middle-age, such as reaching a career plateau, recognizing that one is no longer a promising young man (as happened to Daniel Ellsberg, according to a CIA psychologist) and that the second half of life has begun, the aging of parents, the deaths of them and of friends, diminishing bodily vigor. These things, according to Levinson and his associates, occur very commonly in the lives of men in their early 40's and taken together add up to a crisis or turning point.

Erikson's theory of stages has been criticized by Loevinger (1970) for embracing both embryological and interactionist features, but to me this seems almost inevitable if the theorist bases himself upon clinical observations rather than on tests of abstracted features of the person.

Even if we say that stages, however complex, can be defined, it remains to ask about the practical usefulness of worrying about them, particularly where adults are concerned. There is something to be said for the older behaviorist view that almost any kind of change in behavior can be induced at almost any time provided we can identify and control the crucial stimuli; and that changes in behavior may set in motion developmental changes in personality. However, I prefer the notion, broached above, of challenges that break up structures and lead to restructuring on a higher level of complexity.

Challenge and insight

For practical purposes what we need most to know is what makes a given developmental change take place. I would argue that the ways in which development occurs can be boiled down to two: through challenge and through self-insight. Challenge means simply a situation which requires a new response, or at least a capacity for a new response, which amounts to an expansion of the personality, something which in time has to be integrated with the rest. I would say this process of integration is assisted, crucially, by self-insight. In the case of children and young people, the challenging stimuli are often brought to bear by the process of maturation, which may include some features of cognitive growth. At the same time, we must bear in mind that the normal processes of maturation can be distorted by various kinds of harmful and inappropriate stimuli. When it comes to the study of adults, we need to investigate what mileposts are yet to be passed, and what, on the average, are the major pressures and possibilities of the individual's current stage of life.

What makes it so difficult to get a close grip on the stages of development in adults (as well as in children and youth) is our old friend from chapter 2, the dynamic unconscious. Freud and Erikson have bravely set forth schemes to suggest the times when particular kinds of unconscious conflicts are likely to arise; but no scheme can predict fresh traumata which force something into the unconscious or, conversely, the easing of old repressions.

Recall the 45-year-old woman, who went to graduate school after having built a successful career and having raised three happy children, but who nevertheless structured her academic experience according to a basic pattern established as a child at home, with a talented mother who represented high standards but didn't understand her, and a father who understood but wasn't around very much. Fortunately, this woman was able to modify this unhappy structure during the course of work on her Ph.D. dissertation; but we can well imagine that had she not encountered this special set of circumstances she might still be struggling with this same pattern at 55 or later.

In this case how much of the development was caused by behavior change, how much by self-insight? Before challenging the very form of this question, I want to say that insight need not come only in bright flashes; it may be expressed in quite ordinary conscious functioning.

Yet I suppose the case of the 45-year-old woman could easily be used to illustrate the failure of insight. After years of analysis and immersion in clinical work, she had still experienced no change in the basic structure. Is it not instead a story about the difficulty of attaining insight into deep processes? The insight which finally did come, and which our student valued highly as a contribution to the wholeness of her personality, would not have been attained, I think, had she not left home and come to a different country, escaped from the network of relationships at the clinic where she worked, entered a situation that provided challenges and resisted the projection onto it of old patterns, and engaged in some new forms of behavior while continuing the work of self-analysis.

Nine quite general propositions

We now have enough background to consider a set of general propositions which serve as preparation for the rest of this book:

1. *For a change in personality to occur there must be a change in behavior.*

2. *A change in behavior depends upon the presence of an appropriate and effective challenge, one that is sufficient to upset equilibrium but not so extreme as to induce regression by surpassing the limits of the adaptive capacities we call ego strength.*

3. *In childhood and adolescence there are usually challenges in abundance but adults will ordinarily require a change in general situation—in the social roles, relationships, responsibilities, and reward systems that structure life and are, in effect, external barriers to development.*

In studies of college and university professors (Sanford, 1971; Freedman, 1973, 1980) my colleagues and I have been deeply impressed by the difficulty and rarity of significant changes in behavior as long as a professor lives and works in the same culture and social structure. Major change in an individual professor seems to require either a prior change in the culture and social system or an individual move to a different situation. I believe that the culture and social structure of an academic institution can be changed, albeit by somewhat heroic measures (Sanford, 1971), while changes in people who leave their academic positions are readily to be observed. Two more or less retired professors, a woman and a man, joined the staff of the

Institute for the Study of Human Problems at Stanford (Sanford, 1965) soon after its beginning and immediately began to take a new lease on life. Their gaiety, eagerness to learn, and capacity to find excitement in a new venture contrasted sharply with the grim, know-it-all coolness of the striving academics who surrounded us.

People no longer taken up with making a success in the world have a great deal of freedom: having little to prove, they can afford to take risks. And older people can be sure, too, that they have some developmental deficits, which can now be made up for. Old defensive structures, if they have not disappeared, are at least pretty brittle. Events such as physical changes and intimations of the approach of death provide opportunities to find new meanings.

Some of us were talking about this the other day and one of our students, aged 35, said "OK, I know plenty of swingers in their sixties, but how do I get from here to there?" What she seemed to have in mind was that, although the demands of family and career are often favorable to development and they seem appropriate enough for early and middle adulthood, she sensed other needs and potentialities that were not being expressed, and thus she experienced current responsibilities as barriers to development. However, she clearly recognized that further development is possible; which leads to the next point.

4. *Personality development requires the knowledge, or at least the implicit assumption, that one can develop.*

I remember from our studies at Stanford the amazement and excitement undergraduates felt as they learned that personalities were not forever fixed by infantile experiences or current group memberships. How much more difficult, as Jung has said, for adults in our culture to realize that the second half of life can be radically different from the first.

The 35 year-old student enrolled in my course in personality development while she was working on her dissertation. She said the chance to integrate cognitive theory with her psychoanalytic ideas was very important to the achievement of what she felt was intellectual clarification. It was my impression that she took some lessons from that course very much to heart, finding in our discussions of adult development much that she could apply directly toward the personality integration that she was attaining.

I won't argue that didactic work so formal as this is necessary to adult development or that, by itself, it is likely to have much effect on personality. Our culture puts a heavy value on youthfulness and assumes that the second half of life will be lived along lines laid down in the first. We have defined few respectable roles for old people.

5. *Freedom from external barriers to change, and the knowledge that change is possible, have to be supplemented by positive stimuli to action in order for significant change in behavior to occur.*

The retired professors who joined me at Stanford had not only freedom *from* but freedom *to*. New and interesting things were in fact going on, and their imaginations were captured. They could see opportunities for the use of their special capabilities; and they could see that not only their talents but their wisdom and experience were needed and valued.

Capacity to have experiences

6. *A challenge must be experienced as such, and it must be accepted, if it is to induce durable change in behavior.*

Much of our general knowledge about the succession of developments in personality is based on the fact that we learn from experience and on the possibility, within limits, of predicting when given experiences are likely to occur. But we have to reckon with the individual's capacity to *have* experiences. What the individual responds to is not the situation as such, but what W. I. Thomas (1951) called the subjective "definition of the situation" or what Murray (1938) saw as the "beta press" in contrast to the objective "alpha." If the individual is able to transform new situations into equivalents of what he has experienced before, change in behavior is not to be expected.

Various kinds of motives and cognitive dispositions enter into the determination of how the individual sees a situation. Looming large among them are unconscious processes. The activity of these processes can prevent the effects which we ordinarily expect to follow from the first four conditions described above. For example, an individual can make an objectively new situation familiar by projecting onto it deeply-based fantasies and cognitive structures. Or apparently potent stimuli may fail to strike a responsive chord because the needs to which they would naturally appeal are in conflict with conscience or self-concept and have been made unconscious. Or finally, unconscious needs in various subtle ways interfere directly with knowing, as when a person with a fine intellectual grasp of the possibilities for development in general resists any application of this knowledge to himself or herself.

Parts not dominated

Most commonly, however, the conditions favorable to development do touch parts of the person that are *not* dominated by unconscious processes and, accordingly, the person learns from experience. Moreover, the objective conditions that favor change in behavior also favor self-insight. If behavior changes one can hardly help noticing it; and until conscious effort has brought the new behavior into line with a suitable self-conception, the person will sense the disequilibrium. Arguing from holistic theory, I would say also that if a change in behavior induces change in a part of the personality this will have implications for the whole. If, for example, parts not dominated by unconscious processes expand, the relationship between what is conscious and what is unconscious will change; and the latter may either more readily become conscious, or dwindle in significance.

Nevertheless, a professional who would assist people with their self-development should be prepared to take unconscious processes into account. If we are ever to arrive at psychological laws that are truly general we must learn how to write unconscious dynamic processes into our theoretical formulations.

7. *Steps can be taken to prevent the projection onto new situations of psychological contents from the past, to overcome resistance to the assimilation of knowledge, and to assist consideration of alternative ways of behaving, and to connect new stimuli with inner needs and potentialities.*

The psychoanalyzed graduate student mentioned above was hardly alone in her tendency to structure her graduate school experience in accord with a childhood pattern of conceptions and behavior. Since graduate school offers such a natural stage for the reenactment of family dramas, professors must develop ways to resist being drawn into these dramas. One way, understandably enough, is to remain aloof and stick strictly to business, with the result that students complain about impersonality and inability to "get at" these professors. We cannot expect professors to behave like clinical psychologists, but when a teacher does permit a student to come close, understands the nature of the transference being made but does not accept it, does not get drawn into a fight, does not reject a student who is asking for trouble, he or she can make a deeply significant contribution to that student's development through providing an experience that "corrects" a childish pattern of interpersonal relations and thereby frees the student from it.

An approach of this kind can bring results not only for

undergraduates but for all those who wish to continue learning after college, whether in academic life or outside it. In all these settings we must deal with resistance to certain kinds of knowledge, and must find stimuli effective in assuring interest and moving the learner to fresh action. A teacher will naturally depend much less on techniques of individual therapy such as a psychologist would use, than on resources, often neglected, of the curriculum itself.

Behavior and insight

8. *Personality development in adults requires self-examination aimed at self-insight.*

I think I have shown (or perhaps I should say, have admitted) that great effort to bring about self-insight, as in full psychoanalytic treatment, may fail to bring about personality integration if there are not at the same time, or later, changes in the person's situation and behavior. Now I must add that no amount of situation, or behavior, changing will lead to personality development in adults unless accompanied by self-reflection.

This brings us to a tentative general formulation: *all* the above conditions and processes are necessary to bring about developmental change in the adult personality. Each must be present in at least some degree, although weakness in one may be compensated for by strength in the others. When development is seen in this way, the idea of fixed stages recedes in importance. Their presumed invariance may readily be disrupted by the bringing to bear of potent external stimuli or by the intrusion of unconscious processes.

9. *People develop together.* This holds at the interpersonal, organizational, and societal levels. When elements of one sort of relationship are projected onto a new one, the barriers (now largely internal) likewise are transferred. I have argued elsewhere (Sanford, 1971) that for people in intimate relationships, the development of one depends heavily upon the development of the other(s), whether for parent and child, husband and wife, psychotherapists and clients, teachers and students, or professors and their peers. In a marriage, for example, a wife may find herself unable to develop because her husband can conceive of her only as a child or as a mother.

In an organization such as a school or college, teachers can hardly develop themselves if behavior necessary to start the process goes against firmly established authority or against widely accepted group norms. In the whole society, as Heinz

Werner (1948) pointed out, the development of an individual is limited by the level of social development: in a simple, relatively undifferentiated society the individual who would become complex courts the dangers of deviance. Our society, highly differentiated as it is, must cope today with massive forces toward homogenization due to technology, and toward conformity due to political backwardness.

This general formulation of adult development raises problems for research, but we already know enough to undertake deliberate programs without awaiting the results. Such programs should be addressed to all of the conditions we have just examined, for each of them suggests actions that most adults will find interesting and worthwhile, and that are likely to contribute to personality development.

Research as an occasion for development

The possibilities of this approach were brought home to me by some work with adult women, work undertaken with other purposes in mind and not then conceptualized in the present terms. In the middle 1950's my colleagues and I in the study at Vassar College prevailed upon 50 alumnae of that institution to return to the campus for three days, in groups of 10, to take part in an assessment that would help us learn something about the lasting effects of a Vassar education (Freedman, 1962). Joined by a group of psychologists from the Institute of Personality Assessment and Research at Berkeley, we carried on much in the manner of the wartime pioneers in personality assessment from the Harvard Psychological Clinic (Office of Strategic Services, 1948). From time to time since then, beginning a few months after the assessment, I have heard from more than a few of the women that the three days at Vassar were a profoundly significant experience; for some it was a turning point in their lives, the beginning of courses of personal development in new directions.

In trying to explain how and why this happened I would say now that all of the nine conditions were present in some degree. The women got away from their usual rounds and responsibilities, at least for a little while; they were among strangers who had few expectations concerning them. In taking part in the various assessment procedures such as group tasks, improvisations, games, and directed discussion, they did things they had never done before; they tested themselves in various ways, and had a chance to see themselves as others saw them. Each of the alumnae had at least four interviews by as many different people, covering various aspects of her life. They were not offered interpretations in these research interviews but, as we were to learn later, they seized the opportunity for self-examination and stock-taking, and thereby increased their capacity for continuing self-examination.

Without being defined as incompetent

The most important thing, I believe, was that they had a fully legitimated chance to talk and think about themselves—with people who were objective, interested, and capable of understanding them—without having first to define themselves as ill, incompetent, or in trouble. They were encouraged to talk about their fantasies but not to act them out. The social arrangements for the assessment were, to say the least, unusual: the company consisted of 10 Vassar alumnae and a staff of 11 psychologists and psychiatrists which joined the women at breakfast, lunch, cocktails, dinner and late evening libations, but did not step out of their professional roles and so encourage projection or transference.

Naturally at that time and place we did not offer the women any lectures on the possibilities of development in the second half of life. But the idea was in the air. Since the whole setting was free of any "clinical" actions or expectations, at least as much attention was given to potentialities as to failings. The question "What are you going to do now?" hardly needed to be asked, and I am sure that many of the women got the idea that they could do more with their lives and with themselves. Almost all of those who came back to the college a few weeks later to "hear something of the results" had plans for interesting future activities, which we encouraged.

It would be worthwhile to compare this kind of experience with the various short-term group-psychotherapeutic or "growth" procedures currently in fashion. This is too large a subject to be gone into here; but I will say that all these short-term procedures ought to be evaluated in terms of the nine points set forth above.

For me the big problem about offering groups of adults the kind of experience the Vassar women had lies in how to bring them together without their first having defined themselves as "problems" or having permitted themselves too many great expectations. Perhaps in time the kind of practical theory I have been trying to develop here will find a place in general discussions of education and give rise to various developmental practices. For the time being, my inclination is to start as we did with the Vassar alumnae and as Daniel Levinson later did, by asking people to take part in a study of adult development and then, with the understanding and consent of those concerned, by allowing the research itself to become of a form of "action."

Somebody to talk objectively with

I would focus on activities that are good for almost everybody, not least on providing somebody to talk with. It has been dawning on me recently that not only college students and professors but ordinary people rarely have a chance to share confidences with anyone, to talk about things that really matter to them, to reveal themselves enough in a relationship so that they can get some sense of how they are perceived by others and so that important ideas and plans can be tested through being put into words. Such is the degree of alienation in our society that we have to invent special arrangements for providing what people who live in genuine communities have, and what we used to have, as a matter of course. When I speak of providing somebody to talk with, however, I have in mind something more than can be had from friends or relatives; I mean the assistance of professionals who can be objective and who can bring to their conversations a framework that goes beyond common sense. With their help, the individual is better able to see himself or herself in proper perspective, and to link the past with the present in the kind of stock-taking that prepares for the future.

And so I come back to the interviews for which there should be plenty of time. Along with the individual interviews, a development program might include group discussions, in which themes commonly touched on in the individual interviews are made the focus of attention. Later, perhaps, a program might present special challenges to its participants, or bring to the fore some of their long-buried defenses or strivings. Once the stage is properly set, I would not omit didactic materials on the problems and opportunities in aging or the discussion of practical arrangements.

At any old age

In conclusion, I want to stress that learning after college can occur not only into the middle years but, with the proper conditions, at any old age. But there are special things about adults in the late decades of life and I will mention one: old people, in our culture, are inhibited and unwanted philosophers. (Perhaps they are inhibited because philosophy is unwanted.) Development in the second half of life has been neglected, I believe, because psychologists who study development are a relatively young lot. Bursting with energy and bent on making careers for themselves, they carry out rigorous investigations, using as subjects the people closest to hand—children, students, and people like themselves. Older psychologists interested in development become philosophical about it, but they have no audience or vehicle for transmitting their ideas.

Yet development is very largely a philosophical problem. All along I have been assuming that development is a good thing, indeed an over-arching value, in part because the interrelated virtues that stand high in the great ethical systems depend on high levels of development. I have assumed, with John Dewey (1963), that what we do now for others or for ourselves ought to be evaluated not only according to the short-term satisfaction of all concerned but in the light of implications of present actions for future development, and for our culture as a whole. Am I on the right track? Let us ask the old ones. In imitation of those great cultures that relied and rely on the wisdom of the elders, let us set our older scholars and scientists to work on neglected questions of value.

Graduate
Education

A World We Have Lost

6

"They don't make them like that anymore." This cliche holds for graduate schools as well as for automobiles. But in the case of the former should we be sad, or glad, about the change? The graduate school of the 1930's certainly differed from that of today, but not many people in academic life would wish to reconstitute it just as it was. And even if a majority shared the wish, irreversible changes in the politics, economics, and technology of the society in which American graduate schools exist would bar any return to "the good old days." But even though many values of the pre-World War II graduate school are irretrievably lost, others might be recovered in new ways. If this were possible, which values would we reinstate and how would we go about it?

In approaching these questions I will describe some graduate schools of the 1930's, compare them with schools of today, attempt to account for some of the similarities and differences and, finally, ask how in the light of present knowledge we might take advantage of present conditions in our society to bring about some reforms.

The pre-World War II university will be exemplified by Harvard, where I was a graduate student, and Berkeley, where I began my career as a teacher. These institutions were not typical of all American universities but they certainly were prominent in setting the tone. In describing Harvard and Berkeley from the point of view of a member of their psychology departments, I will rely upon personal observations. Though personal, these observations are to some extent systematic, for I became a student of higher education and began to analyze my experiences while they were still fresh in my mind.

It is a little unsettling to realize that a person who taught in a university before World War II must now be at least 65 years old. Thus, the number of those who can give first hand accounts of the "old days" is small and dwindling. I take this as some justification for the following report of a participant-observer.

By the 1930's the basic structure of graduate education had been around for a long time. As we learned, the American graduate school was modelled after the German university of the 19th century and that, in its turn, still embodied many features of its medieval ancestors. At Harvard in 1930, we became aware of professional ranks, academic tenure, endowed chairs, and an aggregation of assistant professors whose fate was either "up or out." At the bottom of the heap were the teaching assistants, graduate students whose condition was not as bad as might be supposed, for like peons everywhere they could choose to commit only their labor, not their souls. Above them all stood departments, divisions, professional schools, whose chairmen and deans had power and were not afraid to use it. The admission of a student to the Graduate Division was on the recommendation of a department, and more were called than were chosen. To obtain the Ph.D. degree a student passed a comprehensive examination, acquired a reading knowledge of French and German, handed in a satisfactory dissertation, and survived a final oral examination. Degrees were granted once a year.

That's interesting

Certain values were widely shared among professors at Harvard, and it was taken for granted that graduate students would come to share them also. The most important expectation was that all hands should have strong intellectual interests. When scholars said to one another, "that's interesting," the reference, almost always, was to ideas, theoretical issues, or research findings that had significance within a theoretical framework, a point to which I return in chapter 9.

As for *what* a person was interested in there was a great diversity, and broad tolerance for it. The spirit of William James walked abroad. People remembered with what satisfaction he had said, after successfully recruiting a philosophical opponent, that now *all* points of view were represented in his department. Given this nurturance of diversity, based in the conviction that no pathway to the truth should be neglected, professors and students had to learn how to differ; they had to familiarize themselves with their opponents' positions and accord them respect, while forthrightly expressing their own views.

In the 1930's the Harvard Psychological Clinic was housed in a frame building some distance removed from Emerson Hall, the seat of the philosophy department, which included psychology. In chapter 9 I offer a memoir of the Clinic, but I ought to mention here that teaching as well as research and clinical work was done there, and under the leadership of Henry Murray it became a hotbed for deviant ideas. We studied Freud, Jung, Piaget and various other European psychologists, as well as the new dynamic psychology of Murray himself. Students developed strong loyalties to the Clinic and grew passionate about the ideas which distinguished it from Emerson Hall, which many of us tended to regard as enemy territory. I recall one student who had done his dissertation at the Clinic and who prepared for his oral examination in the department by mobilizing his aggression. Expecting to be attacked he spent his time planning offenses that would demolish the enemy. In the event, of course, he was treated with the utmost courtesy and fairness—even compassion. Totally unprepared for this, suspecting some sinister motive behind it, he became completely tongue-tied, flunked the examination, and had to wait a year before trying again, successfully. He had forgotten that the Emerson Hall faculty knew very well what Murray was doing, had in fact brought him in to do it, and regarded their theoretical differences with him as trivial compared with their shared opposition to outsiders who would hinder their civilized way of pursuing the truth.

The wholeness of psychology

An important aspect of truth-seeking, as it was seen at Harvard at the time, was that the "body of knowledge," once it became fully assembled, would be in some sense a whole. Thus the integration of the intellectual life was taken seriously. The setting up of a department of psychology separate from that of philosophy, which occurred at Harvard in the 1930's, was strongly opposed by many professors, who valued the wholeness of knowledge. Once they had won their independence, the professors of psychology worked hard at the integration of their own discipline, and at connecting it with others. The most senior professor taught the elementary course. He regarded it as his solemn duty to show beginners what the core ideas of psychology were, and how new developments could be related to them. This same professor taught the history of psychology to graduate students, going even further than in his elementary course to place contemporary interests and trends within the context of the history of thought. Since the idea of the wholeness of psychology was generally accepted by the faculty, it required only a small number of them to present the whole subject, and make graduate students into psychologists at home in many aspects of the profession.

Getting a job, however, was not the main idea. In the elementary course the professor considered it his duty to prevent students from going into psychology primarily as a profession. He was worried about the poor job market but even more, he was following the tradition of separating ideas and the scholarly life from the work-a-day world. He thought it wrong for students to go into psychology unless they were really caught up by its ideas; and it is safe to say that before World War II few did. Thus to my fellow students and me it seemed a remarkable piece of good fortune that institutions were willing to pay us for being psychologists when we would gladly have done so for nothing. We would have gone on doing what we did as students, earning a living by means of various odd jobs while indulging ourselves in the leisurely life of the scholar. Nobody complained about low academic salaries, for we simply accepted the idea that "psychic income" more than made up for economic deficiency. When I moved to Berkeley in 1940, for example, I was neither surprised nor put off to learn that the man who delivered milk at our door earned more than I did: both he and I took for granted that I was in all important ways better off.

Nevertheless professors at Harvard in the 1930's did worry about the economic survival of their students, both during their graduate school days and after they received their degrees. This was an expression of a general concern for students that had a firm place among faculty values. Students were perceived to be at the very center of the whole academic enterprise. However unpromising they might appear at first, the faculty persisted in the hope that they would become scholars and perpetuate the values of the university.

Highly motivated

Graduate students in psychology at Harvard in the 1930's did appear on superficial acquaintance to be a rather unpromising lot. It seemed to me that almost anybody who wanted to go to graduate school could do so, provided he or she was willing to "work one's way through." But the faculty may have been wiser than appeared, for almost all the students did have one thing going for them: they were highly motivated, by curiosity or a thirst for knowledge mixed with the hope that the study of psychology would help them resolve their philosophical dilemmas or solve their personal problems.

They expected to be put to work, and they never questioned the academic requirements. They accepted the 80 hour week of which their professors boasted. They responded to their professors' concern for them with trust—in the system as well as in individuals—and with deference. Never, until some time after a degree had been earned, did a student call a professor by his first name. (Professors, by and large, called each other and the students by their last names.)

Since the students saw themselves as being in the same boat, swept along in the current of rigorous (and fairly administered) requirements, competition among them was virtually unheard of, and many enduring friendships were formed. Since a majority of the students were unmarried they evolved something like fraternal life, with endless discussion of common problems and burning theoretical issues.

Although many students supported themselves by odd jobs there were a few research and teaching assistantships available. These were handed out, however, not on the basis of a student's economic need but on the basis of a judgment as to what would best serve the student's intellectual interests and development. At least that was the ideal the faculty tried to live up to.

Terms of community

As a general rule the faculty did live up to their ideals, often enough at any rate to maintain the respect and trust of the students. And the fact that students were disposed to look up to the faculty put pressure on them to maintain a reasonably high level of moral conduct. This interaction was possible because values were widely shared among students and faculty. Each of these groups could make effective demands of the other in the name of the common culture. The faculty, in other words, had genuine authority, which they owed primarily to their positions as carriers of values and which they could lose by failure to meet agreed standards of behavior. Students could accept this authority because they themselves felt accepted, and free to make their way in a working system.

Being a faculty member in this system was not easy, for it sometimes meant putting the demands of vocation ahead of needs for status, recognition and power. Conflicts in this sphere were managed by neurotic rather than psychopathic mechanisms: overt self-seeking at the expense of the shared values was "not done."

The psychology department was then very much a community. It was not, however, marked by displays of warmth or good fellowship. The assistant professors, after all, might not be around the following year and a given student might fail the oral examination. Like death and taxes, these unpleasant eventualities were regarded as facts of life.

Within the community, groups organized around philosophical or theoretical positions, and demonstrated solidarity against a common enemy. Since this kind of thing had to be kept within the bounds of civility, there was tenseness. Yet, as late as 1947, the psychology department had a party in which the faculty were satirized in skits by the students, who relished this reminder that professors owed the deference they received in part to their positions rather than wholly to their special qualities as persons.

Become like us

One may ask in how far that department, and the university which included it, owed its cohesion to homogeneity and exclusiveness. It seems obvious that an institution that makes intellectual curiosity its central value is not for everybody. (And I always felt as a student that a university that could take me in was in no way exclusive.) I remember a senior professor of psychology who seemed somehow outside. He had published several ponderous volumes which nobody seemed to have read, and he rarely showed up at Colloquium. There were rumors that the chairman of the department did not like him. He looked more like a businessman than like an academic. Was he too practical, or worldly, or not from a "good college"? Whatever the facts of the matter, I was given the impression that for Harvard some people were "not quite the type."

A faint odor of anti-Semitism persisted at Harvard, expressed mainly in the form of efforts to deny it. And many faculty seemed to fear that Harvard, like other institutions in the area, would sooner or later be overwhelmed by the Boston Irish. In the 1930's Irish youth were arriving at Harvard in increasing numbers; and they were not without good reasons in behaving there as if it were an enemy country. Blacks, Spanish-speaking Americans, native Americans were nowhere to be seen, nor did anyone note their absence. Women on the other hand had already become prominent in psychology, and a small number of them were doing graduate work in this field at Harvard. The tradition that women who became professors would remain unmarried was gradually breaking down. A married woman, the mother of three and an ardent feminist, took her degree at the Harvard Psychological Clinic the same year that I did. Owing to the personality and outlook of Henry Murray, the Clinic was an androgynous society. In psychology generally, however, no effort was made either to recruit or to exclude women. In spite of some male cultism, the university was by no means as masculine either in spirit or in composition as it was later to become. In sum, Harvard in the 1930's was characterized by that form of ethnocentrism which says "we'll accept anybody who will become like us." White women of the college-going class were not systematically discriminated against. To most members of the oppressed ethnic minorities outside the university the idea of being assimilated by a culture like that of Harvard never occurred. Had the issue been drawn, doubt would probably have been expressed that members of various ethnic minorities *could* "become like us."

During the 1930's and up to the middle 1940's, the University of California at Berkeley had the same structure and essentially the same system of values as Harvard. Differences in culture seemed to be mainly an expression of the Western as opposed to the New England outlook and style. Berkeley had more informality, good fellowship, democracy, and department-wide social life. Still, most Berkeley professors had been born and trained in the East, and much of the Ivy League academic culture still clung to them. They were strong on academic freedom—and they could be seen not infrequently at black-tie dinners.

Academic values in another place

Berkeley also had greater differentiation of roles within the psychology department. Some professors published a lot of original work and were responsible for the national (and international) visibility of the department, others served as critics and teachers, while still others were best known as counselors and teachers of students. Thus, that department more nearly approached the ideal of a human community. Berkeley also had more humane personnel policies. Almost all graduate students, many of whom showed no extraordinary abilities, were eventually seen through to the Ph.D. And most assistant professors were eventually promoted. It was not until 1947 that the first assistant professor ever hired by the psychology department was "out" instead of "up."

In Berkeley there was greater diversity in the student body —with respect to social class as well as sex and ethnic background. The Psychology Department turned out its first black Ph.D. in the 1930's, and at that time almost a third of the faculty were women, who more than held their own in the department councils.

In comparing Berkeley with Harvard we are not only comparing a Western with an Eastern university but a public with a private one; and, what was certainly significant for its humane personnel policies, a university in an expanding economy (for much of the time) as compared with one in economic depression. In this light it is striking that the traditional university values were sustained as well at one place as at the other.

The structure of graduate education seems to have changed hardly at all since the 1930's. Perhaps there has been some loosening up of requirements, such as requiring only one foreign language instead of two and permitting students to take their degrees when ready instead of only once a year, but in general the structure has been remarkably durable.

What has changed are the purposes for which the structure is used and the spirit with which it is managed. The motives of professors and graduate students are less purely intellectual and more professional. The academic man or woman is less often taken up with satisfying curiosity than with gaining recognition in his or her professional field, less concerned with deepening human understanding than with enhancing the status and power of a chosen discipline. This means that problems are defined and inquiries conducted less often in accord with natural curiosity and more often on the basis of what can be researched by existing methods, what will fill a gap in knowledge as conceptualized in the terms of a subspecialty, or even what is fashionable.

With increased loyalty to disciplines goes decreased tolerance of diversity within them. When it comes to the question of who is to say what the discipline is, differences often become polarized. And they become politicized, in the sense that they are made the basis for seeking money and power: civility tends to go by the boards. In place of open discussion of important differences, we find the withdrawal of department members into like-minded groups which have little to say to each other.

In these circumstances efforts at integrating the intellectual life of the department or the university are reduced from everyday practice to embarrassed rhetoric. Success in a discipline requires specialization; and successful professors, even assistant professors who promise to be successful, are permitted to teach their specialties. Hence the curriculum proliferates, and since money and power go to the specialties, no one with the necessary authority remains to undertake integration.

Struggle of all against all

The general climate of today is one of competitiveness among universities, between departments in a given university, and between sub-groups and individuals within the same department. Students are regarded less as potential intellectual leaders, and more as resources to be used in professorial struggles for a place in the sun.

Students for their part, come from a greater diversity of backgrounds than before, and have a greater variety of motives for going to graduate school. During the 1950's and 1960's the economic benefits of the Ph.D. became very clear. We began to receive a flood of applications to graduate school. The students we accepted engaged in an unrelenting contest for grades and for good evaluations, thought to be required for the best job opportunities. Thirst for knowledge is not absent, at least not at the beginning of the graduate career, but most students focus sharply on preparation for a fairly well-conceived professional role. Naturally enough, student community, mutual help, and friendship all declined.

Student-faculty relations also deteriorated. If faculty see students as resources and students see faculty as gatekeepers, then it follows that not much love is lost between them. Students no longer showed the kind of faith in the faculty that was common in the 1930's. With considerable accuracy students began to perceive the degree to which faculty were out for themselves. While some still found professors who supported them in a genuine quest for knowledge, many adapted themselves cynically to what was, after all, the only game in town; and many others became disillusioned and withdrew.

But not all is so grim. The modern multiversity may look bad to some people on the inside, particularly to old-timers with nostalgia for "the good old days," but more and more people have "wanted in," and have got in. World War II led to a movement toward the liberation of hitherto suppressed minorities, and their rising expectations helped to swell the ranks of those going to college. Once in college these first-generation college-goers could see the advantages of graduate school and, despite the resistance of those who run our universities, most graduate departments and schools today can boast of at least a sprinkling of "third world" students. The ethnic and sexual mixes on many campuses today may be regarded as a triumph of democracy. And the presence in the university of such a diversity of people has created a force for more democratic governance, and produced some significant achievements in this area.

The overwhelming demand for what the university has to offer has led to enormous increases in faculty salaries, without this preventing professors from doing just about what they please.

During the twenty-five years following the end of World War II the university (particularly its graduate and professional schools) sought to maintain its structure and culture while responding to massive social changes. These changes have led to almost overwhelming demands upon the university, most notably to demands that it help to meet various economic, military, and health and welfare needs of the nation, and to demands that more and more people be given a chance to participate in the good life as depicted in the romanticized version of the liberal arts college.

Both of these demands arose in considerable part from the success of the pre-World War II university, which not only presented an attractive picture of a way to live but showed that it was prepared to make important contributions to the prosecution of the war.

After the war the federal government, the states, and the private foundations began pouring money into the universities. Research and advanced training were expected to raise the standard of living, to improve health and welfare, to keep us safe from attack by foreign powers. Great faith was placed in the analytical methods of science, which seemed to deserve most of the credit for our great advances in technology. These advances helped to spread the idea that one had to go to college in order to obtain a good job, and that a good way to attain status and power was to go to graduate school and so find a place in the "knowledge industry." Parents, firm as always in their belief that children and young people should be useful, were more than willing to foot the bills.

The softer the money the harder the noses

The university responded to the new demands upon it in the way that the federal government responds to demands from the populace: by adding programs on top of those already in operation while effectively resisting any fundamental change in structure. Many entrenched professors assumed that the new institutes, training programs and so forth would go away as soon as the "soft money" gave out. But the money kept on coming and professors in psychology and the social sciences busied themselves in gaining control of its distribution. Thus they were able to use funds intended for new programs or for the improvement of existing ones to do what they had wanted to do all along, to strengthen the academic guilds through departmentalism, proliferation of specialized courses, and imitation of the successful natural sciences.

The influx of federal funds for research the government wanted done was strongly opposed by some humanities professors at Berkeley who retained the values of the pre-War university. But then, as now, it was hard for a university to turn down money. Visions of overhead danced in the heads of professors as well as administrators. Although humanities professors did succeed in blocking some new ventures in social science, they could not prevent the establishment of the Radiation Laboratory.

By 1950, programs such as the "Rad Lab" had become well institutionalized, and they were given a great boost by the orbiting of Sputnik in 1957. Administration expanded to meet the available overhead. In thus entering the marketplace and competing for grants and contracts to do research desired by government agencies and large corporations, the university imitated the ways of business and military organizations. Professors in large numbers became grantsmen and operators within large bureaucratic structures. Even the pretenses of moral leadership were abandoned. As the values of competitiveness, toughness in dealings with others, hard-nosedness in research, and efficiency in production gained the ascendancy, the university became increasingly masculinized, first in its spirit and then in its membership. The proportion of women in academic positions actually declined during the 1940's and 1950's.

If this new multiversity culture was not cordial toward women it was downright inhospitable to students identified with the ethnic minorities. With the university of the 1930's, it seemed to be saying, "we'll take anyone who will be just like us," but for women and minority students, the costs of undergoing this acculturation, in terms of selfhood and identity, were great. In time many, perhaps most, students came to see that the university's great pre-occupation with the market, with the production of knowledge that could be paid for, had led to the serious neglect of their interests. What was felt by women and minority students as social discrimination was in fact neglect of the needs of most students. The disappointment and frustration to which this neglect led, and the disenchantment with established authority which followed upon the escalation of the Viet Nam War, were enough to provoke the student protests of the 1960's.

After disenchantment, what?

Ironically enough, the university's efforts to meet outside demands for research and service has not done much, as far as the ordinary citizen can see, to meet the real problems of society. In spite of much talk about "the knowledge explosion" its most spectacular advances have been in techniques for keeping some people alive a bit longer, and for killing or threatening to kill others. Distrust of the knowledge industry has been growing apace: George Wallace got his biggest response when he spoke of "throwing the intellectual's briefcases in the Potomac river."

In part because of public disenchantment with higher education, in part because of economic hard times, the years of multiversity expansiveness are over; and the values that supplanted those of the pre-war university are themselves thrown into question. The times call for a fresh examination of the goals and structures of graduate education.

There is no going back to the "elitist" university of the 1930's, as we began by saying. Yet it seems clear that some of its values, such as intellectual passion, tolerance, and concern for students, are fundamental to any good society. Can they be revived under present conditions of expanded democracy and academic entrepreneurship? Can we have both quality and equality, both leisure and involvement in the problems of society?

It may be possible to take advantage of the present phase of retrenchment to move toward some needed reconstruction (Comstock, 1974). Since it is now clear that going to college is no guarantee of a job, and that advanced degrees are no guarantee of bigger jobs, it may be possible to revive interest in more fundamental goals of education. If the primary goal of education is not to earn a living and to go up in the world, then what is it? There are various goals, honored at various times in the past and still capable of revival today: to enjoy life, to be a good citizen, to contribute to society by means other than paid work—goals which belong together in the sense that they are reached by developing each individual's potentialities as fully as possible. These goals were very much in view during the years of the Great Depression. Why not now? They are as meaningful to the poor and the oppressed as to anybody else. Perhaps more so; for these citizens still find hope and inspiration in the most traditional democratic ideals, while to them the "Protestant work ethic"—so important to an industrializing elite—is of no more than marginal relevance.

The suppression of interest in goals of development has been responsible for much of the grimness of graduate school. It ought to be possible, at a time when the problem of numbers of students is not so great, to provide for careers in graduate school that are broadening and humanizing, and in the course of which students learn a variety of skills and values needed for intellectual leadership. Such a career would serve society as well as the student better than the present socialization in narrowly conceived disciplines.

If the university is to continue responding to the demands of the real world it should, while being realistic, make a greater effort to conduct itself in accord with democratic values. No one will deny that the great resources of the university ought to be brought to bear upon the great human and social problems of our society. But if this is to be done at public expense it ought to serve the interests of all the public. By giving first attention to the interests of those who can pay for its services it tends inevitably to shore up the status quo.

A peculiar incompetence

In offering services to the federal government and the corporations, the university has oversold itself. Professors bring a peculiar incompetence to the world of affairs, tending simply to carry over formulae derived from the laboratory or from a theoretical scheme belonging to a single discipline. The trouble is that the formulae never quite fit the concrete case. Managers cannot make day-to-day decisions on the basis of organizational theory nor can classroom teachers make much use of what they are taught in schools of education. It is not that the formulae are wrong, for they can be shown to hold in a general way, or when specified conditions are present; it is rather that they are not adequate to the complexity of the real situations to which they are applied. Too many relevant factors are left out of account, too many relationships ignored; and, what is perhaps most common, too big a gap often remains between abstractly conceived and mathematically manipulable variables and the real processes they are supposed to embody, as when "body count" is used to stand for the fact that people are being killed, or when "behavior" is substituted for experience.

If professors are to contribute to the solution of our great human and social problems they must find new ways of coming to grips with them. "Applied science" (as it is usually conceived) won't do. Instead of generating some knowledge in the laboratory and then looking around for some way to apply it, professors should organize inquiry around the problems themselves, observe them at first hand, participate in the more precise definition of them, and ask what actions would have desirable effects without producing too many undesirable ones. Once we recognize that problems are complex and interconnected, we must also accept that solutions require attention to facts and principles of various disciplines, and that action can almost never wait until all the facts are in. This kind of problem-oriented inquiry would be very attractive to many graduate students.

Rigor and compassion

The trouble with disciplines now is that they have been corrupted and misused, adapted to the needs of faculty or to those of a few powerful clients, rather than to the needs of students and of society. The task is to reduce disciplinary parochialism; which derives from the need of faculty to identify themselves with their disciplines in the pursuit of advancement in their careers. Here we may look again at the pre-war university where, in less stressful times, deep intellectual involvement with problems defined in disciplinary terms was common, and where there was community with people similarly involved in other disciplines.

We must be careful, of course, not to mistake the mere form and rhetoric of pure inquiry for the genuine article. As most graduate students know, and others are learning fast, professors are capable of using these forms and this rhetoric to shore up the whole system of departmentalism and careerism, to make the most trivial research seem important, to put down colleagues and students, and to exclude from academia people better than themselves. There are some tests by which the genuine can be detected. Its distinguishing feature is purity of motive. The great motive is curiosity, which brings the excitement of the quest for knowledge and the hope of knowing the joy of discovery. Is it the case that when a professor gets up in morning he or she can hardly wait to get to the lab, the library, the field? That he or she makes no sharp distinction between work and leisure or play? Would the professor behave in the same inquiring way in less comfortable circumstances, such as having a heavier teaching load or being a member of a less highly rated institution?

Another way of making the judgment is to examine the context of attitudes and values within which academic activity takes place. The spirit of true inquiry is conveyed not by the use of any particular method or by protestations of seriousness and rigor, least of all by arrogance; it is conveyed rather by a set of capacities which rest upon character as well as trained intelligence and are to be found only in highly developed individuals. Is the professor able to risk much in the service of an hypothesis while admitting that he might be wrong, to hold firmly to certain views while respecting different ones? Unless these values prevail, truth cannot be found.

Training in a setting where these values are dominant is surely the best way to promote the intellectual and moral development of students. Most graduate students aspire to become, and are capable of becoming, genuine scientists or scholars. They want to be shown the way. Their greatest need is for exemplars. The creation and maintenance of settings in which such exemplars are plentiful is the great task for the future. But the university of the future cannot and should not be sequestered or aloof: not only graduate students but the momentous practical problems of our times require well-developed adults who have been imbued with the values just described. Professors with these values would respond to demands for service to outside agencies and interest groups, which are usually no more than requests for engineering skills, by first examining the terms in which the "problem" has been defined and the priorities set. This kind of involvement with practical problems, far from downgrading the intellectual values of the university, poses the greatest challenge to the mind and spirit, for it requires that things be seen in their whole context, and that rigor go arm and arm with compassion.

Out of the Masculine Wilderness

7

When affirmative action seems about to bring more women faculty to university campuses, we begin to hear rumblings of uneasiness among male faculty who firmly believe that hiring women will mean lowering their standards; who just don't want to work with women; or who simply fear that their tweedy, pipe-smoking male preserve will never be the same. It won't. But just how will it be different? What are the sources of the fear and hostility male professors may sometimes feel towards women? And what might become of these feelings if women were integrated into the university? With these issues in mind, I would like to examine two educational settings in which women and men are equal in numbers, and more so than usual in status and power. The only places I know at first hand that approach this situation are The Wright Institute Graduate School in Berkeley and the California School of Professional Psychology in San Francisco. These two schools have been stumbling out of the "masculine wilderness" of higher education. They make one realize all the more strongly that had the modern university been as much in the hands of women as in the hands of men, or had it been guided by a conception of the shared destiny of women and men, its structure and functioning would have been very different from what it is today.

The Wright Institute is an independent, multi-disciplinary, problem-oriented organization primarily concerned with action-research on human problems. Early in May, 1969, less than a year after the Institute was incorporated, Mervin Freedman proposed to me that we start a training program, at the Ph.D. level, in clinical psychology. I agreed, and the program was begun about 20 weeks later.

Uppermost in Freedman's mind were the facts that Stanford had abandoned clinical training, and the University of California at Berkeley was admitting only five clinical students a year; that the situation in the Bay Area reflected a national trend as psychology departments pressed toward "scientific purity" despite rising demands for clinical training and clinical services; and that in consequence many highly qualified college graduates who wanted clinical training had no place to go. I had primarily in mind the production of what I call "problem-oriented generalists," and David Krech calls "clinicians to society", but I saw that if we defined our program as "*social*-clinical psychology" we could bring in much that was worth teaching about society and about the person, and still allow our students the practical advantage of being able to call themselves psychologists.

Feasibility studies

Freedman and I toyed briefly with the idea of a period of planning—a "planning grant" is always nice—but we decided we had better start the program at once and plan it later, after the students had arrived. Accordingly, I telephoned 15 kindred spirits. In the course of a few meetings, we worked out the economics of the program on the back of an old envelope, prepared a brochure for distribution in the Bay Area and among our friends nationally, and soon were faced with the pleasant task of interviewing an extraordinary variety of talented applicants to the program. Instead of attending primarily to courses and grades in psychology and the reputation of a student's undergraduate institution, we looked for signs of a good general education; we were particularly interested in students who were changing to social-clinical psychology after having tried something else and in students who had seen something of life. And naturally we looked for curiosity about people, self-awareness, and the capacity for humane feeling. As soon as a person was admitted he or she assisted with the interviewing and selecting. We took 13 students that first autumn.

The California School of Professional Psychology was another response to the increasing demands for clinical psychology and the increasing unfriendliness of university departments toward clinical work. The development of this school has been the work of the California State Psychological Association, whose members for several years had discussed the idea and the plan for the school at innumerable meetings, and in over 40 printed articles, before opening its doors to students. With a staff volunteering their services, the CSPP was opened in the fall of 1970.

The brochure for our school, and other written material available to students, put the emphasis on training for research and action on human problems, and on the interaction of individual and social processes. Understanding of this interaction, and integration of theory and practice, were to be achieved largely through field work, begun in the first quarter of the students' first year, and through seminars organized around field problems. Paid employment for students on the Institute's own research projects was to be arranged whenever possible. A wide range of Ph.D. dissertation topics was not only allowed but encouraged; in place of the usual overconcentration on experimental studies we encouraged research based on case studies, participant observation, and theoretical work. At the same time students would learn a common core of psychology and acquire the usual clinical skills.

Influence of students

Before the first year had ended, by which time the students numbered 21, we had full student participation in the running of the school. All policy decisions were being made by consensus of those present at meetings of the student-chaired Executive Committee. We had individual learning contracts and humanistic administration in contrast to the usual mechanical theory of management. The young woman who ran the school office approached decisions, of which she soon made hundreds, with first attention to the people concerned—those who should be consulted, those who had a direct interest in the matter, those who would expect to be notified in advance, those who would have to be placated—rather than to existing policy, or rules, or abstract principles, or the demands of efficiency. This has been crucially important to such success as we have had.

The CSPP began with a carefully planned and highly structured curriculum, one designed to give full coverage to the content of professional psychology. I know this program only as a visitor, not through any official connection with it. At the beginning theirs was a six-year program (three trimesters a year) leading from college freshman to Ph.D., which means that they took responsibility for providing students in the first three years with humanistic studies as well as psychology. Field studies, coordinated with classroom work, were required from the first year. When I visited the San Francisco campus of this school, students expressed great satisfaction about their power to change the curriculum. They had a sense of adequate participation in the school's government, although their responsibilities in this respect were not nearly so great as those of students at The Wright Institute. As a matter of principle the CSPP employed only part-time faculty, and all core faculty members were paid at the same rate. At The Wright Institute teachers were at first paid by unit of instruction, all at the same rate, but we later developed a core faculty.

Both schools have heavy admixtures of women students: as of 1972, half of our students, and 40% of those at CSPP, were women. By comparison, of all graduate students nationally one in ten were women. The proportion of women in the Psychology Department at Stanford had only recently climbed to 25%; and at Berkeley only a third were women. The faculties at our school and at the CSPP likewise had a larger than usual proportion of women, about 40%. Administration was another story. The President, the Dean, and the Associate Dean of the Wright Institute School were men; and so were the President, the Deans, and three out of four Assistant Deans at CSPP. It will take a little research to find out whether the high proportions of women students had more to do with the large number of women who applied or with a trend in selection from among applicants. Very probably both of these factors have been at work.

Attractive to women

I shall argue that the programs of these two schools as well as their egalitarian structures were from the beginning particularly attractive to women, and that the attraction increased as the numbers of male and female students approached equality. At The Wright Institute we made no particular effort to recruit women students during the first two years of the school's life; our concern was to find the best qualified people. After three years, it was pretty well understood that a "balance" with respect to sex is a good thing.

Both of these schools, when compared with university departments I have known, have been happy communities: the atmospheres relaxed and informal, people open with one another, concern with status minimal.

Women seem to thrive in these schools. There seems to be no sex differentiation with respect to the kind of field study undertaken or dissertations planned. In some kinds of behavior, traditional sex differences do seem to continue. When the administrator of the school, the woman referred to earlier, had a baby and began bringing him to work, a careful observer could note that the women made more extravagant comments about his beauty, spent more time holding him and hovering over him than did the men. They also showed more concern about setting up and managing the Day Care Center (which, however, has been in the daily charge of a young man). It seemed that women tended to look the other way not only when used coffee cups had to be removed, but when cartons of books had to be carried upstairs or when the furnace or fuse plugs had to be attended to.

Women have taken the larger role in doing the committee work necessary to the running of the school. They have chaired the budget committee, the admissions committee and others, served as student representatives on the Board of Trustees, carrying out these tasks with devotion and thoroughness. Personal relationships (close friendships, sisterhoods) entered more largely into their schemes of things, played a larger role in their approach to the affairs of the school, than was the case with the men. I have seen women students display what I would call a fierce maternal protectiveness or sisterly solidarity toward another woman student. In general (there are large individual differences), the women seemed to worry more than the men about the school as a whole. They wanted it to survive as a community in which no one would be neglected or unhappy.

Making a family of the school

Some of the women have spoken of their self-consciousness about this tendency to make a family out of the school. The dean has assured them that they should feel free to continue what they are doing. This was not, I hasten to say, because he was disposed to leave the humanistic aspects of the school to the women, as if this were their special province; it is rather because in this day and age one is grateful for any contributions to the humaneness of an organization, whatever their source. As a matter of fact, the dean was at least as humanistic as any of the women; and this favored humanism in all concerned. Our administrator, for example, could not have used her distinctive talents in an ordinary bureaucracy; she needed an organization in which her way of doing things was appreciated and supported. And there was nothing in the situation at the school to prevent women from being as unsocial or privatistic as they needed to be for the sake of their creativity; at any given time there were enough of us not in the mood to be creative so that adequate community was maintained.

It should be clear, too, that the "watching-over" activities of the women were not something that they did for men. The things I have been describing were not "stroking" in Jessie Bernard's sense of that term. What the women did, they did for everybody, not least themselves. And they were hunters as well as keepers of the camp. When they were in hot pursuit of funds, all hands turned to the support functions.

I am not saying that our School or the CSPP was a model of an ideal community, or that the way our women students behaved is the way they should behave or would behave in an ideal society. Nor were all of our male students completely at ease in the situation in which they found themselves. One still heard jokes putting down women's liberation. I do believe, however, that we were moving in the right direction; and that our women students offered a fair representation of what, in the present period of social change, is to be expected of highly intelligent, professionally oriented women under conditions of relative freedom; and that our men students were moving, though too slowly, toward acceptance of women, and of their own full selves.

In my opening paragraph I borrowed a phrase from Carolyn Heilbron (whose *Saturday Review* article, "The Masculine Wilderness of the American Novel," also says much of what I want to say by way of theory). In company with philosophers and literary figures such as S. T. Coleridge and J. B. Priestly, she assumes that masculine and feminine tendencies exist in everybody; that wholeness, or full humanity, in the individual requires the integration of these tendencies; and that their interaction nurtures creativity. This state of affairs in individuals favors, and is favored by, group and organizational life in which men and women cooperate closely in pursuit of shared goals.

What would be gained?

Many women, as they seek to improve their status and as they become socialized in male graduate or professional schools, seem merely to "want in" on the present system of production, service, and education, without asking how these systems ought to be changed. And there are captains of industry or education who regard their entry into these systems merely as a matter of "utilization of women power." With the advent of the women's movement, however, other women, especially young women, are realizing that they cannot simply join the professions as they now exist, since their present structure and mode of operation are inimical to feminist goals.

The fundamental question is, how much would be gained if, in the process of liberating women from men, both women and men were dominated by technological modes of organizing production and human relations? It has been suggested that women may avoid this fate by remaining on the fringes of the professions, saving much of themselves for other things. If this perception is sound, it applies to men as well as to women. Professions as now defined are not well suited for anybody. Women and men must cooperate in the redefinition of professions, and in the design of new ones.

This is true, most certainly, of work in the university, an institution that has been made by and for men. A British educator, visiting recently in this country, was surprised that a woman scholar he and I knew, who was developing educational programs for poor people, was attending only to cognitive functions. He "should have thought," he said, that in this day and age such a program would be concerned with all aspects of the person and that in affluent and automated America more attention would be given to education for leisure. But then, we agreed, our acquaintance was a mannish woman, a product of the masculine university, working in a male-dominated organization, and using research designs developed in accord with masculine principles.

Masculine style

What is meant here by "masculine"? I suggest the following things as examples (although women can do all of them as well as men, and in the present cultural situation they often do): stressing analysis, to the neglect of how things fit together; separating thought from feeling, inquiry from action, teaching from inquiry and action, work from play; abstracting functions for purposes of study, and then basing practice on the abstractions as if they were separate in reality (for example, focusing on the learning of content, inventing teaching machines, and then treating students as if they were learning machines); putting science and technology ahead of other values, and adopting for human behavior and human affairs the kind of science that underlies technology; focusing on a single purpose and then making everything else instrumental to it (for example, determining to turn students into social scientists, and to this end putting aside all concern for students as human beings, presumably so that they may ultimately contribute to humanity);

adopting for the running of the university the mechanical theory of management, with its emphasis on differentiation of function, specialization, precise role definition, efficiency, and on the use of status competition as the motive force for keeping the machinery going; and engaging in grim, concentrated shop-talk relieved only by weekends of pro football.

I am not saying that under present conditions in our society males and females differ as groups with respect to these tendencies. I am saying that these tendencies can be derived psychologically from what can be conceived as basic masculinity, the sort of thing we see most vividly displayed, perhaps, by the boy engineer.

What we really want

The changes in society just described have to be arrested, and we have to set a different course in accord with an understanding of what we really want and need. Instead of viewing the development and exercise of talent as a manpower (or "womanpower") problem, we should see it as the highest purpose of democracy. Personality development depends heavily on the development of the individual's talents, just as talent, in its manifestations, depends on the total development of the person. Such development, which occurs mainly through graded challenges and through self-insight, implies complexity and wholeness; and in particular, the generation, liberation, and integration of male and female impulses.

Let us begin with the idea that dispositions to femininity and to masculinity are present in both sexes. These dispositions begin in body feelings occasioned by anatomical-physiological characteristics and fantasies that arise in connection with these feelings. They grow along with the perceptions, misperceptions, inferences, and fantasies that are stimulated by the presence of people having contrasting anatomical-physiological characteristics. They are shaped by the complexity of feelings, fantasies, and beliefs occasioned by being brought up in a family, or by adults of both sexes, with different roles taken by the two sexes.

Probably most men and women achieve sexual identity mainly through conformity. They are products of, participants in, and at the same time creators of the American male-dominated culture. They are at the "conforming" level of ego development, according to Jane Loevinger's scheme. (Lower levels include the pre-social or impulsive and the self-protective; higher levels are the conscientious, the autonomous, and the integrated.) They seem to act according to the stereotypes and role definitions prevalent in our culture and distilled in commercials and popular movies.

The androgynous society

In contrast, truly mature men and women are psychologically free to have the satisfaction of dependence, passivity, and tenderness without any loss of competence or the capacity for action or mastery. Mature people are sufficiently secure in their sex identity so as to be capable of role-flexibility, and to have a sense of self that does not depend entirely on social role. The individual is freed from inner fears and compulsion, and can do many kinds of things, including non-paid work, regardless of how they may have been culturally defined as masculine or feminine. This is a matter of personality development in general, in the direction of self-awareness, acceptance of feelings, self-determination, and self-control.

Although personality development may be set on its course by childhood circumstances, there are probably no structures or tendencies in the person that cannot be profoundly altered by later education and training. Personality characteristics, indeed, are nurtured and sustained by the person's culture and social situation. We know how to enable people to become aware of, and to accept, their opposite-sex tendencies, and how to help provide constructive and gratifying modes for the expression of these tendencies. But the social situation can make or break efforts to carry out these procedures.

Consider the negative side first. If one partner in a couple has a childish sex-identity and a primitive stereotype of the opposite sex, it is extremely difficult for the other partner to develop. If in an institution of higher education the women are treated like girls in a mining camp, all education is severely hampered. New experiences are simply organized according to old stereotypes.

How are we to break into such a system? Or better, how do we develop a system favorable to individual development? We must assume the mutual dependence of personality and social process. It won't do to say only that the man who projects his own (feared or hated) femininity onto women must be made aware, as in psychoanalysis, of what he is doing. His conceptions of women will still depend to some extent on what women actually do. For this and other reasons we must focus on building the androgynous society.

"Coeducation," even with equal numbers of males and females, by itself won't do. Nor will "equal opportunity" in the ordinary sense of that term. The androgynous society requires "equitability," a condition in which nobody feels unjustly treated. Above all, it requires a deliberate effort to create social structures which embody individual development as the highest value. Precisely because the femininity or the masculinity that people reject in themselves is represented by people in society, individual development requires a social structure in which each person's humanity is fully appreciated. Our school wouldn't have worked unless each student felt that she or he participated fully in all decisions affecting her or him. Nor would it have worked unless the women felt free to voice openly any sense they had of being put down. These circumstances make for the liberation of women from men, which I would call the first stage of liberation. Like any other condition of justice, this is an end in itself. But it is at the same time a precondition for higher stages of liberation, which involve changes in the whole system of sex-roles and sex-identities, as well as development toward wholeness and creativity in individual women and men and in androgynous collectivities.

8 Early Years of the Wright Institute

To the extent that development of such qualities as creativity, discipline and independence of thought depends upon the complexity and wholeness of institutions in which education and training take place, the big question for graduate deans is how we can achieve higher levels of integration in our universities. How can we connect what happens in the classroom with what happens in other areas of the student's life? How can we facilitate the continuing development of faculty members, upon which the development of students depends? How can we build community on the campus, and thus prepare ourselves for building community in the larger society?

In approaching these questions we must have our eyes open to the difficulties. American universities have been expanding and becoming differentiated at a rate far beyond their capacity to achieve the integration which is necessary to any living system. Particularly in the years since World War II we have seen a fantastic proliferation of departments, specialties within departments, institutes, centers, and programs each of which, in the major universities, has behaved as an independent principality, bent on its own aggrandizement, related less to other parts in the same institution than to outside constituents, markets, and sources of funds. This has been going on long enough so that this model of a university is widely regarded as a phenomenon of nature, something that the good Lord intended.

Enormous interest is vested in these present structures. Only a few of us old-timers remember the humane and humanizing universities of the 1920's and the 1930's, some of which achieved greatness even without huge inputs of funds from Washington or elsewhere. As I argued in chapter 6, their greatness depended on a clear vision of goals and a willingness to organize effort in their pursuit.

In my more despairing moments it seems to me that the modern university has succeeded in separating almost everything that belongs together. Not only have fields of inquiry been subdivided until they have become almost meaningless, but research has been separated from teaching, teaching and research from action, and, worst of all, thoughts from humane feeling. In practice we often neglect what very few would openly deny: that knowledge of how things fit together is at least as important a part of science as knowledge of how things may be divided for the purposes of analytical study. The processes of nature exist in contexts of other processes, and are to be fully understood only when seen in their natural setting. Although inquiry proceeds by analysis, and by the intensive study of parts that have been abstracted from the wholes in which they are naturally embedded, the wholes must be reconstituted if they and their parts are to be known well.

Splitters ascendent

In accord with this basic wisdom we have always had "lumpers" as well as "splitters" in science. But splitters have tended to gain the ascendency, no doubt because of the enormous pay-off from specialized inquiry in the physical and biological sciences. When the great flow of federal funds to the universities began in the 1940's, it was the splitters who profitted and were able to institutionalize their way of doing things. But this success has not proved to be an unmixed blessing, especially to the extent that it held out an alluring model to the disciplines that study human experience. For example, a model that seemed to work well in medicine—finding the cause, hopefully a single cause, and prescribing treatment—has been extended to such areas as alcohol and drug addiction, crime, and violence, even social deviance, where it is not only ineffective but actually stands in the way of amelioration.

The splitters seem to have been particularly busy, and well regarded, in psychology and other social sciences. They have succeeded in virtually eliminating the concept of the person. In its place we have "researchable man", an aggregate of separable part-functions which can be studied by existing methods in ways that lead to quick publication.

When this notion about human functioning is carried over into practice we have a wide range of specialized agencies and professionals, each attending to some particular problem or function and nobody attending to the person himself. As I showed in Chapter 4, most professionals focus on particular symptoms without regard to the possible implications of their actions for other areas of functioning for that person. A mother on welfare might spend days traveling by bus to various parts of her city seeking out the special agencies set up to cope with the problems of herself and her children. In academic culture a similar system encourages students to find a specialty, stick strictly to its own methods and intellectual style, stay out of other disciplines, and keep values out of the work.

Success through loss of self-esteem

Since students come to graduate school today from various backgrounds and with diverse motives, it takes a great deal of pulling and hauling to shape to these requirements. Our interview and questionnaire studies with hundreds of graduate students in various institutions and departments shows that a majority experience the required socialization as a loss of self-esteem, some as a loss of the sense of self. When the Wright Institute held a literary contest in which we offered $1,000 for the best autobiographical essay on the experience of graduate school, the dominant theme, one that appeared in more than half of the essays received, was concern about whether students could maintain their identities while undergoing the hardships that graduate school imposes.

These hardships are greatest, according to our studies, for members of ethnic minorities and for women. This, as I argued in Chapter 7, is because academic culture is masculine and exclusive, and particularly so in universities below the first rank but striving to reach it. In a culture that says "we will accept anybody who will be like us," what happens to those who aren't? Often, it appears, they face a choice between giving up too much of themselves and dropping out. Members of the minorities have to give up the most, while very little attention is paid, except within the group, to their unique contributions. Not all of them have that "future orientation" which enables some white males to put up with a lot while focusing on the rewards to come.

Members of the minorities often believe their hardships in academia are due solely to discrimination on the basis of their color or sex. Actually the ethnocentrism of the departments is more all-inclusive than that: everybody who would belong must learn and accept the catechism. Thus, in my view, justice for minorities will not be attained solely by arousing the guilt feelings of professors and administrators through insistent cries of institutional racism or by depending on "affirmative action" programs to admit many students who will later become alienated and drop out; justice will come instead through broadening the definitions of the disciplines and lowering the barriers among them so that they allow expression of, and can gain from, wider ranges of human talents and aspirations. This would help not only the minorities but everybody else.

It is fair to say that many students, far from losing their identities, actually find themselves in their discipline, grow to love it, and become productive scholars and teachers. But far too many either drop out or become cynical system-beaters, telling themselves (forlornly, I am afraid) that once they become well placed in a job they will accomplish what they really want to do, something for humanity. I worry, too, about those who adapt themselves whole-heartedly to the system without knowing what is happening to them, and who will discover ten or fifteen years from now that they have come to a dead end, that they have been wasting their lives.

An alternative to the system

Against this background how could we fashion a more successful setting for the development of young adults? In 1968 those of us who started The Wright Institute faced not only this general question but, as I mentioned in Chapter 7, the paradox that university departments of psychology were down-grading or abandoning altogether clinical training at a time when society's need for it, and young people's demand for it, were at all-time highs. We saw this lapse in psychology as an expression of failings of the university system as a whole; and as long-time critics of this system we wanted to conceive an alternative and to show that it would work.

In the Institute our focus was upon human development in social settings. The basic question was how we can modify or create settings—ranging from the family to the whole society—so that they will maximally favor the development of the individual. We started with open-ended conceptions of what people can become, but we thought of ourselves as *practical* idealists. Our graduate school was started to train students in this alternative approach, in the hope that we could meanwhile favor their development as creative persons.

Inquiry and action addressed to our fundamental question were based in a value-orientation, a philosophy of science, a theory of personality and its development, a theory of organized settings or "social systems" with special reference to the ways in which they influence individual development, and a strategy for action and research. The "newness" of our approach was less in any of these ideas themselves than in the way they were combined.

We were more or less committed to the idea that "man is the measure"; a problem-centered, field-theoretical, holistic, and pragmatic scientific approach; a comprehensive and holistic conception of the developing individual; and an approach to subjects of research as clients who should benefit as much from the processes of inquiry as from its results.

How we drew together

Our values turned out to be shared by a very impressive and eager group of applicants. After the first year with 13 doctoral students, in the second year we had 35, in the third about 50, in the fourth 68, already close to our intended maximum of about 75 students. This translates into some eight to ten Ph.D.'s per year.

In terms of their professional goals, our students seemed to fall into four categories: (1) clinical practice; (2) social activities such as working in social agencies, community programs, evaluation positions, or combinations of these; (3) intellectual careers of a less applied nature, similar to more or less traditional academic careers; and (4) combinations of psychology with other professions and careers. We have among our alumni, for example, a dental surgeon who has an appointment at a medical school where he works on the service which operates on victims of cancer of the face and mouth. In order to carry on effectively in his work, he decided that he needed a Ph.D. in psychology to gain some knowledge of such matters as the social psychology of hospitals and the psychology of response to dying or physical mutilation.

In admissions we gave preference to applicants who had experiences beyond the role of student. Thus our students ranged in age from the early twenties to the early fifties. The mean was about thirty-three.

During the first three years of the Graduate School's existence faculty members served on a quarter-to-quarter basis. They taught seminars which met weekly, and served on student contract committees. Only three of us, Mervin Freedman, Edward Opton, Jr., and I were present most of the time. At the beginning of the fourth year a "core" faculty was hired, four faculty members on a quarter-time and two on a half-time basis. In two years the "core" faculty grew to eleven quarter- and half-time members.

These men and women shared our vision of innovation and change in education, research, and action in the discipline of psychology. We thought we could do some things that large universities couldn't do, or weren't doing, or were doing badly. Abjuring the anti-intellectual trends of the "counter culture", we sought to restore some of the best features of the pre-World War II university, and to help reform the multiversity, rather than to abandon the model altogether. Even in those early years our faculty had impeccable credentials, as researchers, writers, teachers, and practitioners, in such disciplines as medicine, psychiatry, psychoanalysis, social welfare, sociology, political science, and anthrotlogy as well as psychology.

Structures for freedom

The structures of the Graduate School evolved organically over the early years of its existence. The first agency to appear was the Executive Committee, consisting of all members of the community, both students and faculty, a direct democracy of whomever had the time and patience to attend. During the first two years most matters of moment were decided by the Executive Committee—the courses to be offered quarter to quarter, the faculty to be hired, the number of new students to be admitted each year, the disposition of the budget. As the school became larger, various committees evolved out of the Executive Committee, to supervise budget, curriculum, personnel, and training. During the first three years, decisions of the Executive Committee were made by consensus of all persons present. As the school grew larger and became more diverse this consensus procedure became less efficient. It was replaced by a smaller Executive Committee consisting of various officers of the school—the Administrator, the Dean, and Managers of the various committees—and elected representatives of the faculty and of the students.

The management of the school rested on a sharing of faculty and student power. Since the school was supported primarily by student tuition the needs and desires of students could hardly be ignored. On the other hand, demands of legitimation and academic and professional recognition were such that faculty concerns had to receive their share of attention. For the first three years in the life of the school conflict between faculty or administrators and some students surfaced from time to time.

The conflict centered basically on structure versus freedom. To what degree were students to be free to determine their own programs and establish their own standards of performance independently of faculty?

While the faculty and administrators were committed to recognize the uniqueness of each student and of his or her professional and academic development, they likewise agreed on the necessity of having curriculum guidelines, for example, and established procedures for evaluating the performance of students. Probably three-quarters of the students agreed with this point of view, and curriculum and contract guidelines were adopted. A student was expected to attain some competence or mastery in each of the four areas called by us the self-system, interpersonal systems, organizational systems, and social-cultural systems.

The individual contract system is the mechanism by which we implemented the contract guidelines. Before the end of his or her third quarter at the school, each student assembled a committee consisting of at least two faculty members, one of whom had to be a core faculty member, and one student. Membership on the contract committee could be changed to correspond with changes in student goals. All the members of the committee assumed responsibility for developing the best possible educational program for the student involved. In particular, the committee required that the student give serious consideration to his or her educational goals, specify ways toward the attainment of these goals, and indicate the procedures for evaluation. The contract committee was a joint venture.

Achievements of the first five years

It is fair to say that during its first five years our school achieved a modest success. We turned out 13 Ph.D.'s, all of whom are employed. Some of the dissertations were first-rate, fully in accord with the institute's ideal of integrating action and research. Other dissertations, I have to add, were marginal but their authors are nonetheless doing useful work and doing it well. Some of our students developed remarkably well as individuals. I am particularly proud of our work with some lower-class, culturally deprived, poorly educated white students who after two or three years of defensive struggle with what they perceived to be a middle-class institution, emerged as mature professionals, prepared to work effectively in social settings where Ph.D.'s from our great universities could hardly enter. After only five years we already enjoyed a good reputation locally, and an excellent one nationally, distance lending enchantment. The number and the quality of the applicants to the school had mounted each year—rising to 350 a year, of whom only 12 could be chosen.

We also had problems. After five years the issue of freedom and authority was not altogether resolved and may remain with us indefinitely. Having started our school in the climate of the 1960's, and having wished to be ideologically as well as ethnically, sexually, and socially diverse, we became something of a magnet for white radicals. Some of these were the sort who, during the 1960's, tried to turn our universities into bases for political action. It seems that they subsequently lowered their sights: what they could not do at the University they would try at the Wright Institute. In their efforts to gain power, they inflamed the passions of third world students and women and generated no end of excitement. I can testify that small size and deliberate efforts to achieve community are no guarantees against paranoia. But we survived all this.

More troublesome and persistent was the problem of how to integrate the clinical and the social. We learned that even a small institution set up, as it were, "outside the system" remained very much under the influence of forces in the larger society. The separation of the clinical from the social, like the separation of research from action, has been so institutionalized in our society that it has been difficult for our students to find paid field-work placements, and for our graduates to find jobs to do the kinds of work that we have primarily in mind. Jobs tend to be either clinical *or* social, or even further specialized. Graduate programs such as ours need to be supplemented by educational programs designed to acquaint various public officials and administrators with the services that professionals of the sort we produce can render.

Murray's Clinic as a Place to Learn

9

In chapter 5, I quoted Henry Murray on the concept of personality, and here I want to recall the way the personalities of would-be psychologists, including my own, were developed by the academic center that Murray did so much to create. I have already mentioned this setting, the Harvard Psychological Clinic, in chapter 6, as part of a much broader account of university life in the 1930's. In chapters 7 and 8, I described the early years of a social-clinical program of the 1970's, and in this chapter I will suggest certain continuities as well as substantial contrasts between the Wright Institute and Murray's clinic.

During my years at the Harvard Psychological Clinic (1931 to 1940) we always had a Christmas party, the annual regression as it was called, when, as we knew through staying up to listen, "the bird of dawning sangeth all night long." For these occasions Harry always prepared a special literary work—flights of fantasy, graceful toasts, elegant orations. For one party, which turned out to be especially memorable, Harry wrote a play, which he entitled *Clinicus*. Filled with virtue and somewhat naive, the young hero had been chosen to carry out some great mission, perhaps to lead psychology out of the wilderness, perhaps to discover great truths that would liberate us all. Clinicus had surrounded himself with a highly diversified band of more or less talented eccentrics and misfits whose devotion to the cause made up for the fact that they were not always helpful.

The invented names of these characters conveyed at once to the company their real identity and at the same time signified an essential and salient character trait. For example there was "Queen Morganatica", who had in her charge one of the group's most potent instruments of magic, the Thematic Apperception Test. I wish I could remember more of those names.

I do of course recall "the Reverend Sangfroid", a particularly lovable figure. Brought up a Southern Baptist, this fellow knew the importance of the difference between private and public sin, but was otherwise quite confused. Without any clear idea of what was going on he tried, without ever quite succeeding, to meet each situation by playing it cool.

In this fashion everybody at the clinic was neatly but gently satirized.

Forces of darkness

The action of the play was set at a meeting called to see what could be done about the enemy, the forces of darkness, who seemed to be completely taken up with efforts to spoil Clinicus' mission. This was the Emerson Hall Junta, the main line psychology department, an aggregation of elementarists, introspectionists, behaviorists, experimentalists, and extraceptionists. They too were neatly caricatured. (Another prominent figure was an old whore named Harvardianna, whom Clinicus couldn't quite take, or leave alone.) The upshot of the meeting was a decision to carry out an enormous collaborative investigation of personality, one that would do justice to its complexity and wholeness. This investigation would confound, if not convince, the enemy.

If resurrected and studied, this play could reveal much of what life was like then at the Harvard Psychological Clinic. Those were the early days, a fact lost on me at the time. All this imagery of a new and fragile institution, the survival of which was in doubt, and which had to contend not only with wrong ideas but with all kinds of academic pathology, didn't really get through to me. I thought of the Clinic, as of everything else at Harvard, as old, firmly established, shrouded in tradition. Actually, if I am right in thinking that the play was produced at Christmas, 1935, its hero was only eight years old. Morton Prince had founded the clinic in 1927 and Murray, having been brought to Harvard as Prince's research assistant, had taken over as director a year later. He was without academic tenure.

Several years ago I wrote some recollections of Harvard in the 1930's, the basis of chapter 6. It was really a story about what the place *should* have been, but quite close to what I was fortunate enough to experience. When the recollections appeared as an article in the *American Psychologist* I got quite a lot of mail. A man who was at Harvard a little before I was, wrote that my account had left out one important thing: money. I knew that money was important in New England, the evidence being that it was never talked about; but I had not heard, as my correspondent assured me, that "Morton Prince bought his professorship for $80,000." If so, Harvard appears to have driven a hard bargain. In any case, the starting of the Clinic exemplifies the way new things usually get started in academia. Can you image a group of professors getting together and starting something really new? Probably not. New ventures in the academic world require action from the top, often with the aid of outside money. The trouble is we don't have any university presidents like Lowell, or any more psychiatrists with Prince's combination of vision, resources, and opportunity.

A place in personology

Prince and Murray were out to bring medical psychology, the psychology of the clinic, dynamic psychology, into the university. They also wanted to integrate their kind of psychology and the academic psychology of the day. For Murray this meant that psychology had to be redefined as the organismic study of persons. Hence his term *personology*. Around 1960 I published a piece in one of the Koch volumes, *Psychology: A Study of a Science*. At the editor's behest, my chapter was called "Personality: its place in psychology". Harry wrote me at once to express his indignation. My title, he said, was meaningless. Why not say "Psychology: its place in personology" or "Personality: its place in personality"?

Murray agreed with Whitehead when he wrote that "an isolated event is not an event". Thus the task of personology was to study the relationships (and the patterns of relationships) among processes in the person, arriving ultimately at a formulation of the whole personality. This "vast and intricate architecture" as Murray once called it, was to be studied in its interactions with the environment. To Murray it was painfully unscientific for a psychologist to measure a particular process in thirty subjects, to assume that it owed nothing to context but was essentially the same in all thirty, and then, upon finding that the process was correlated with an environmental stimulus in nineteen of the thirty subjects, to speak of a general law. Murray asked, what about the other eleven? You could find out about them only by studying their personalities. The only truly general laws would have to include personality variables in the formulae.

Some of the most vivid and exciting writing in *Explorations in Personality* comes when Murray attacks the already established model of experimental research. For example, "he who clings to the hope that the results of his research will approach in accuracy and elegance the formulations of the exact disciplines, is doomed to failure. He will end his days in the congregation of futile men, of whom the greater number, contractedly withdrawn from critical issues, measure trifles with sanctimonious precision" (Murray, 1938). If you think this was going too far, you should have seen the manuscript before it was edited.

Although the psychologists at the Clinic and those in Emerson Hall had major differences in theory and philosophy, they still talked to one another. There was controversy, sometimes quite bitter, as intense as there is today; but these various disputes were conducted with a kind of civility that was really quite extraordinary and is rarely found today. Everybody kept control: often we students could sense their passion only from the flushed faces. Those of us from the clinic witnessed many colloquia in Emerson Hall where Murray more or less had to defend his points of view singlehandedly. He never hesitated to do so. People would prepare for the most devastating sort of attack, but nevertheless keep their voices down, stay polite, and even summon up a sense of humor. Murray's students of course felt proud that he was able to give as good as he got.

Don't want to go higher

I remember an interchange between Murray and Fred Skinner at one of our weekly colloquia. During a discussion of levels of analysis, someone had drawn some examples on the blackboard. At the top level was the person, below that the syndrome or complex, then the need or trait, then the conditioned response, then, I suppose, the nerve impulse. Skinner, who as a graduate student had already worked out most of the ideas that would make him famous, thought one ought to focus at about the level of the conditioned response. Murray said he thought we should go higher. When Skinner said, "but I don't want to go higher," Harry replied, "I know, you're afraid you'll go to heaven."

Skinner, I think, enjoyed the joke as much as anybody. As a matter of fact we saw him at the Clinic more than a few times, once when he gave a formal report on one of his studies of verbal behavior. He thought it would interest us, and it did.

Murray was not only tolerant toward ideas he argued against, but diverse in what he absorbed and made available to his students. In the initial course in dynamic psychology we were introduced to the great triumvirate of Freud, Jung and Adler, in considerable depth. We had to read this stuff, as well as listen to lectures on it; and after 1933, when the refugees from Germany and Austria began to arrive, we had an opportunity to meet many of them as they passed through Cambridge or Boston. Psychoanalysts, field theorists, Gestalt psychologists all appeared at the Clinic or at Emerson Hall, came to lunch, stayed around, and looked over our work. Having Kurt Lewin visit my experiment was a big event in my life. Lewin had a fantastic capacity to be interested in things, genuinely so. He wanted to know everything about the experiment and made me feel as if I were doing something of importance, as if I were one of his colleagues, which I really found quite inspiring.

Going into clinical

At the time, the one thing absolutely required by Harvard culture was that you have some kind of strong intellectual interest. It didn't matter *what* you were interested in, but you had to be able to identify it and tell others about it. Looking back over the years, this seems to me rather important. All of us in the Clinic program were there because we shared a deep interest in psychology. I say this to contrast it with the way some people have gone into clinical psychology in a later period. I remember being shocked in Berkeley in the early 1950's when I encountered a family whose son was studying clinical psychology primarily in order to prepare himself for a private practice of psychotherapy. I hadn't previously encountered this idea of going into psychology the way one went into medicine, and it shocked me that this student's family should have such vivid imagery of what his practice was going to be like. The later quest for licenses led students to place a different type of demand on their instructors—namely, that they be trained for a specific job they wanted.

By contrast, the extremely variegated bunch of students at Harvard had only one thing in common, and that was some kind of intellectual interest in the issues of psychology. In many cases this came out of an early interest in philosophy. At Harvard, philosophy and psychology were then in the same department, in the tradition of William James. Some people, like myself, got interested in psychology because it offered the possibility of an empirical approach to philosophical issues, which in turn had their roots in religious issues.

Despite the various divisions that were developing in psychology, it was still fundamentally one subject, and not all that many people were needed to present it. The faculty in psychology at Harvard was made up of only nine or ten people; we took something from virtually all of them and had a sense of being psychologists by the time we got through, which meant we could move into any kind of position in the field. This flexibility also had something to do with the Depression. People who had been trained as experimental psychologists did seek and find jobs in clinics. I also recall a trained animal psychologist who taught at Harvard as assistant professor, and then took a Depression job with the Oakland School system, where he remained. The notion was that if you were a psychologist, you were prepared to do anything: school work, clinical work, anything. What you didn't know, of course, you were supposed to pick up on the job. I hardly need to make the comparison with the kind of proliferation that exists today, where people specialize in the most narrow kinds of things.

Perhaps what lay behind the passion that enlivened the competition between Emerson Hall and the Clinic was not so much differences in ideas or point of view as the way in which Prince and Murray were brought into Harvard. They had not turned up in a search, or gone through the channels prescribed by the faculty. As interlopers brought in by the President, their presence was a constant challenge to faculty power. By and large faculty can tolerate a fairly broad range of ideas, but they will come out fighting in response to any threat to their power to run the university for their own benefit.

It's my narcissism

Back to the cast of characters at the clinic. We were remarkably diversified: a poet who made his living as a psychiatrist, a psychiatrist who didn't need to make a living, an artist who had wandered into psychoanalysis. All these people were at the Clinic because they were attracted by Murray's ideas and were willing and able to accept his leadership. And he, not unnaturally, tended to think well of people who were smart enough to see the value of his work. If you had called this to his attention at this time, he would have said, "of course, it's my narcissism."

One of the first things I learned from Harry was to make small confessions: you may be spared having to make big ones. Or give a name to a behavior pattern (or to its hypothetical source) and it sounds almost as if you were talking about somebody else. You can easily turn that into permission to do the same thing again. A favorite example arose during Murray's Freudian analysis in the mid 1930's. Every day he would arise from the luncheon table and say, "well, I'm off to see Foxy Grampa," his name for Franz Alexander. He conceived an enormous curiosity about Alexander's wife: having caught a glimpse of this dark beauty, he took steps to find out something about her. "It's my voyeurism," he said. I think Harry won't mind these somewhat gossipy remarks. In any case I expect to be forgiven. It's my envy, you see.

Same conceptual scheme

The diversified group around Murray, including the 28 authors of the *Explorations*, all agreed to use the same conceptual scheme in their study of 50 Harvard men. (Erik Erikson, I think, had the most trouble with the scheme, probably because he was working on a scheme of his own, but he bravely stayed with the ratings on needs and traits.) Murray was our undisputed leader. He worked harder than anybody else. He had the ideas, the background, and the charm to win people to his cause. More, he was not afraid to be in a position of authority. He ran the Clinic. It struck me only in recent years that in all the many, many meetings, luncheons, private conversations that we had, I never heard any mention of the administration of the Clinic. Surely most of us just assumed that Harry took care of that sort of thing.

Thus, the Harvard Psychological Clinic in my day followed the model of a small organization—whether clinic, institute, or laboratory—operating under the leadership of one person with seminal ideas. We have seen a number of highly productive organizations of this type during the last half-century. They do not last very long. What happens is that, as they expand, people with different views, purposes and ambitions inevitably come in. Bureaucratic procedures are installed, decision-making bodies formed, and pretty soon more time is devoted to administration than to creative work.

Along with the quiet intensity of the Clinic, we also enjoyed what I called, in chapter 7, an androgynous society. The proportion of women was higher, I think, than in any other psychological center of the time. They were not in the majority, but they were as likely as men to occupy central roles. All a person had to do to be admitted to the group was to be interested in the ideas, and to show some promise of being able to make a contribution. These women were, of course, of various types; and among them were some ardent feminists.

The setting for the Clinicus drama was the library of an old house on Plympton Street in Cambridge. This room, like others at the Clinic, was furnished with handsome antiques and oriental rugs. The important books on psychology were there, as well as photographic portraits of the great forebears, often with letters and autographs. Aesthetic sensitivity was to be observed throughout the building. My favorite hang-out was an upstairs room whose walls were lined with books, especially biographies and novels. I spent a lot of time in that room browsing, reading, and borrowing books from there—some of which, probably, haven't been returned. I remember one of the boys at Emerson Hall saying, "I hear Murray thinks the study of literature is a part of psychology." He thought it was amazing that we were expected to read biographies and novels. But I was struck by the conception of what it meant, and what it could mean, to be a broadly educated person as well as a psychologist. When I asked Eric Trist not long ago how people are introduced to the systems way of thinking—to the idea that you start with a kind of reconnaissance of the whole and get a sense of it before you begin zeroing in on particular features you want to study intensively—Eric said he had learned it from the study of literature.

Write a story

When I took Harry's course, in 1930, he had been reading Thomas Wolfe's *Look Homeward, Angel*. He brought this with him to several of his lectures, and I knew he was very familiar with it. About the same time he produced the early version of a projective test based on a set of evocative but ambiguous drawings, a "thematic apperception test," or what was intended to be one. Later I had time to read *Look Homeward, Angel*, and discovered that the character Eugene, at school in Asheville, North Carolina, is asked along with his class to write a story about a picture they had been shown of a girl walking along a dusty country road by herself. In typical Wolfe fashion, Eugene wrote a story that went on and on, revealing much of his character not shown by his other behavior. I've always thought that the Thematic Apperception Test was inspired by this incident in Wolfe.

It was in the library that the famous Clinic luncheons, as well as the serious celebrations, were held. Every working day at noon the Clinic regulars gathered there, often with a guest from among Murray's extraordinarily wide band of friends and acquaintances. We met Katherine Cornell and Felix Frankfurter, for example, and numbers of famous psychologists and psychoanalysts from Europe. Harry's broad-mindedness was such as to overcome even small differences; hence Talcott Parsons and Clyde Kluckhohn were included.

I once undertook to describe life at the Clinic in the 1930's to Murray's second wife, who had not been there to witness it. I mentioned the surroundings, the luncheons, the extraordinary visitors, the constant, entertaining discussions, and then added, to her great amusement, that I thought all this was normal operating procedure, just what any graduate student of the time had a right to expect.

In the preface to *Self and Society* (Sanford, 1966) I set down a list of quite specific things Murray did for me as my mentor and friend. All this and more came back to me recently when I read Daniel Levinson's *Seasons of a Man's Life* (1978). It's a marvelous book—really in the tradition of the *Explorations*—although the stress on definite stages didn't ring bells for me quite as much as it did for many people. I have no sense of having negotiated these stages. Instead I have a sense of major events, externally determined, that brought about changes in my career and my life: getting a job at the Norfolk Prison Colony; getting psychoanalyzed; becoming director of a study of child development for the General Education Board at the Shady Hill School, which led to my landing in California; going to the Tavistock Clinic; becoming coordinator of the Mellon Program at Vassar College. These were important happenings that led to enriching experience. I have been heard to say that chance was the great determinant. Actually, Murray was behind all these happenings, putting in the right word at the right time with one or another of his friends and acquaintances. So he has been not only my mentor, friend, and exemplar, but my guardian angel.

The need schema and beyond

I'd like to say a little more about Murray's work and how it affected me. The "need schema", I suppose, was the most widely known aspect of his work: Murray spent years elaborating this fantastic inventory of needs and traits, which owed a lot to McDougall and what he had called instincts and later "propensities." I took to Murray's schema right away, because I had discovered psychology as an undergraduate by reading McDougall. (For some time I had thought I was the only other person in the world who had thought about these things.)

In his need schema Murray developed McDougall's general approach into what amounted to an enormous system of classification. Although it was of limited use in working out a dynamic theory of personality, this scheme was extremely valuable as an invitation to us to include everything. Once you had seriously worked with the need schema, it was impossible to focus on some sliver of personality as if it were the whole thing.

Murray's most basic contribution was his organismic point of view, which was expressed directly in the Clinic's assessment procedure. In the *Explorations* Murray quotes Ritter and some other British biologist on the organismic point of view, which is pretty much the sort of thing put forward nowadays under the heading of "general systems theory." Likewise, Murray drew heavily on L. J. Henderson's work, especially his discussion of the blood as a vast system which can be analyzed into diverse elements, but which would be changed, as a system, by a change in any one of its elements. At the same time a change in the larger organism that affected the blood would, naturally, affect every element into which the blood could be analyzed.

If you take this idea into the field of personality, it becomes clear why these principles are so important. What it does is to permit us to study personality with the understanding that what is happening in a particular experiment is in fact being in part determined by processes going on in the larger personality. And the personality as a whole is more than simply an assembly of the particular measures we've been able to obtain.

Levels of functioning

Another fundamental notion we developed at the clinic was that of the levels of functioning in a person, the unconscious. Here we were guided by the typical psychoanalytic account, in which we refer something at the surface, like some kind of aggressiveness, to an underlying fear, or underlying passivity, which we then refer to an underlying homosexual attachment to the father, which we then refer to a castration anxiety (of which the father was supposed to be the source), which we refer to an even deeper aggression against the father, and so on. This moving from one level to the next, using some kind of mechanism to explain the interaction of things on one level with things functioning on deeper levels, was fundamental in the work at the Clinic.

In my view, most of our most fruitful theory about personality lay precisely in that area between what was manifest and what was latent. In our ratings we couldn't rate something hidden unless we did so on the basis of a conception of what it was that prevented it from being overt—or, if it were manifest and somehow related to what was latent, unless we knew the means by which the relations had been set up.

Let me end with a question: if the *Explorations* was so great, if Murray and the Clinic turned out so many promising Ph.D.'s, how come the enemy to whom Clinicus gave battle seems stronger than ever? It is true that personality research in the grand tradition flourished for a time in the 1940's, and many psychologists brought up in that tradition are still active. But if you try to get government money today for personality research of any complexity, you will probably be disappointed. The experimental social psychologists, who have the power, will work nights to find reason for turning you down. If money for research is what you want, you had better stick to the model we thought Harry had demolished in 1938, the year he published *Explorations in Personality*.

Concerning that book, I remember two early reviews: one by a man at the Psychological Corporation who found nothing good to say about the book but was impressed by Murray's getting all that money from the Rockefeller Foundation. It was $500, I believe. The other review was a friendly but critical one by Richard M. Elliott, the dean of Psychology at Minnesota. He found the psychoanalytic leanings of the book hard to take, but was impressed by its scope and profundity. He said it should be required everyday reading for anybody who worked with people and Sunday reading for academic psychologists.

He wound up with a literary quotation that has stuck in my memory for forty years. He was thinking of people who refused to attend to the *Explorations* but who might wake up later to find that Murray was right. I use it in speaking to personality psychologists who don't know their history, who underestimate the enemy and who think that by breathing words like humanism or holism they can overcome; and to those who make discoveries without knowing that they have been made before, in a work that was before its time. The words are those of Henry IV of France: "Hang yourself brave Crillon; we fought at Arque, and you were not there."

Academic
Culture

Opening the Way to Faculty Development

10

Educational researchers have not altogether neglected the subject of teachers and teaching, but most of their inquiries have been directed to rather superficial aspects of "how to do it" rather than to the really important matters of attitudes, values, and ways of conceiving of the teacher's role and functions. For example, N. L. Gage's comprehensive handbook on teaching has an authoritative chapter on college teaching by W. McKeachie, who includes a section on attitudes and values but is forced to write on the basis of his impressions: he can cite no research on this topic, whereas his bibliography for the chapter as a whole is massive (Gage, 1963).

Criticisms of teachers and teaching come from people at all levels of the academic hierarchy. We have heard from education policymakers such as John Gardner, who has written sharply and with a note of urgency about the "flight from teaching" (1964); from college and university administrators, who in recent years have been taking blame for student unrest which really belongs at the door of faculties; from faculty members, who though they make no judgments of their colleagues, comment freely upon the uninspired teaching to which they were exposed as undergraduates; and of course, from students whose complaints and routine dismay are now generally admitted to be not wholly without cause.

Apart from actions at the level of exhortation, however, little is done to meet the problem. At some institutions prizes are given to popular teachers, but without evidence that a few prizes can raise the level of performance in the institution as a whole. From time to time we hear of a plan to change the "reward system" for faculty members, such as by linking promotions and salary levels more to teaching and less to research and scholarly publication; but nothing comes of these plans, in part because we lack an adequate way to evaluate teaching but more because reformers soon discover they can't change the reward system without restructuring the whole set of academic values.

My ideas about what is wrong with college teaching have been derived largely from interviews that my colleagues and I have conducted with around 600 professors in eight different institutions. Guided by a comprehensive outline, each interview lasted, on the average, about three hours.

We found it is mistaken to assume, as many observers do, that college and university professors do not like to teach or that they neglect their teaching duties in favor of research. Most of those we interviewed were working hard at their teaching; very few regarded themselves as poor teachers, and almost all wanted to be seen as effective. Very few, however, could say on what basis they evaluated themselves, nor could they offer any rationale for what they did in the classroom. Most appeared to be carrying on in the manner they had learned as students. At distinguished institutions teachers are oriented not to their undergraduate students but to their disciplines. Their self-esteem depends most heavily upon the esteem of colleagues in their field and their actual advancement within it. They want to present their subject rather than to influence the development of students, and they prefer graduate to undergraduate teaching.

As if it had no discipline

This adds up to saying that undergraduate teaching is not, for professors at four year colleges and universities, a true profession. When such professors assemble informally or formally, they almost never discuss teaching; this is not the "shop" they talk. Nor, for that matter, do they discuss the philosophy of education, a subject in which they generally have little background. When professors meet to discuss educational programs or reforms, they usually proceed as if the field of education had no discipline, no shared terms or organized knowledge, and as if no such discipline were required. They discuss it as would any educated adult, on the basis of a few opinions and biases and some knowledge by acquaintance.

Instead of a profession, college and university professors have a kind of "culture," a set of shared ways and views designed to make the ills that they have more bearable, to prevent any flight to "others they know not of," and to contain their anxieties and uncertainties about their competence as teachers.

I will not undertake to describe the whole academic culture

here, but only to indicate some features that might have to be changed if college teaching is to improve. For example, professors often identify with their discipline or specialty rather than with the role of teacher. They respect norms concerning how much time one may properly spend with students or how much interest in students one may display, and in most institutions the norms are pretty low: if a teacher becomes popular, he courts the danger of being ostracized by colleagues. Similarly he must beware of giving away too much of the mystery upon which support of his discipline depends. In conversation with colleagues or other professionals he should not go beyond the bounds of his own specialty, and if something outside of it comes up for discussion he should always defer to other specialists, even though this puts an end to the conversation. He should always exhibit a devotion to the highest standards in matters of appointments and promotions and admission of students, and let somebody else suggest that a risk be taken in particularly interesting cases.

Widespread unhappiness

It all seems pretty grim, unnecessarily so. Since academic men are fundamentally free to read and study and look into whatever we like, always have interesting colleagues to talk with, and are surrounded by eager students waiting to get the word, why aren't we all happy as kings? Instead we live amidst widespread unhappiness and cynicism. Indeed, academic culture seems to decree that it ought not to be otherwise. Since faculty members are devoted to such high purposes, it seems almost immoral to take any pleasure in pursuing them. Nor does it help to be stationed at a prestigious institution. Following Groucho Marx, who said that "happiness won't buy you money", we can add that it won't get you a job at Berkeley, or Stanford, or Harvard either.

Academic culture also seems to discourage communication among professors who are interested in students, and to deprive the individual teacher of means for evaluating his work. Without terms for describing student development, without even a perspective from which the student can be seen as a person, the teacher of undergraduates is denied the most elementary satisfaction of professional activity—seeing desirable things happen as a direct result of planned action. Although academic culture has rational elements in it and serves various personality needs of professors, it does not promote educational purposes as well as it might and it puts severe and unnecessary restraints upon the satisfaction of other personality needs.

Stages of liberation

The liberation of professors from contemporary academic culture requires the achievement of three interrelated goals: (1) greater awareness on the part of professors of themselves and what they do, of their philosophies, objectives, and styles of teaching; (2) familiarity with alternative ways of attaining their objectives; and (3) recognition of the legitimacy of being interested in students and taking satisfaction from work with them.

Of these goals the first is the most basic. If the professor's alienation from himself and his classroom work can be overcome, it will be easy for him to see new possibilities in the classroom and in work with students as individuals. Increased awareness on the part of the professor leads to his seeing students in a new light. The more familiar he is with his own feelings, his anxieties and misgivings as well as his satisfactions, the greater his ability to understand what students are thinking and feeling; and the greater the latter, the more conscious he will be of his classroom behavior, the more able to evaluate his work.

Teachers and teaching are almost never discussed in the way we have just illustrated, whether on campuses, in scientific papers, or in popular writing about education. This largely defines our problem and sets our task. We must expose, and begin the process of breaking up this conspiracy of silence. In our work along these lines I suggest that we conduct intensive and comprehensive interviews with faculty members, use our analysis of these interviews in leading discussions among groups of teachers, and observe teachers in their classrooms and then submit their work to joint analysis with them.

Talking with outsiders

In the work we at the Wright Institute have done with faculty, interviews center on issues which, as we know from experience, are deeply relevant to the work and the lives of college professors. All of the questions are open-ended. This frees the professors to dwell on what is uniquely relevant and spares him the feeling that he is being classified or that what he has to say is being catalogued according to somebody else's preconceptions.

In the conduct of the interviews the professor's confidence in the process rises as he sees that the interviewer has genuine interest and compassion and has brought no axe to grind. Apart from these considerations, the interviewer who comes to the professor from outside the latter's department or school has certain distinct advantages: he is not a competitor, or an authority; unlike the professor's colleagues and professional associates, this interviewer has no way of holding what the professor says against him. More, the interviewer is there to talk about subjects in which the professor has deep interest but which he never has a chance to talk about, except possibly at home with his spouse.

Almost without exception, those we interview say they enjoy the experience and derive benefit from it. In particular, they are given a rare chance to reflect on certain important matters; they do a certain amount of personal stock-taking; and they discover, often with considerable relief, the possibility of talking about troublesome and revealing aspects of their experiences with students.

To increase the likelihood that the benefits of the individual interview will be sustained, we seek to stimulate campus-wide (or, in large universities, department-wide or school-wide) conversations and discussion about our program and the issues it raises. By interviewing a relatively high proportion of the teachers in a given academic unit, we can count on conversations springing up spontaneously about the interviews and their content. We go further. After all the interviews have been carried out and we have had a chance to study the material obtained, we schedule group discussions at the institutions. Sometimes in small groups and sometimes in meetings to which the whole faculty is invited, we report tentative findings in ways that invite discussion. If the teachers present have not already discovered how widely their anxieties are shared, and the existence of viable alternatives to unsatisfying ways of doing things, they often do so now.

The idea of self-study is, of course, an old one in the world of higher education. But it takes a special sort of approach to be effective. In recent years, many self-studies have turned out to be expensive exercises in self-congratulation. Rarely have they resulted in significant changes. In the approach I am proposing, the agency of change is in the process of self-study itself, not in some academic body that makes up its mind to do something (or, more likely, not to do something) only after the so-called facts are in. In contrast we start with the assumption that professors have needs and aspirations not being fulfilled under present arrangements but which, once brought into full awareness, can be fulfilled, without loss to other values, under different arrangements. As outsiders our job is to help increase this awareness, first in individual professors and then, as a social fact, in groups.

Today's subjects, tomorrow's interviewers

We do not suggest, however, that raising the consciousness of American professors is to be accomplished only by having teams of professionals visit one institution after another. What we have in mind, rather, is a process of change which, started at one institution, could spread to others. It has been our experience that among the professors interviewed at each institution there were some, not necessarily psychologists or social scientists, who were well-qualified to serve as members of an action-research team such as ours. It could become a part of our work to train such people as interviewers and to organize them into additional interviewing teams preferably for work at neighboring institutions. In large, complex institutions, however, a team from one department, school, or institute might interview professors in others. At Stanford, for example, a group of students who were taking a course with me at the Institute for the Study of Human Problems interviewed professors in the School of Arts and Sciences, with good effects all around.

What I have described is a way of beginning a process which could make our institutions of higher learning more human. Not only students, but millions of people who work in large organizations, are alienated from their work and suffer from the impersonality of their surroundings. It is ironical that our colleges and universities which are supposed to teach us how to live and which could be models of human communities, tend to go the way of other bureaucracies.

My analysis puts the emphasis on change in consciousness. This is not to deny the importance of change in the academic structure or in techniques of classroom teaching: it is merely to put first things first, for the best laid plans for academic reform will go awry unless they accord with faculty attitudes and wishes.

Teachers who are honest with themselves will admit, I think, that the era of student protest taught us how much we had relied upon authoritarian structures and methods and, of course, upon submissive students. But if pathology in relationships is a product of interaction, so also is development. As students become less submissive we must become more differentiated and flexible; else we will either sink deeper into authoritarianism or surrender such genuine authority as we have. As we become more flexible, adapting our behavior to the needs of particular students, exercising the authority that comes of knowedge and experience without insisting on immediate or total conformity, students will become more self-determining; and more of them will consider us as possible models. In sum, if students are developing, the faculty must develop too, or else go backward.

Competence and discovery

Our studies indicate that college professors develop as individuals in much the same way that other poeple do, in distinguishable stages which are only loosely related to chronological age. A particularly important stage is the one we call the achievement of a *sense of competence* in a discipline or specialty. The way in which this developmental task is approached and accomplished depends, of course, on what has gone before. It depends, for example, on whether the professor was, as a child, "isolated" or "social." Perhaps we should not have been surprised to discover that the overwhelming majority of the professors in our samples were isolated children. Indeed, half of those we interviewed in one liberal arts college were only-children. Whether prodigies or plodders, they learned early to enjoy being rewarded by adults for academic achievement and they learn late, if at all, to participate in the rough and tumble of campus politics. The mischievous and sometimes disobedient social children who were to become professors were relatively late in discovering their academic potentialities and, though they are likely to wind up in charge of the important committees, and to relate easily to students outside of classes, they have a hard time getting over the feeling that they may not be doing the right thing in the classroom.

Until a professor has achieved academic competence he is not ready, as a general rule, to pass on to the stage of *self-discovery*, in which he gives attention to other abilities, interests, and aspirations, and so expands his personality. Even when a professor is ready to change, however, he finds that he has made commitments and must defend what he has done, while also dealing with the expectations of family and colleagues who, often at some pain, have grown used to him as he is. Our experience is in line with the finding of Kurt Lewin that it usually takes a "group decision" to sustain a change.

Ideally, self-discovery is followed by *discovery of others*, much as, in Erik Erikson's formulation of stages, identity is followed by intimacy and generativity. Now the professor is prepared to use all of his skills in genuine relationships with other people; he may find it enjoyable and even appropriate to take a parental role with some students.

Standing pat

The developmental status of the faculty member is expressed, we have found, in various aspects of his life and work. An example in the 1960's was the way he responded to new value-orientations of students, and especially to expressions of skepticism and rebelliousness. Michael Bloom and Norbert Ralph of the Wright Institute have separately described three patterns of faculty reaction to the new forms of student behavior (Bloom and Ralph, 1971): first, standing pat, sticking rigidly to the pattern of values and behavior toward students that existed before the appearance of campus unrest; second, radical accommodation to new student values and behavior, a kind of total flipping over to a new outlook, almost an identification with students; and third, a kind of integration of the new values into a scheme of things broad enough and flexible enough to embrace the new without total rejection of the old.

In the first pattern the professor clings, in the face of changing reality, to the system of thought and action to which he has grown accustomed. The more importunate the new demands upon him, the more totally does he reject the new values, the more rigidly does he reaffirm his longstanding position. One encounters this response in much writing, perhaps especially social scientific writing, about higher education. Traditional institutional forms are treated as if they were a part of nature. Instead of thinking of ways to change these man-made and culture-bound structures in order to meet student needs generated in a radically changed society, the writer simply assumes it is up to the student to do the adapting: if he can or will not, he is pathological, or possibly just responding to a pathological social condition which will pass away in time.

Perplexed, rejected

Although the stand-patter continues to present himself with characteristic self-confidence and authority, our interviews show that in reality he is perplexed and threatened. He may fear that all he has worked for is being undermined. Knowing that his prestige has diminished, he struggles to maintain self-esteem. But he does not change essentially his way of teaching, unless to reassert his authority, to show his complete mastery of the facts, to isolate himself further from the students.

Students, increasingly, reject this type of professor. They are inclined to see his authoritarian ways as a sign of weakness; they are less and less inclined to model themselves upon him as a person; often they are not looking for the kind of technical competence he has to offer. Rejection by students may lead to more authoritarianism.

We believe the stand-pat professor is most commonly in the developmental stage of establishing or maintaining a sense of competence. His concern is mainly with the approval and recognition of his professional colleagues, and his status within the academic world. Thus it is that his self-definition and self-respect depend heavily upon his adherence to the traditional academic beliefs and ways. This adherence is also a matter of conscience. He regards the academic value-orientation as a guide to life, and would feel guilty if he failed to act in accord with it. Professors differ in the degree to which the stability and integration of personality depend upon the stability of the academic culture, but many professors experience attacks on the university as if they had caused serious wounds in the personality itself.

The traditional value-orientation is assimilated and held to in different ways. In one case, it may be a matter of conformity, the professor changing as the external climate changes; in another case the values may have been assimilated in accord with the professor's best thought and judgment, and so be deeply based in his personality. Some teachers, having been intellectually awakened at the hands of a particular devoted instructor, now want to be that kind of teacher themselves, and thus find rebelliousness or lack of deference on the part of students particularly hard to take. Why should they, who really care about students, be subjected to insult and a lack of trust? The case is different from that of the professor who simply embraced the academic values when he was in graduate school. Since he cares primarily about his subject and his discipline and the structure which sustains them, and since he knows he is right, the indifference, skepticism, or opposition of students may be a matter for some regret but nothing to be deeply disturbed about.

Joining the students

The second type of professor with whom we are concerned deals with the new values by embracing them and modifying substantially his frame of reference. He may make a total commitment to the new values and become radical with a vengeance. Sometimes it appears that his new orientation has the same absolutism as did his old one; sometimes it seems he feels he has at last found himself. Or when students have asked, "What is the relevance of this?" or "Why should I know this," he may have lost faith in whatever answers academic culture had offered and therupon joined students in their search. In all of these cases, the professor becomes anti-establishment, sometimes even anti-intellectual. Students who espouse the new values become his major reference group, and sometimes he identifies with them in the psychodynamic sense.

Students generally accept this type of professor at first, and he may become popular. They feel he understands them. He relates to them as a peer, shares their interests, makes friends among them. But they soon see that he is searching for answers in the same way they are. They can accept him as a peer but not as a guide; they see little to be learned from one who regards his past as a waste of time.

At first glance it appears that these professors have attained a sense of competence and are now embarking on a voyage of self-discovery. In some cases this is indeed genuine. A young professor has performed brilliantly in the terms of his discipline and specialty and risen rapidly. Faced with the strong appeal of new values he begins to test them in action; but at the same time he begins a period of soul-searching which may end with an integration of the old and the new.

More often, it seems, he embraces the new values with as little self-insight, as little "self-actualization," as marked his acceptance of the old ones. Perhaps he came along too fast, as universities are wont to make able people do, defining himself too early and too narrowly in terms of his specialty without benefit of a more ample education that could have prepared the way for self-discovery. Now, he wants to discover himself, but is starting at about the same place as the students. Like them he feels that the system has let him down, and like them he is against it; but he is hard put to it to know what to build in its place. Like most professors, he has never given serious thought to a theory of education.

When a professor's acceptance of traditional academic values was absolute, we are led to wonder why. Perhaps he accepted the system under pressure and, while conforming strictly to its demands, barely controlled his rebellious impulses and had a barely conscious feeling that he was going against some parts of himself. Or perhaps the rebellious impulses were fully conscious; he was in some way really alienated from the academic community and is now seizing an opportunity to liberate himself from it. In professors of this type we commonly find a remnant of a cynical adaptation to graduate school. They "played the game" without any genuine commitment of self, enjoyed the benefits of outward conformity and are now coping with bad conscience.

One of the most poignant cases is that of a young professor who, as in the 1960's, would be driven into the camp of the students by an ambitious and rigidly traditional department. With much student unrest on the campus, such a professor believes that, since he has good relations with students, he may serve the community by becoming a member of some committee concerned with student complaints. This takes much time, and though he continues to publish in his specialty, his rate of publication declines. After a couple of years of this the department "lets him go." A spirited young man might regard such treatment as quite sufficient reason for joining the rebels.

Ways to integrate

The third type of professor, as suggested above, reacts to student skepticism neither by rigid reassertion of his existing scheme nor by radical change but—without losing his equilibrium—by finding ways to integrate the two. He is not upset by the skepticism of students because he has remained skeptical himself. He has guidelines that he has found useful and enjoyable, but he does not regard them as absolute or good for everybody. He is willing to change his beliefs if he finds more satisfactory ones. He wants to share what has given him satisfaction and believes he can learn by discussing alternative views. Far from neglecting facts or the technical aspects of his field he sees them as integral to the work that he loves. He rather dislikes the role of authority, but is willing to assume it when necessary. He believes students might well learn something from his experience, but he does not expect them to accept what is not relevant to their lives.

This professor does not come on strong, and may well be in the background during periods of unrest, but he endures. Students in his classes do not abandon their skepticism about the university, but they come to see that he is deriving satisfaction from his style and outlook, that he has dealt successfully with some of the questions they face, and might even be a suitable model. Self-contained, he is cordial toward but not intimate with students.

The key fact about this professor is that he is still developing. He is still incorporating his past within himself and entertaining concepts of what he might yet become. What he wants to share with students, as a developing person, and what they see (however dimly) can be useful to them, is his own experience.

More than a role occupant

This professor's sense of himself owes much to a fortunate past. He is a professor because he has found in the forms of academic life suitable means for self-actualization, rather than because he has found in academic norms a source of identity where none existed before. In short, he does largely what he wants to do rather than what, as an occupant of a role, he ought to do. He respects the academic norms because they serve him and others reasonably well but he does not regard them as absolute. In fact, he can imagine himself getting along quite well with a quite different set of norms; he can see value in various ways of being a professor, and in being various other sorts of person.

In the terms of our developmental scheme this professor is most open to development because he has already developed more than either of the other types described. His discovery of self probably began early, when he gave thought to what he was to become, probably trying several alternatives, and now usually has more than one string to his bow. His renewed work of self-discovery prepares the way for discovery of others.

When we turn to the question of how matters might be changed, how teaching might be improved and how colleges and universities might become more humane and enjoyable places, we might easily find ourselves at a loss, for our analysis has suggested that we have to change both personality and culture, and that the two are so intimately bound up together that we can hardly think of changing one without changing the other. I am going to suggest, however, that we summon new courage and resources and see what can be done about changing academic culture. Perhaps the way to begin is to imagine in some detail what we want, as in Chapter 11, and then to discuss in some detail, as in Chapter 12, how a young person might best proceed within the system we actually have.

Specifics for an Academic Utopia

11

Apart from whatever degree of faculty development we can directly encourage, the university in America urgently needs a new model for itself. Numerous large institutions in the second rank are struggling bravely in the mistaken hope that they can somehow be like the great multiversities. They need to realize that in the perspective of history the multiversity must be regarded as something of an anomaly. In chapter 6 I described how it was not until the end of World War II that the universities began the scramble for government money, developed the "knowledge industry" and, while encouraging mass higher education as a means for placing their Ph.D.'s, used their power to promote the idea that the multiversity and the nice little liberal arts college were the only models worth serious attention. What is now called "retrenchment" is in part a timely withdrawal from the excesses of the 1950's and early 1960's, excesses which helped to make a shambles of undergraduate education and contributed heavily to subsequent student protests.

In developing our vision of an ideal university we should be willing to learn from the past. It seems appropriate enough that a section about graduate education should include a vision of an ideal university. For one thing, the realization of such a vision would require a prior reform of our graduate schools and departments, for they dominate the rest of the university's life. But when we ask how schools and departments are to be reformed, we soon discover that what they can become depends heavily upon university-wide values and processes.

What characteristics are to be desired, and why? To answer this question we must have a conception of the purposes of the university. For me the major goal of education is the fullest possible development of the individual, and all aspects of the college or university should be evaluated in terms of the degree to which they favor or hamper the attainment of this goal, whether for students or the professors who teach them.

Within this goal we must distinguish between personal development and professional development, which may conflict one with the other or be mutually supporting. We have much to learn about the way they interact. Meeting the professional requirement of focusing upon a narrow specialty can cut an individual off from experiences necessary to the development of creativity or wisdom, while preoccupation with self-development (or doing things thought necessary to it) might easily get in the way of professional development.

Improvement of teaching seems most likely to follow from changes on the level of attitude, value and self-conception and, since changes at this level would make for better performance and more satisfaction in various spheres of working and living, we will do best to invest our efforts in assisting self-development in general. But as I have already explained, self-insight will not make much difference in an individual's life, or even be sustained, unless it is followed by changes in behavior. Activities that heighten the self-awareness of groups of faculty will only add to their frustrations unless the institution permits changes in its structure to enable these faculty members to do what they now want. The question then is what kind of structure, in the departments or in the university as a whole, will be most favorable to the self-development of those who work and study there.

Basic trust

1. The ideal university envisioned here is first of all a human community, in which trust, justice, and care are fundamental values. When they do not prevail the free pursuit of truth is severely impaired, and the institution cannot in good conscience undertake to instruct the young. These values were taken for granted in some pre-War universities where it never occurred to a graduate student or assistant professor that senior professors could not be trusted or would not, however sharp their differences of opinion, behave in a statesmanlike way with respect to the business of their department or university. Today the restoration and maintenance of these values has to be worked at. Thus the ideal university would, in its continuous self-studies, work hard to understand and to create the conditions for trust and justice, in full recognition of the widespread erosion of these values during the last 30 years.

Sponsored mobility

2. The humanity of the ideal university is expressed in, even as it gains from, its care for its assistant professors as well as for its students. Barring malfeasance or something like that, *all* assistant professors are promoted eventually. Whether or not they win increases in salary depends on the university's financial situation, which is well enough known to all. The expectation of being kept is basic to community in a department, a division, or a whole university. It does not endanger the quality of research, unless we believe that quality depends more upon the fear of being thrown into the cold than upon the social and intellectual conditions under which a professor lives and works.

A former president of the American Psychological Association reported not long ago that when he was an assistant professor at the University of Chicago in the early 1950's he competed with eleven others for one of two tenured positions in the graduate psychology department. While he and his fellows looked desperately around for projects that would lead to quick publication, young professors hired to teach in the College, where the pressure was far less, were serenely producing more and better published work.

It was not until 1947 that the first assistant professor hired by the Psychology Department at Berkeley was "out" instead of "up." The Department at that time had a fine national reputation—perhaps it was great as psychology departments go—whereas under the system in which everybody is supposed to be a star researcher it has lost something of its distinction. Before tense professionalism took over, the new assistant professor became, almost immediately, a member of the family. If it appeared that he was not doing enough research to make a good case for promotion the senior professors worried with him and each other about how they could help him overcome the deficiency. Likewise with teaching. The climate was such that a young professor's difficulties in teaching could be discussed and thereby reduced. In sum, senior professors in that human community, out of their security and fullness, were generative toward assistant professors as well as toward students, and they were rewarded with trust, gratitude, and loyalty.

Division of labor

3. Consistent with this practice affecting assistant professors is the understanding that a professor's job, for which their

university pays a full salary, is to teach, do research, take part in campus affairs, give service to the larger community, but not necessarily all of the above. A norm that research is to be done out of curiosity or other inner needs, not because of formal external requirements, serves as an important condition for truly significant work and a safeguard againt triviality. In this time of over-specialization, it is well to recall that many professors before World War II found it uncomfortable, somewhat undignified, to have to define themselves in terms of a discipline. It was enough to be a university man or woman. Before the educationists came along it was even all right to define oneself primarily as an educator, to say, "I teach at State." Many professors were content to be "locals," who devoted themselves to making their university a better place. Naturally in that climate, inter-departmental seminars and various other kinds of collaboration across disciplinary boundaries were taken for granted.

A task in common

4. In the ideal university teaching is organized by divisions (of humanities, natural science, social science) and by departments—but not necessarily the same departments, or all the departments, now found in a large multiversity. Each course is taught as a liberal subject. It is up to the divisional deans and departmental leaders to insure that all offerings can be justified on the ground that, whatever else they might do, they contribute in some way to the students' intellectual and moral development. (The two go together: the professor of physics who by precept or example can induce a student to do what he promises, finish what he starts, subject himself to the right way of doing things, abandon a favorite idea in the face of facts is, like the football coach, engaged in character-building.) Thus held together by its educational task, the university accepts that professorial activities without educational value are just as well done elsewhere and paid for by some agency other than the university. Professors may have difficulty in communicating with colleagues in other fields about their research interests, but everybody can talk about education.

In recognition of the fact that education is the first business of the university the most distinguished professor in a department usually teaches the elementary course. The human significance of the whole undertaking is highlighted by demonstrations that men at the top of their fields of research can make their subjects meaningful to the uninitiated. They care both about their ideas and about the young.

Senior professors and some of their colleagues also work hard at the task of holding the discipline together; by constantly making judgments about the significance of new research they separate the wheat from the chaff and thus help to show that the department has a discipline, and is not merely a conglomerate of specialized inquiries. The expensive and disintegrative practice of permitting each professor to teach his own research interest has little place in undergraduate education. (His special interest might find expression in a graduate seminar or tutorial.) So common in the multiversity, this focus in undergraduate courses upon a narrow field of research marks a department run more for the benefit of professors than for the benefit of students; indeed, it is a giveaway of the use of students to further the departmental aim of becoming a success in the eyes of the academic world.

Need for models

5. In the ideal university the norm is for professors to think of themselves as primarily teachers of the young. They accept the fact that, like it or not, they are not mere organizers and dispensers of information but people whom students may want to admire and emulate. They try to understand the students whom they know they are likely to influence in one way or another. Recalling their own student days they know that students need and want someone to look up to, someone who knows them personally and expresses faith in their potentialities as scholars and as human beings, someone who will help make them do and become what they are capable of. Such professors know the limits of what they can do to meet urgent, sometimes global student needs, and they are somewhat amused that fate should have chosen them for the role they have, but they try to do the best they can.

Already full members

6. Entering graduate students are treated as if they were already full members of the academic community, on the assumption that the various hurdles in the way of the Ph.D. will eventually be overcome. Also regarded as future teachers, the students are encouraged, and shown how to take some responsibility for younger people. Since professors are secure, they can uphold the traditional value of tolerance, and this means that

students have a good chance to work at dissertation research that really interests them rather than at something that accords with the current fashion and will get by the dissertation committee.

Human problems as a focus

7. In the ideal university the deans or vice-chancellors of divisions have real power, delegated by the president or chancellor, with whom they share a vision of a civilized university and the determination to bring it into being. It is the task of the Divisions to reform the disciplines, and to search for better ways to organize teaching and the search for knowledge, such as by interdisciplinary, problem-oriented inquiry. The authorities recognize that any serious field, taught in the right way, can help the young to attain inner discipline, and thus to expand and enrich themselves through the assimilation of culture. If a teacher's object is to stimulate the imagination, to develop sensitivity to the poetic, to increase self-awareness, it might be better to use Shakespeare than some new "interdisciplinary package."

Any serious attempt to come to grips with the human and social problems of today, however, probably requires interdisciplinary work, for which the ideal university has a special division. In place of a group of traditional subjects, a division might gather together various kinds of applied work and focus on the combination of action and research, or provide a home for various other kinds of experimental programs at the graduate (and undergraduate) levels.

A structure for experimentation

To do something new and different at the graduate level has become a must for American higher education. Governing boards are casting a baleful eye on the duplication on smaller campuses of what is done on the large ones. Graduate programs informed by the ideas of Thomas Jefferson, Cardinal Newman, and A. N. Whitehead would be breathtakingly new and radical, even if they were carried forward in the existing departments, but we also need some fresh structures for inquiry. The tolerance and flexibility of the ideal university would be favorable to educational experimentation: thus, if a group of faculty wanted to make sure that some freshmen got started off right by having a two-year program in human problems, ecology, energy, or futurology, they would be encouraged.

Having established the sound core outlined above, the ideal

university is well prepared not only to offer small experimental programs but to incorporate on a large scale the best contemporary educational ideas and practices in, for example, field studies and university-town relations. All such activities, plus others such as advising, counseling, and athletics, are held together by an educational philosophy and by knowledge of how students learn and how community is developed and sustained.

Such a philosophy and such knowledge make clear the vital role of leisure in the ideal university. Nothing is more needed in American higher education right now than a slower pace. How is this to be achieved? As I suggest above, a faculty starts by giving up the idea that students have to be entertained or have their hands held; more important, they understand that the quality of education does not increase in direct proportion to how much is taught. Knowledge of how students actually learn explains why it is that some liberal arts colleges attain first rank while offering no more than half the courses to be found in the catalogues of other good and not-so-good institutions.

In the ideal university, departments achieve their educational goals through the integration rather than proliferations of their offerings, which allows sharp reductions in the number of courses professors would otherwise teach in order to advance their careers. These circumstances favor leisurely scholarship, deriving more often from inspiration than from external expectations.

Time for a shake-up

It is often assumed that universities cannot be changed deliberately, that they merely adapt themselves to forces in the society at large. And even among observers who recognize the possibility of change through deliberate effort, many assume that the impetus must come from outside and above. Professors, in this view, respond to rewards and punishments: "change the reward system and their hearts and minds will follow." In contrast I believe the change must generally come from inside and above, from a President and other academic leaders who are willing to use power if necessary. They would gain their objectives mainly through persuasion and moral authority, and gather about them the most highly respected professors, but they would have the means and the will to take decisive action when necessary. The use of their authority probably would be necessary at times in order to initiate and maintain the practices vital to the ideal university.

They had best be blunt and open about it; for given the

mood of today any attempt to use power invisibly seems almost bound to arouse suspicion. The fact that authority is everywhere discredited in our society today, so that even grown-up people have to make a show of dislike for it, only makes it difficult for people in positions of leadership to use such authority as they have; it in no way diminishes individual and organizational need for it. The president and deans could take heart by recalling that just fifteen years ago it was not uncommon for deans in first-rate universities to "shake up" departments that had become ingrown, or divided into warring camps, or allowed their curriculum to proliferate, or displayed too great a passion for trivial research. And the university was better in consequence. A demonstration of the proper use of power and authority by a university today, for something other than retrenchment, would be perceived throughout academia as a stunning innovation, and would go a long way toward building that community which everyone desires.

Advice to a Recent Ph.D.

12

I like to give advice to young people about practical affairs, and as I get older I become less inhibited about it. Giving advice is even more fun than imagining an ideal university. Perhaps each of these activities offers perspective on the other. Unfortunately, the opportunity to give advice does not occur often enough. Every year I explain carefully to our new students at the Wright Institute that the side door of my office is always open; if they see that I am alone they should just come in; and if they feel inhibited they should just ask my secretary for an appointment.

It is hard for me to believe, since I still feel most alive when I am tangling with the establishment, but most of our students see me as the big authority, the "power structure" or as one particularly irreverent young woman put it, "the great white father." With very few exceptions then, they are prevented from coming to see me either by rebelliousness or by deference, or by some combination of the two.

Thus when a young man from another institution recently did come to me for advice I was delighted, and proceeded to go far beyond the call of duty. As it turned out, we got into a whole set of problems that confront those who do academic work, and I thought in the end that the advice I gave him might well apply to others.

Artie had received his Ph.D. from a prominent school of education a few months back and was applying for jobs. Two places wanted a social psychologist, a third someone to work on adult development. All three, he believed, assumed that their new assistant professor would work within the conventional social-scientific paradigm: do highly specialized, narrowly focused, value-free research and produce a stream of publications in scientific journals. He can do this. As a matter of fact his dissertation was right down the line. He could do it without feeling compromised because he has a genuine interest in personality determinants of political attitudes, and he has felt himself becoming well-adapted to life in the computer room. Dangerously so, in fact, because he has a range of deep interests—in alcohol and drug abuse, in clinical work, in the analysis of social systems. The question: should he tell the dean of the school of social welfare, by whom he was about to be interviewed, about his generalist inclinations or should he restrict himself to his research attainments and his ability to "do what they want"?

Suppose he adapted

He feared that the conventional paradign, as contrasted with the Wright Institute's holistic, problem-oriented, action-research approach, was actually gaining ground in academia and would soon exclude all other forms of inquiry. Very likely it would never again be possible to produce a work like *The Authoritarian Personality*. Suppose he adapted himself to what appeared to be the only viable professional role: where would he be in five or ten years, what would have happened to him? He had read some of my writings on academic life and faculty development, including what appears here as chapter 10, and he had looked about him. He had been troubled by watching those who as graduate students tell themselves that as soon as they have degrees they will do what really interests them, who then must postpone it "until they get tenure" and who, once tenure is attained, find themselves defending what they did in the past and making sure the next generation of graduate students have to go through what they did.

I told Artie what he wanted to hear. I was pretty sure of my ground because I knew him well. He has a first rate mind, was an academic star as an undergraduate and, during the 1960's had risked everything in the interest of what he thought was right. He barely avoided being caught in the counter-culture but after two years of soul-searching decided he could live "within the system".

I suggested that things might not be so bad as he thought. Scratch an academic zealot or even a 9-to-5 educational psychologist and you may reveal an idealist or, at the least, may uncover a wide range of frustrated aspirations and humane concerns, lively remnants of motives that led to the academic life in the first place.

This reminded me of a story. When I was a graduate student our ranks were joined by a man who had been a priest. This seemed to me very interesting. I thought we would get into some discussion about the nature of man and of social reality, and, above all, about how psychology might be useful to a man with a demonstrated concern about human needs and potentialities. Not at all. This man became the most hard-bitten behaviorist around, experimented with animals, and would discuss issues only within the context of these interests. What, I asked myself, became of all the dispositions and modes of thought that had led him into the priesthood, to all the knowledge and skills he acquired in the course of being trained for it? They had to be still there, somewhere within the structure of his personality, even though obviously held in check. I have often wondered whether he ever succeeded in bringing together his old and his new selves and thereby becoming a whole person.

Many of our academic friends, I told Artie, were not unlike this priest. They had been "socialized" to within an inch of their lives, but behind those "countenances gruff, frowning, and terrible," all kinds of noble passions might still lurk. We could hope that ways may yet be found to liberate them from themselves and especially from each other. As a matter of fact the very conceptual impoverishment that Artie had described was bound to set off a reaction. Psychologists had already been left about 30 years behind by physical scientists and biologists who had altered the old paradigm of scientific inquiry. Anyway, a man as smart as he, and with as much self-insight, did not have to define himself in terms of some particular kind of work that he did or identify himself with it. If he kept himself brushed up on the skills and perspectives that went into his dissertation while he explored the possibilities of holism, systems theory, clinical investigation, and action-research, which would become increasingly easy to do as he matured, he might well find synergistic resolutions of the issues we were talking about.

Lapses from authenticity

Then I recalled that when it was my turn to seek tenure at Berkeley I took some time off from my work on authoritarianism, in which I was engrossed, to do a couple of experimental papers. It seemed strategic to show that I could do that sort of thing. I have been ashamed of that ever since. No doubt there were other instances of my choosing expediency, but probably not many, for as I have explained in chapters 6 and 9, it was far easier and safer before World War II to do what I had really wanted at least at Harvard and Berkeley, than it would be today. Perhaps what troubled me was the belief, which grew on me later, that I would have got tenure without bothering with those experiments. Anyway, these lapses from authenticity have bad consequences. It was sad to contemplate how many academic men and women had based their whole careers on what was at first a strategy like the one I adopted.

So what should Artie say to the dean? I advised my young friend to lay all his cards on the table. This dean, whom I happened to know, is a wise old bird who has seen just about all there is to see in the university world. He would be sympathetic, he would be delighted to talk about the issues raised, he would tell a few stories illustrating academic skullduggery, he would learn that he was talking to a good man; and he would advise playing the game, without taking it *too* seriously.

Strategy for a career

Then, having got the job—this one or some other—our assistant professor should do nothing in the way of intellectual work unless he was highly motivated to do it, and should plunge into as many as possible of the things he really wanted to do, even though this might get him labeled as a generalist. Each paper should, of course, be of such high quality that a refusal to promote him would have to be on the ground that he was a generalist. Do all that and he might well be an inspiration to others. In the academic world moral courage is so rare that even a small display of it, if it is not plainly self-destructive, can have impressive effects. He would of course have to face the possibility of not getting tenure. The social welfare department to which he had applied for a job is polarized, and Artie might very well disappoint both the "let's imitate sociology" wing and the "let's do something about people's problems" wing. If he did not get tenure, he should find a job in some altogether different setting, and thereby develop himself as a person.

Work in a different setting would bring new challenges, which would evoke new ways of behaving. There would be new skills, sensitivities, interests, attachments, all of which would have to be integrated in an expanding personality. The range of choices would be widened, and the capacity to make appropriate ones would be enhanced. This would be very favorable to a high level of morality, for he would be able to find things to do that were at once enjoyable and beneficial to others.

Jung on mid-life crisis

I also reminded Artie of the old Jungian notion that almost any kind of success in the world requires the full exercise of some dispositions and competences, the neglect or suppression of others. The latter remain very much alive and with increasing age they become increasingly insistent. If they are denied, depression is likely to follow. He should remember too, that life, though all too short, is much longer than young people can easily imagine. Perhaps by the time he is 45 this Jungian view will have become a part of our culture. Tenured professors will be expected to make radical changes in their work and styles of life. Some might even have a go at work in the outside world, and he might change places with one or another of them.

Artie said he was really pleased with the advice he had been given, and I was enjoying our discussion—or near monologue—very much. He said enough to show that he understood completely what I was offering; indeed it was my impression that he already knew it all but had not heard it put into words before. So we continued; not so much with advice-giving as with an effort to analyze some important features of academic life and to suggest what he might expect, not only during the struggle for tenure but after it was secured.

I said I would not offer the advice given him to everybody, probably to no more than a few in his position. We should not underestimate the vital importance of tenure: for most young scholars and scientists it was the only game. By what right was I inviting him to take risks?

The ethics of giving advice

This brought to mind the days of the loyalty oath controversy at Berkeley when Edward Tolman, the leader of the non-signers, strongly advised some of his former students, and some young faculty members and teaching assistants, not to join him in open opposition. Whereas he was near retirement, had financial resources to fall back on, and would have no trouble finding other positions, they had much too much to lose. I was troubled by this at the time but not sure about what was involved. Now it seemed to me that Artie was entitled to some support, from a trusted friend, for the moral position he wanted to take; and knowing him as I did I was sure that self-betrayal would go harder with him than with most. But I did not believe we were being quixotic about this. He could afford to take risks for the sake of his integrity because he had alternatives. He had a deep intellectual interest in psychology and would no doubt pursue it whatever his circumstances, he would indeed have a good chance of getting a job in a clinic, and, for that matter, I would bet on his getting tenure without having to become the very model of a modern academic.

More than that, in giving the advice I did I was in fact offering to take a share of the risks, just as I would have a share of the guilt if I helped to set him on a course that led to bad conscience. If he took my advice and things went badly he would have a right to come back to me for substantial help. But this prospect did not trouble me for I would have some resources that could be put to use. In sum, moral behavior by him or me depended not only on our ability to see what was right but on our competences.

All professors admire competence, of course, but they disagree on what kinds are necessary or even tolerable in academic life. What was most important, as suggested earlier, was to have a wide enough range of things we could do to good purpose and with satisfaction so that we had a good chance of finding synergistic resolutions of opposites. This was a matter of personality development. Artie wanted to go more deeply into this and I was very glad to do so. I began with a story.

"Productive bigots"

I had recently been a member of a committee working on guidelines for the evaluation of graduate programs. Our draft stressed close supervision by professors so that they could appraise the student's understanding of his discipline, which was "so necessary for developing a scholar." I observed that this was the only thing we had said about the requirements for becoming a scholar, and I asked if we ought not to insert something to indicate our belief that a scholar needs to have some other qualities, such as devotion to the truth, ability to admit that one might be wrong, respect for different points of view. A philosophy professor from Berkeley said immediately, with intentional irony, "But some of our most productive scholars are bigots."

I had to allow that that was true, adding that some universities could tolerate a fair number of bigots but it would be sad if bigotry became the norm. Our committee was in a hurry, so it was quickly agreed to insert "and other qualities of the scholar", and we went on.

The episode had stayed in my mind. I thought at the time of various "bigots" I had known in academic life, people who were absolutely sure they knew what science or psychology was—meaning the particular paradigm they had adopted—and who regarded all who differed with them as fools or knaves.

I had thought since then of something more general: of people who make it in academic life through concentrating on a single pet idea, or through going to an extreme on some one dimension. I recalled from Sartre's "Portrait of the Anti-Semite": "This is Uncle Jules. He hates the Jews." In academic life there were many opportunities to paraphrase that: "This is Professor So and So. She hates fishing expeditions," which is to say, exploratory studies. Or he hates the revisionist historians, or the new look in perception.

This brought to mind the numerous polarities found in academic life: William James' "tough-minded versus tender-minded", reductionism versus holism, "splitting" versus speculation or inspiration. In psychology the split between the experimentalists and the clinicians was of long standing. I recalled a passage in my *Issues in Personality Theory* and proceeded to look it up: I had written of those "zealots" who regarded themselves as guardians of all that was holy in science, "who terrorize the clinicians and personality researchers by their righteous insistence upon exactitude and rigor and so forth, while indulging in utopian dreams of a general psychology that can explain everything."

Schismogenesis

Gregory Bateson had coined the term "schismogenesis" (literally "growing split") to describe this sort of thing. What he found in his anthropological data we can also see in academic life: focus on a single idea or virtue together with the assumption that if the approach has any merit then the more of it the better. The beauty of the concept of schismogenesis was that it permitted the linking of personality dispositions and the structure of social relationships without subordinating the individual to the system or the system to the individual. Schismogenesis could be observed in personality, ideology, human relationships, organizations, and culture.

I was inclined to believe that many, perhaps most, schismogenetic patterns in social systems as well as in personalities could be explained in psychodynamic terms. The political science department in a great university was a case in point. It had achieved notoriety some years ago because of its success in resisting pressure to add one or more women to its membership, and had more recently been called on the carpet in connection with affirmative action. There was a wide and growing split between its "behavioral" wing and its theoretical-philosophical wing, the former being clearly the stronger. Why, then, were the behavioralists not satisfied? Why had they to go on and on, demanding more and more quantitative rigor of themselves, requiring more loyalty of their members, suspecting the worst of their opposition?

My hypothesis was that shortly after World War II, when the university entered the market-place and its departments began going after the big money, leaders of the department in question experienced, almost as a threat to their masculine pride, the derivature nature of political science and its weak position relative to sociology and psychology (which had begun to enjoy great material success through their imitation of 19th century natural science). In other words, we dealt here with genuine "machismo." In response to threat, the insecure male flexes his muscles, hardens his nose, and tightens his research design in a strenuous effort to build, on an immovable data base, an impregnable scientific fortress. His colleagues are impressed. He wins academic tenure and gets a handsome grant. But lo and behold, he still feels insecure.

The trouble is he has a soft side. On a deeper level of his personality he would like to take it easy, worry about human values, even be in a submissive relationship with stronger men. Often unconscious, these needs can't possibly be satisfied by his masculine strivings, even when he redoubles his efforts. He rejects or condemns anything that reminds him of his softer side. Bringing in a woman to do work like his would be the final indignity.

Of course, once polarization has started in a department it is not necessary to resort to psychodynamic explanations of members' behavior. The heroics of the male cultists are enough to force the opposition into an extreme position and from there things escalate as in any arms race.

Both fair-minded and creative

The developmental task, then, for a social system or for an individual is to build a structure sufficiently complex—so expanded, differentiated and integrated—that conflicting ideas and dispositions can have place, can qualify, moderate, balance one another, where the benefits of one-dimensional extremism can be had without too much loss to other values, where, in sum, synergistic resolutions to conflicts can occur.

I supposed that someone looking at the university from outside would think it a great place to develop one's personality, what with all the challenges and varieties of experience to be had there. It seemed clear that if one wanted students and professors to become intellectually independent and committed, open-minded, able to deal courageously but fairly with opponents and to admit it when they were wrong, creative and productive, concerned with the development of students and younger colleagues we would do best to expose them over time to an institution in which these values were deeply based and widely held. Indeed, in institutions where this was the case we should expect most faculty to behave in conformity with the norms, apart from the level of their development as individuals. And this would pose for the "productive bigots" the developmental task of becoming mature enough so that they could be both fair-minded *and* creative.

Rewards for not changing

But experience suggests that the attainment of such maturity is extremely difficult. Professors are rewarded for being what they are already. In a sense they are already in ruts by the time they get their first jobs, having selected and been recruited by an institution and department that suited their personalities. Professors as a group seem to prefer a protected environment, and to avoid the rough and tumble of the real world. It seemed highly likely that the political science department discussed earlier pulled certain types of people, while excluding or separating those that did not fit in. It was a fairly safe bet that the woman they finally brought in was at least as tough-minded as the men, and probably more so.

At the same time that the university system rewarded professors for not changing, it placed various barriers in the way of further development, including certain features of the job itself, of the academic culture, and of the various academic professions. Artie and I agreed to look at some of these features. Perhaps he would gain a better view of what he was up against, while at the same time we addressed ourselves to a major social problem.

One feature of the assistant professor's job, I thought, was finding out just what its requirements were, what was the actual basis for tenure. Artie had already demonstrated a very clear understanding of what would be expected of him in the universities he was applying to: not only was he to do research but he was to do research of a particular kind. What about teaching? He had thought about that too. It held no terrors; in fact, he had enjoyed his work as a teaching assistant. I wondered if, when he began giving a course of his own, he would try to tell everything he knew in his first lecture. He was not worried about that, or about being lured into doing more than his share of committee work. All right, suppose he failed to get any one of the jobs he was presently applying for and wound up instead at an institution which put a lot of emphasis on teaching in its recruitment interviews but in fact would later evaluate a candidate primarily on the basis of research. This was the pattern in many institutions, particularly in prominent liberal arts colleges and universities that aspired to be in the first rank.

Things could be even more complicated. Many departments have conceptions about the kind of person who "fits in." Those conceptions are highly subjective, vague, and obscure; but they are operative. For example, how much interest in, or concern for, students is considered proper? Institutions have implicit norms to govern behavior in this area and assistant professors ignore them at their peril. At a prominent private university I had known a professor who got along well with students and enjoyed their trust. During the time of student protest, with encouragement from members of his department, he accepted membership on the Student Affairs Committee, and became very much involved for two years. Although he had a fine list of publications and he continued to publish, his rate fell off too sharply and out he went.

"Simple, clear and unfair"

One of the most difficult situations for the assistant professor I had known was at the University of California at Santa Cruz. This institution is known nationally as a place that really cares about teaching and expects all its professors to be active members of the faculty-student communities that are supposed to exist in its eight colleges. At the same time the university had the usual structure of ambitious academic departments where professors are supposed to teach and do research or scholarly work. Each teacher was evaluated both by the college and by the department. There was much tension in this dual system, with strong differences of opinion concerning what the structure of the institution should be. I had a friend there, a highly gifted man, who was up for tenure. He didn't have a clue as to what his fate would be. He thought he was in trouble, mainly because his scholarly writing, while good enough by most standards, was not in line with the modes of inquiry dominant in his department. As for the system for deciding on tenure he much preferred that of Harvard, which was "simple, clear, and unfair."

Life for assistant professors everywhere could be soul-trying. It was not easy to get support from peers in the same department because they were likely to be in competition, while the tenured professors kept their distance because they would have to evaluate their young colleagues' work, or because it was already known that they would not be around next year—which was about the same as their being dead.

Artie was not frightened of any of this. He recalled a survey which found that urban university professors more than any other occupational group, 93 percent of them actually, would choose the same line of work if they could start over again. So academic work has its rewards. As a matter of fact neither Artie nor I had considered for a moment that anything we had said would shake his determination to apply for those jobs. Certainly the chances of being able to throw oneself into work that one really wanted to do were as good in academia as anywhere else. University professor was a high status profession, and much better, in real terms, than when I had entered. One also enjoyed the comforts of sinecure. Even for those professors who had been disillusioned early and could no longer get excited about scholarly inquiry, the privileges and the prestige of full membership in the establishment, the deference shown them, and the power that goes with membership on important university committees, were enough to give reassurance.

Around for a while

This imagery of the older, tenured professor evoked the idea that perhaps tenure ought to be abolished. The system was instituted in the first place in order to insure that professors would be free to speak and write as they pleased, but it had been a long time since I had heard a tenured professor say anything to which a board of trustees were likely to take exception. Actually, it had seemed that untenured professors were more likely to stir up controversy.

But we decided to face the likelihood that in the leading universities tenure would be around for quite a while and it was best to be prepared to deal with it practically. Artie knew a professor who produced a steady stream of little quantitative researches of the kind educational researchers love so well but who, the moment he got tenure, dropped that sort of work and never touched it again. Some years later he produced a very significant book, one that made use of the technical skills that had served him at the beginning of his career but embodied a totally different philosophical outlook. We could not put that down. Dealing with the intractable university system was somewhat like surviving a natural disaster. The important thing in doing what one had to do in order to get tenure, we thought, was to maintain a sense of self as separate from the required instrumentalities, and to sacrifice no more of one's genuine interests than absolutely necessary. It was well to remember, too, that work undertaken because it seemed necessary could turn out to be interesting once one got into it.

Suppose one got tenure, then what? As I said at the outset, Artie was interested not only in landing a job or the right to keep it forever, but in what would happen to him over the whole course of an academic career. I thought it most appropriate that he should be. In the middle years professors were likely to tire of the specialized work that had brought them that far and yet it was then very difficult to change areas of inquiry and teaching. Perhaps this is part of the reason that, despite their strong inclination to choose the same profession again, many professors complain so much, and an air of gloom hangs over so many campuses. A young man applying for admission to the Wright Institute had said he looked over the department at a great mid-western university and "they had a good program but everybody was depressed." Artie had made the same observation, and he pointed out that the survey he had mentioned didn't ask the professors whether in starting over again in academic life they would plan and follow the same career patterns. I confessed my impression that something had gone terribly wrong with our universities.

Hard to live up to

For one thing, the freedom that seems to be so highly valued in academia is also experienced as a burden. Universities go to great lengths to protect the freedom of professors who, as a group, have in the past fought for these protections, in part on the assumption that truth would be discovered (and best helped to prevail) by truly autonomous moral persons. Probably only Supreme Court justices have been accorded as much freedom or had such high expectations thrust upon them.

Young people who later became professors had visions of greatness. In effect, they promised their mothers, or a teacher who seemed to exemplify greatness and showed faith in them, that they would some day make great contributions to knowledge and help people younger than themselves catch and carry on the vision; but they found that it was very hard to live up to such ideals. Almost everything in academic life seemed to conspire against their efforts to produce great work.

I recalled that professors at the Center for Advanced Study in the Behavioral Sciences had often suffered from acute and continuing anxiety. They had told themselves that once free of such distractions as teaching duties, committee meetings and telephone calls, they would really produce something. But the ideas had not come, or too many ideas had come at once, so that they had found it impossible to apply the seat of the pants to the seat of the chair. They had looked around for ways to reinstate the conditions they said they were trying to get away from; and had at the same time tried to find some way to make themselves work, or somebody who would do that for them. Most professors had long since taken care of this conflict by substituting external structures and controls for the inner conscience that goaded them in their youth, and would goad them now if they should free themselves from their "duties".

I proceeded to expand upon the theme that the burden of freedom was a major determinant of some features of academic culture and of the way some professors relate themselves to their profession. This required some attention to definitions.

A shared set of values

The editor of *Daedalus* and several writers in its big issue on higher education (Fall, 1974) had spoken of "the academic profession." In the same issue Donald Light had taken the position, however, that according to the generally accepted definition of a profession, academic life is not a single profession but an aggregate of professions-in-the-disciplines. I agreed with Light but argued as in chapter 10 that what does exist is an academic culture, a set of shared values, ways, and views which are uniquely patterned on each campus, but which pervade our university system.

Academic culture changes with the times. Some of the Pre-World War II values such as intellectual curiosity, tolerance, and concern for students, persist; but there have been changes in the dominant conceptions of man and of social reality, in root assumptions about science, in beliefs about the relations of the university to society, and so on.

The way to get a good sense of the culture on a given campus is to observe professors in action at a faculty meeting. Here individuals one knows to be very decent and reasonably relaxed can be observed exchanging a few "in" jokes and then tightening up as they put on long faces and proceed to demonstrate their knowledge of the catechism of the church of science and scholarship and their dedication to its tenets. Some, who could be expected to express dissenting views, remain silent, and by their silence give assent. Actually—what is probably most common—a minority of particularly stern, self-appointed culture-carriers display the dominant values and see to it that they prevail.

What are these values? Most important in the university system of today, I told Artie, are the beliefs that all knowledge belongs to one or another of the existing academic disciplines, that the way to make discoveries is through specialized inquiry, and that the discovery of knowledge is more important than its "dissemination" or "application." Interdisciplinary inquiry or teaching, undergraduate teaching, applied work, general studies are out, or at least severely downgraded. Some other common elements of academic culture are ethical neutrality, the use of language understandable only to a chosen few, avoidance of encroachment on another expert's territory (at least in his or her presence), the belief that education is merely a matter of exposing students to facts and principles, and the belief that graduate students are already educated enough and need only to be trained and "socialized."

Academic culture thus constitutes a pervasive set of controls over a professor's behavior. To these controls have to be added the ones imposed by his or her particular profession-in-the-discipline, such as history, psychology, or physics.

Not sufficient but necessary

Although the professions generally had been taking their lumps in recent years, it seemed to me that we could hardly do without them. For a young person starting out to be a scholar, scientist, or practitioner, they seemed to provide some necessary guidelines; and they still served to help bring behavior up to some minimum ethical standard.

As a graduate student and young professor I was inspired by a fairly clear idea of what psychology was and by the accomplishments of the psychologists I admired. I had a sense of finding myself in psychology, which showed me how to do what

I most wanted to do. It was the same when I became a psychoanalyst—only more so. I felt that I really needed the profession, not so much to be accredited and get patients, as to know people who would lend moral support and help me figure out what to do in particular cases. I was later to learn that distinguished analysts didn't know that much about what to do either, and that organized psychoanalysis embodied as many ills as any other profession, but if I were to practice analysis again I would still want to belong to the profession.

In order to understand the present-day role of the profession in the development of the professor we have to examine what is happening to the professions themselves and then look into the different ways in which individuals can relate to their professions.

We could agree with what Artie had been saying at the beginning, that as competition within academia increased, the professions had become narrowed and rigid in their demands for conformity. In the 1940's I could do anything I wanted to—get involved in long-term comprehensive studies of personality, practice psychoanalysis, even get into education, and still call myself a psychologist. Today, in contrast, a young person was under great pressure to find a specialty within a sub-area of a discipline and stick to it. Artie was absolutely right in sensing that this puts enormous constraints upon people who would develop their personalities.

Ways of relating to a discipline

Still there were different ways in which professors managed the problem. I thought I could identify at least three ways in which professors relate to their disciplines, styles roughly analogous to something I discussed in chapter 10: the ways professors relate to students.

The first was authoritarian. We had already seen this at work in my stories of the "bigots" and of the political science department. Just as graduate students have to submit to "socialization" in their disciplines, however little they might like some of its requirements, so with assistant professors. Many young Ivy League professors did not submit wholeheartedly, as shown by those who, coming to California in the 1960's, became surfboard enthusiasts or identified themselves with hippie culture. But many professors, perhaps most today, suppress their rebellious tendencies, and keep them suppressed by becoming zealous defenders of the system. They kick over the traces only in special circumstances, as with a group of pals at a convention. In psychoanalytic terms the profession serves as an external superego, the source of that academic viciousness every insider knows so well from the behavior of colleagues if not from his own. When acting in the name of the superego one can justify any kind of punitiveness toward deviating colleagues, rebellious students, or potential nonconformists who try to worm their way into one's department.

"What's with you guys?"

One of the least pleasant aspects of academic life, for me, has been having to listen to colleagues debase people better than themselves who were being considered for appointments or promotion. I was reminded of that scene in John Hersey's novel *Too Far to Walk* where in the course of a visit to a prostitute the student hero said he would like to ask her a question. She said okay if she could ask him one first. Her question was "What's with you guys?" It seemed to her that the men at his university had everything to make a good life and yet they were always complaining and having at one another. Their coming to see her was a way of celebrating some poor fellow's failure to get his promotion.

Authoritarian professors seem to have little enough to celebrate. Having escaped from freedom, having based their careers on early strategic decisions, they have the task of convincing themselves that what they did was of great importance, which easily leads to identification with the profession and all its works.

Little boxes

Another way of relating to one's profession is to put it in a compartment of its own, while finding satisfaction in other activities. These are the professors who close up shop at five o'clock and never give another thought to their work until the next day. Some who make this adaptation are quite cynical about their work and the whole university scene, and they devote their spare time to pleasure. Others value their work but are far from allowing it to dominate their lives. I had a friend who had made a career of neat quantitative studies in child development and in the administration of research, and yet he had a wide range of lively intellectual interests, including psychoanalysis. I could discuss anything with him. He also had highly developed interests that extended far beyond academia. Yet he never did anything to change the professional image that he had built up by the time he was 40. Few of his associates or students knew of his interest in psychoanalysis.

Finally, and in the happiest cases, professors find true vocations in their disciplines, exemplified by what I said about my relations to psychology and psychoanalysis. I added that I had always considered myself lucky to have gone to graduate school when I did and to have been at Berkeley in the good old days. It seemed much more difficult today to find professional roles that encouraged or even allowed professors fully to express and expand themselves. Still, it was being done. We had been talking mainly about features of university life that needed to be changed. We should not forget that within that vast complexity there were still opportunities to do what one wanted. Our Wright Institute interviews with faculty members had turned up more than a few who had been quite resourceful about that. The marks of their success were the joy they found in their research or scholarly work and in their mutually satisfying relations with students.

How to handle teaching

How had they managed? Or better, given the academic situation today, how could young people such as Artie manage? I thought we had pretty well covered the general principles: preserve a sense of self apart from the socialized self, do enough of what was necessary to survive in the system while using the rest of one's energy to do bold work that the system discouraged or failed to support, and expose oneself to new experiences in order to insure that learning and development continued. But could we not be more specific?

Well, learn how to teach; learn well enough so as not to have to waste time preparing for classes and so as to develop a continuing source of enjoyment. We could assume that young Ph.D.'s had mastered their subject; indeed, that it was coming out of their ears. Instead of focusing solely on content and cooking up something that was sure to go over the students' heads, they should think about how to get in touch with the students. If the teachers do not remember what it was like to be an undergraduate they should study up on student development. In fact, they should do that in any case. Most important, they should feel free to reveal something of themselves; they should allow their values to show, without making too much of them. Since most questions that students ask are, at bottom, questions of value, teachers who can put their subject matter in such a context are bound to arouse interest and get the response they want.

But now the young teacher courts the danger of becoming popular. Any tendency toward glorification of him or her on the part of the students should be countered by giving them a lot of work to do. And any impulse to talk about teaching among the departmental culture-carriers should be firmly inhibited.

Natural colleagues

Here, however, is a basis for communication, even friendship, with other assistant professors in the same departments. As teachers they are far less in competition than as scholars. And teaching is also a basis for association with the most interesting people in various other departments. They, typically, are people who have found their vocations and who, as we had seen, show interest in students and in teaching, continuing intellectual curiosity, and a sense of themselves as learners as well as teachers. Very likely they have more than one string to their bow.

These are the people to whom young academics like Artie could look for support of their research as well as of their teaching. I knew a professor who was interested in engineering and in art, both of which he saw as modes for apprehending reality. More than that he believed that general systems theory was as adequate for the analysis of works of art and literature as for the analysis of those congregations that molecules saw fit to join. People like this had long since abandoned the 19th century model of physical science. They were interested in field theory, general systems theory, holism, and the application of Heisenberg's principle to social science. At least a few could be found in almost every department of the university, and chances were they were somewhat lonely. Artie should seek them out; he might actually be the instrument for bringing some of them together, thus helping to organize some of the intellectual work of the university around domains instead of departments. If, as a matter of fact, a dozen or so assistant professors took that same course and worked together the result might be a truly significant change in the university.

Once again, faculty development

All this could follow from learning how to teach. But how was one to do that? Artie had not seen *Faculty Development in a*

Time of Retrenchment, a well-known and widely acclaimed publication by the Group for Human Development in Higher Education (Comstock, 1974). This volume contained all the really good ideas for the improvement of teaching that I had ever heard of—take part in studies of students, be interviewed by outside consultants, join a group of faculty who observe and criticize one another's teaching, and so on. It might be a good idea to look into some of the "faculty development" programs that had been springing up around the country. Some of them were good as far as they went but almost all suffered from the lack of a sound basis in theory. Unlike the authors of the report just mentioned, most organizers and supporters of faculty development programs did not fully understand that in order to change personality you had to change behavior and that this was exceedingly hard to do without a change in the faculty member's situation and culture.

So we had come, finally, to the question of change in the university itself. I thought that a major reason why ideas for faculty development were welcomed so eagerly by educational leaders, was their low estimate of the possibility of change in academic structure and culture. With these "citizens beyond reproach," it was hard to disagree. To bring about such change we should have to liberate the suppressed desires of these citizens as well as those of faculty and, more than that, we should have to deal with the remarkably un-suppressed desires of corporate power in America, which had just about the kind of university they wanted and deserved. Still, Artie and I agreed on the importance of knowing what was happening to us in academia, and on the method of understanding corporate structures like universities by trying to change them.

Action-
Research

A Talk to Psychology Graduates

13

When invited to give a commencement speech at the Psychology Department of the University of California in Berkeley, I bent tradition by starting with a criticism of the very group the graduates were about to join:

Commencement exercises are a bit depressing. What troubles me is not only that we are all a year older and have to face yet another change, but that another generation of students has turned into alumni. Organized alumni constitute one of the more reactionary forces in education. Warner Brown, a well-remembered colleague in this Department, used to remark on this during the loyalty oath controversy. He had thought we were not doing too badly as teachers, but felt that some alumni cast doubt on the whole academic enterprise by supporting the oath. They showed they had learned little of democracy, had not the faintest appreciation of what the university was about, and wanted to impose on it a set of values that seemed to have come out of the Middle Ages. Perhaps there are not many readers of the *Stanford Observer* among us today, but more than any paper published largely for alumni it tells the plain truth about happenings on the campus. What is shocking are the letters from alumni, which are often appalling in their violence and irrationality.

Everybody in Berkeley knows alumni who want to perpetuate at the university the fun and games they knew as adolescents, which is not so bad; I'm calling attention to the type of alumni who want to make sure contemporary students suffer as much as they did. But hope springs eternal. Surely this year's graduates, who have gone through so much, and to whom we already owe so much, are going to do better.

I am expected to talk about the social relevance of social science, or about the integration of science and action. I will undertake to do this, but I can't resist the temptation to talk about something else first—about science as an end as well as a means.

Let us agree that a great purpose of science is the promotion of human welfare and that social science should be put into the service of man, should be used in building the sort of society in which each individual is able to develop his full potential. What would such a society be like? One of its features, I submit, would be the freedom of its members to pursue their deepest interests, and where this existed we would find some of its most highly developed members devoting themselves to science, just as others devoted themselves to poetry, art, philosophy or religion. Here I am talking about science as a human achievement and as one expression of what is most humane in man. I am talking about pure science, the chief mark of which is the purity of its motivation. The great motive for science, of course, as for other forms of scholarly inquiry, is curiosity, the excitement of the quest for new knowledge, and the hope of knowing the joy of discovery.

Intellectual erotics

Love of a discipline or of a subject is one of the more interesting developments of the erotic life. Love of these things is like the love of anything else, or of anybody; and it has its special benefits: unlike the love of things its object cannot be lost, stolen or worn out; and unlike the love of a fickle person it will never let you down. Difficulties about changing a curriculum are often put down to the cussedness of professors. This is not totally wrong, but we should remember that when we speak of eliminating a professor's course or specialty we are threatening him with the "pangs of disprized love." Many students, unfortunately, do not have the experience of falling in love with a subject, of being excited by a course, of having their imaginations captured by a line of inquiry. Whether because their courses are not taught in a way that is relevant to their inner needs and developmental problems, or because these students insist on learning only what they know already, they remain culturally deprived.

Pure science, like modern art and music, is bound to appear mysterious if not downright ridiculous to the uninitiated. One sure way to embarrass a graduate student is to ask him in a company of non-academicians what his Ph.D. dissertation is about. I was asked this question more than once as a graduate student, and when I said I was studying the effects of abstinence from food upon imaginal processes my wife always added amid gales of laughter, "he means he's going to prove that when you are hungry you think of food." My efforts to explain the great theoretical significance of what I was doing always sounded a bit lame, as would such efforts today. Suffice it to say that I found the whole inquiry quite fascinating, as did more than a few other people, and I took enormous satisfaction in the fact that I had advanced our knowledge of needs and images a little beyond the limits of common sense. I would happily undertake the same kind of investigation today if I had not found other problems that seem even more to my taste.

Distribution of power

One thing that has seemed more interesting in recent years has been the social-psychological study of group processes, as in large organizations like colleges and universities. We study them in order to improve them, of course, but studying them in this spirit is also a means of advancing science, of extending and deepening our knowledge of social processes in general. The stubborn fact is that the inner workings of an organization like a university cannot be fully revealed unless, as I concluded in Chapter 12, we make a deliberate effort to change it in some widely desired way. If this effort has any potency at all it soon reveals the distribution of power, it lays bare all kinds of entrenched interests and implicit purposes and their relations one to another and most important, shows the ways in which the organization as a whole mobilizes its defenses against change.

This kind of work, carried out in the right spirit, is pure science. It is not applied science, but is or can be as pure as science ever is or ought to be. To be sure, the scientist who engages in this kind of activity influences the object of his inquiry, and thus he has to be sure that his work does more good than harm, but this is true of almost all investigations of human subjects. All this being so, the social psychologist who rejects this sort of inquiry on principle is simply being unscientific.

One more point about science. Those of us who think that social scientists ought to get out of their laboratories and address themselves to practical problems have to realize that the great bulk of federal funds for social science already goes to applied social science. If we never hear much about this work, and if all the great social problems not only remain but grow worse, one of the reasons is that most of what goes forward in the name of applied social research is not good science.

The need for structure

Those of us who are engaged with social problems and are willing to use our intellectual and moral resources to solve them, have assumed that pure science is safe, and that the best place (but of course not the only place) for pure science is the university. If this institution didn't exist it would have to be invented. As I have already suggested, great universities will be one of the crowning features of that ideal society we hope to create, partly through the proper use of social science. More than any other institution we now have, the university is a place where everybody is free to pursue his interests, where any kind of idea can be entertained and discussed. It is in fact the major source of radical ideas.

Those of us who are building new institutions assume that the university will continue to exist, even if it doesn't improve. We at the Wright Institute are out to modify some of the university's structure and functions; we are out to build some models that might well be adopted within the university, and we are developing a new kind of institution to stand in between the university and society's agencies of action. Of course, we are against the establishment, but not to the point of wanting it to disappear. Let me suggest to all the members of the graduating class who are thinking of starting new schools that sooner or later you will have to have some structure, and that this structure will inevitably resemble in some respects something that has existed before. It wasn't long after we had started our graduate program at the Wright Institute before students and faculty alike discovered how accustomed we had been to blaming things on the administration and to expecting the administration to perform various uninteresting but necessary functions. We finally discovered that we had met the establishment and "it was us."

With all this said about the ideals of science and the university, let us face some realities. The trouble with academic science is that it has fallen into the hands of scientists; that is to say, science is a difficult human enterprise and is thus subject to a variety of human failings. It is very difficult to be sufficiently conscientious about one's work without becoming intolerant of the work of others; it is difficult to be impeccably rigorous without tending to restrict oneself to narrow or relatively simple problems; it is difficult to become expert in the testing of hypotheses without sacrificing some of the imagination that goes into the forming of hypotheses or some of the breadth of view it takes to tell which hypotheses are worth testing.

Psychology, which is not as sure of itself as it has the right to be, constantly courts certain familiar dangers: apparent soundness of method at the expense of substance; narrowness and over-specialization; and an over-accent on analysis of phenomena into finer and finer parts to the neglect of the context in which phenomena appear and of the ways in which things in nature relate one to another.

As an organized human activity, psychology, like other academic disciplines, sometimes strays from purity in its motives. It enters into competition for power, status, and money and thus encourages activities which, though they conform with professional standards, are a pretty far cry from those of the man who can hardly wait to get to his work and who leaves it reluctantly at the end of the day.

Beyond parochialism

A failing of psychology that I particularly hope none of this year's graduating class will display is parochialism. I have had the experience, going back over 20 years, of dropping out of the councils of psychology. I became involved in higher education and over the years have spoken on the subject at many universities. Psychologists, including old friends, stayed away in droves. We might say that they had their minds on higher things; but is it too much to suggest that they didn't want to be mixed up with anything of such low status in the academic world as education? Recently, becoming involved in a new psychology training program I thought it the better part of wisdom to get back into the councils of our national association—and so I accepted an invitation to join one of its boards. If you are going to do something radical (and not merely look that way or make sure that everybody recognizes your radical identity), it is a good idea to retain at least a few marks of conservatism—without, of course, carrying the matter too far.

As a member of that board, and once again among old friends and colleagues in psychology, I was very much struck by the way they viewed the world and the future with first attention to what would advance psychology as a science and as a profession. It was as if they considered that what was good for psychology was good for the nation. Psychology is of course a great discipline; it is at the very core of the social sciences. Surely we can overcome this defensive parochialism; surely those of this graduating class who remain in the academic world will see that we do. The problems of our society do not sort themselves out by academic departments, but require the closest collaboration of various disciplines; and membership in a professional fraternity is not a sufficient basis for identity in a highly developed person.

These critical remarks add up to saying that academic science is not scientific enough; it too often accents the methods, the manners, the outward forms of science at the expense of its spirit. But the shortcomings I have mentioned are not, or not yet, dominating, and they can be corrected. The corrections will have to be carried out by the academicians themselves, but students can help by insisting that academic learning be relevant to the human condition and to the problems of contemporary society.

Out of the labs

I think academic psychology could refresh itself or participate more fully in the spirit of the enterprise, if a higher proportion of the members of the departments left their laboratories for the field or the clinic and addressed themselves to problems as defined by the man in the street. (This is the part of the elephant that I have hold of.) An important corrective also would be for psychologists to take far more seriously than they do their duty as scientists to communicate with people who are not scientists. Nobody will deny that the reporting of scientific activity is a part of science. What is not fully enough recognized is that the audience for reporting should include not only our fellow scientists but many others who could be helped by what we are finding. We should, I think, talk with our public, or as much of it as will listen, about what we are proposing to do and why. I have already made speeches and written articles about the research I want to do on human destructiveness. If I should succeed in getting a research grant I would announce this to all who would listen, taking the occasion to say something of what is already known about the subject, to convey something of the perspective in which the problem was being viewed, and invite feed-back on the issue of whether the right questions were being asked.

If scientists have sometimes failed to behave in accord with their highest ideals, so, it must be admitted, has the university. It has come under a great deal of criticism in recent years, at the same time that more and more is expected of it. My favorite criticism is that the university is too responsive to criticism and yields too readily to external demands, instead of being guided by its own light. There are still no better general guides to life than the traditional values of the university—tolerance, universalism, freedom, truth, unity amid diversity. The university should not only cling to these values, but it must strive to arrange them in the right order, recognizing that men cannot seek truth unless they have freedom, will not care about freedom unless they have justice—that even a longing for justice depends upon care and trust.

The university cannot do everything that is asked of it today. It used to appear that it could. When I came to Berkeley in 1940 it seemed that everything was possible. The air of grimness that seems to hang over the campus today is due not only to an unfavorable political climate in the last few years; it is due as much to the earlier decision to limit enrollment at Berkeley. If the university can no longer develop by adding new programs, it must finally get its priorities in order; and to do so it needs a clear critierion.

Students at the center

I believe the highest priority should go to whatever can be meaningfully related to undergraduate teaching. The only way to have unity in a university is to place the student at the center, to be concerned primarily with what is good for students, and in the same spirit to keep asking more generally, what is good for man?

Conflict over this issue is at the very heart of our social troubles today. Young people and members of ethnic minorities no longer believe they must fragment themselves, or surrender their personalities, in order to adapt to required roles in organizations like universities and industries. The great problem is how to develop, sustain and protect the humanity of all concerned without abandoning legitimate corporate purposes.

Social science, particularly psychology, here has a special role to play. It should state research problems in terms of what is good or might be good for man, and what social or institutional arrangements will best serve man's development. It must then involve itself in designing and promoting those arrangements, all in an experimental spirit of course. Learning about social processes cannot be separated from doing something about them; our studies of people, singly or collectively, affect those people, and we must see to it that what we do as investigators must be favorable, now, to their welfare and their development. Any interview, whether with a welfare recipient or a suburbanite, should be instructive and rewarding, now, to that person as well as to the researcher. Likewise, any study *of* students should be a study *with* students. They should take part in formulating the questions, gathering the data, interpreting the results.

With this kind of work as its focus the university could safely and wisely reduce its involvement in certain kinds of activities. Other institutions such as governmental and quasi-governmental institutes for research and development, industrial research organizations, voluntary agencies, professional societies, and independent institutes can well perform some of the tasks now expected of the university.

A well-established law states that as universities become great in the ordinary sense of that word, they necessarily alienate themselves from their local communities. The sciences and scholarly disciplines become increasingly specialized and mysterious, and the scientists orient themselves to Washington instead of to Sacramento or Berkeley.

Independent institutes

It would be a help to the university, I think, if we set up a large number of new institutes that stand between the university and our agencies of social action. The university cannot act both as a center for free inquiry and as an adversary in political struggles—except in defense of values upon which its life depends. Some of the problems centering about war and peace, race relations, poverty and welfare are so controversial as not to be suited to the academic style of work. Our society needs, both for the amelioration of social problems and for the advancement of social science, a type of agency that can define a problem, make inquiries into how to attack it, take action affecting it, and evaluate the effects of that action before deciding what to do next.

All the complex social phenomena that call for study and action exist, at least in microcosm, in the immediate neighborhood of the university, or even within its own body. Interdisciplinary, problem-oriented institutes within the university could not go as far as independent organizations in advocating and carrying out actions, but they could make hard-hitting analyses of problems and issue policy statements. They could even go as far as to build models of ideal social arrangements; for example, an institute for research and development should by all means have its own experimental school.

Another highly promising way to connect the university with its community is through a great expansion of field studies for undergraduate students. There is no better pedagogy, and no better way to reduce the town-gown hiatus. What the students learn from this work in the community can be passed along to the professors who help them conceptualize what they have learned. Probably it has to be added that if the university is to work in such fashion with its local community, more than a few of its faculty may have to abandon their status needs, and acquire greater sensitivity to those of others.

Continuing education

Finally, there is another heretofore low-status activity that must be vastly expanded—and that is continuing education. It will help keep the alumni enlightened if arrangements are made for their continued learning in the university, and if they are invited (particularly the cantankerous ones) to come and lecture from time to time.

This brings me to something I might say directly to the graduating class. Today we realize, with a new seriousness or a new enthusiasm, that education must be continuous. This is not only because skills acquired in college or graduate school soon become outmoded, or because one must continuously learn in order to adapt himself to the changing demands of his work and other roles; it is because we understand that developmental changes can occur at any age, that a person has many chances to further his development toward full humanity. We are not bound by our childhood experiences or by our contemporary memberships in groups or by our roles in society. We can change at any age through having experiences that challenge our adaptive capacities. The reason adults, in contrast to youth, seem not to change very much is because they get into ruts, into situations that are sufficiently rewarding and comfortable.

We must understand, and accept, differences in rates of development toward maturity; and today, one cannot help but be impressed by the greater speed with which young people reach a kind of psychological maturity. When I was in college my classmates and I took no interest whatsoever in the affairs of the larger world. We were totally taken up with problems much closer home—football, girls, and relations with each other. But at last when I was in graduate school, I began to pay some attention to political and social problems, found them interesting, and arrived at a level of sophistication comparable to that found in the average freshman of today.

So, if anyone in this graduating class feels that he hasn't developed enough, or as much as he might, let me remind him that there is still plenty of time, and that there will be plenty of opportunities. Let him remain open to experience; let him look at his life in a long time-perspective, seeing it not as a fixed course already determined, but more as a voyage of discovery that might bring important changes of direction.

Recently I met a man, a dean of a graduate school at a great university, who offers an example of what I mean. He started out as a physicist, went into engineering during World War II, thence into industry where he became a member of the top management; now, after several years as dean of a graduate school, he is planning to go into social science. He suggested, what is certainly true in many cases, that if a man wants to be creative after the age of 50 it is a good idea to change his field of concentration.

I hope also that you will take risks, and not be afraid of failure. Our culture has adopted a peculiar and, I think, inappropriate view of success and failure. We have made worldly success into a sort of moral imperative, and we have arranged things so that almost anyone with any talent at all can be some sort of success within our organizations, by doing what he is supposed to and not causing trouble. Hence, in critical times we become aware of an enormous passivity; it seems there is nobody to take the lead or even to stir things up.

If you have not made any trouble in college—well, it's still not too late. If you have been a critic of the status quo, a seer of visions of what might be, stick to your guns.

Training of Clinicians-to-Society

14

Apart from recruiting established people whose desire to work on human problems is left unsatisfied by the demands of their several disciplines, where are we to find what David Krech has called clinicians-to-society?

The jobs to be done require not only noble purpose and high-minded will, not only wisdom, and not only the approach of the psychologist to problem-solving, but also some special kinds of skills and knowledge and experience. Consider, for example, a problem facing many of our colleges and universities: how to prepare themselves for an influx of students belonging to various racial and ethnic minorities. Whoever took the lead in attacking this problem would have to attend to the competences and outlooks of the minority students, to subtle forms of prejudice to be found among personnel of the institution, and the nature of faculty resistance to any possible threat to their academic standards. He would have to be able to see his problem against a background of events on the national scene and in its relations to the social structure of the particular institution, and he would have to work with others in setting goals in accord with a philosophy of education. Not least, he would have to be enough of a scientist to learn by evaluating the effects of his actions, his mistakes as well as his successes, and to make his lessons available to others in terms that would permit tests of their generality.

Here, as well as in various other problem areas, in police-community relations, the welfare system, the struggles of farm workers, and so many others that the spirit droops, there is an absolute need for a *practical* as well as theoretical grasp of personality and social events. How can we train young men and women with a sense of values, humane feeling, disciplined intelligence, particularly the capacity to assemble and evaluate evidence from various sources, and the confidence to act?

This is a large order. It cannot be filled by training that consists almost entirely of how to do specialized research in narrow, albeit theoretically valuable, areas of social psychology. If we agree on the need for effective social action by social and personality psychologists, then let us consider seriously, and urgently, how large numbers of social clinicians and problem-oriented generalists can be trained in departments of psychology. We might begin with the question of recruiting and then discuss ways in which trainees might be helped at various stages of their careers as graduate students, to relate theory and action.

Much of what is required for the sort of activism we are talking about should be present in the student by the time he graduates from college. Our first step toward a solution of our problem, therefore, starts with recruitment.

Criteria for recruitment

Graduate schools of psychology could take an important first step toward turning out action-oriented Ph.D.'s if they were to do what they have often spoken of but rarely carried out in practice: recruiting college seniors on the basis not of what they "have had," but clarity and ingenuity of thinking, richness of imagination, breadth of interests and openness to experience.

The beginning of this practice would come as something of a shock to psychology departments in the better-known liberal arts colleges. These departments evaluate themselves mainly on the basis of what proportion of their students get into graduate school and believe the best way to increase that proportion is to teach what will be taught again later on. However much we bemoan the failure of our most expensive colleges to provide the liberal education they promise, we do not expect these colleges to initiate change. The system within which they operate is dominated by the graduate schools, and as long as these latter institutions want (or appear to want) junior specialists, that is what they will get.

Nor do I expect the graduate departments to change fundamentally either—not until we have produced a few hundred social-psychological activists with an interest in education or until the departments become far less able than now to give immediate material rewards to graduate students willing to go along with the system. I hope, however, that in at least a few departments the faculty in social psychology wants to move toward greater social relevance and has some power and room to maneuver. For them, I venture these suggestions concerning recruitment and selection:

(1) Look more for signs of a good general education than for top grades in psychology.

(2) Instead of giving automatic priority to candidates from well-known colleges, who, according to old friends and colleagues, "have already done graduate work," look more closely at applicants from more obscure institutions who might be just as bright as these apprentices and have had a much better exposure to liberal education.

(3) Give special preference, "other things being equal," to applicants who want to change to social psychology, after having been seriously involved in another field such as classics or history or engineering. Perhaps we may yet turn up another James or Tolman or Boring or Kohler. In any case, this is probably the best assurance we can get nowadays that our candidate will have some breadth.

(4) Give special preference to candidates who have seen something of life, especially those who have worked for a few years in programs or agencies directly concerned with social problems and who now have good reason to believe that more scientific training would help them reach their goals.

(5) Be a bit wary of students who are activists first and scientists or intellectuals only secondarily, in particular those already totally committed to a social program or ideology. It would probably be better if they went immediately to the action front, returning to the academy only when they felt a strong need for the types of training and understanding that can be had only there.

(6) Look for curiosity about people, self-awareness, and humane feelings, rather than visions of oneself filling some particular, well-rewarded social role.

Restoring a core program

Let us move to our second step: the psychological training of our clinician-to-society, or problem-oriented generalist. Nothing that has been said (or will be said later) is intended to suggest that our activist does not need the discipline of psychology. I do urge, of course, that he be something of a generalist, a man who is able to see problems in context and to bring to bear upon them a range of perspectives and kinds of knowledge. Yet some highly desirable and useful skills and intellectual powers can be developed only through intensive engagement with phenomena, systematic knowledge, or method, and this sort of engagement is possible only if the student's range is, at least in the beginning, relatively narrow.

Thus, for example, if a student is to understand the experimental method in science, he must experiment; and if his experimentation is to be meaningful, he must first acquire a good measure of the discipline of a particular science. It would appear also that for the development of confidence in himself as a scholar or professional, a student needs a sense of having mastered some area of knowledge or method, and obviously this area must be relatively narrow if the sense of confidence is to come early, when it is likely to be most needed.

Within the space of a more or less normal Ph.D. program, can a student acquire this discipline and also what it takes to become a problem-oriented social psychologist? I believe that he can, but only if graduate programs are reformed in accord with some elementary principles of pedagogy.

Acknowledging an open secret

Reform would have to begin with at least a tacit acknowledgement by the department of what has become an open secret: that much of what is taught in graduate schools has no place in any defensible philosophy of training but has been inserted into the curriculum for various other reasons. One reason, deriving from the department's wish to compete successfully for "able faculty," is the practice of allowing each professor to "teach his own career." If graduate training in "core" psychology were put on a sound philosophical footing—if it were agreed that its basic function is to give a student the necessary attitudes and inclinations, the knowledge of how to learn and the approach to understanding peculiar to his discipline—doctoral programs would be less expensive than they now are, less frustrating and more favorable to students who wished to prepare themselves for the practice of social psychology (or any other specialty).

Somebody must take the responsibility for this core, sorting out the essential from the trivial and connecting the new (or, more likely, the apparently new) with the established. Since the chairman, good fellow that he is, is probably neglecting this critical task, those interested in training problem-oriented generalists might as well take the lead.

They might begin by reminding their colleagues, with suitable tact, that much of what is taught in under-graduate courses, and even in some graduate courses, is not really decided upon by anybody, but just happens, often as a result of the activities of publishers and a few text-book writers. Publishers persuade their writers to write what market research shows that most teachers want to teach. But how is a teacher caught in a market survey to decide what he wants to teach? After due attention to his own research interests he is likely to look around to see what others are doing, or what text-book writers are writing about, or what has caught the eye of the opinion-makers with their uncanny way of knowing what is about to become fashionable. This highly competitive business can become very tricky. Just the other day, one of our opinion-makers spoke of "the corpse of cognitive dissonance." This will get around, and it is sad to contemplate its impact on the man who is earnestly updating his text and has just devoted nine-tenths of his chapter on attitude change to this now-panned "flash in the pan."

The updating business is a story in itself, one that is both funny and tragic. Like other consumer products, textbooks sell better if they are obviously "new," and what better assurance of apparent novelty than to cite only research published within the last five years? This explains why so many revisions are less interesting and less useful than the original; and it helps to explain why so many graduate students in social psychology have such narrow and otherwise peculiar conceptions of the field.

Field studies from the start

In reforming a graduate program, it is not enough, of course, to eliminate the non-essential, no matter how new. What is taught must be relevant to our activist, and be taught well. And now we come to our third difficult step. Most students who enter graduate school today have already been exposed to various set fields of knowledge and they have learned more or less by rote many concepts that remain largely meaningless. There is no point in offering more of the same. What we want for our future activist is a large experience with field studies that enable him to confront directly some of the phenomena of life in all their complexity and immediacy. He should have this at the beginning of his graduate training. He should have this at various times during his training. He should have this after his graduate training.

We would start him off right by involving him in problem-oriented research in this field, in the first year of his graduate work. Since most of such research is in a comparatively early stage of development, the student could begin participating creatively in the search of knowledge. Through being given a chance to use his mind actively early in his career as a student, he could "learn how to learn," instead of being required to devote himself exclusively to set fields of knowledge, many of which will shortly be outmoded anyway.

With urgent questions already formed in his mind by field experience, he would approach didactic work wishing to connect concepts and experience. If he were fortunate enough to be able to work with faculty engaged in the study of new kinds of empirical phenomena, he could see the work of conceptualization performed, as it were, before his eyes—and could take part in that work himself.

Little of the wasted motion

Field study would have the additional advantage of helping the student to see his scientific and scholarly work in a context of values. The field work of a student would be bound to have implications for the welfare of the individuals or groups he was studying, which would lead him to ask questions not only about the nature of what he observed, but about what he ought to do.

It would be precisely the student's concern about what to do in a practical way that would give him experience in synthesizing knowledge. Forced to consider the various possible consequences of any action he might take on a human or social problem, the student would begin to gain an understanding of some of the ways in which things cling together, and of the ways in which they can be brought together intellectually. A student thus engaged would be unlikely to raise questions about the "meaning" or "relevance" of what he is studying; on the contrary, he would probably have high motivation and morale, and exhibit little of the wasted motion so common among graduate students.

If we are to offer field work in the first year, faculty may, of course, worry about how students are to assimilate that core of psychology we mentioned previously. I am of the opinion that if we do a good job in paring down the core, and an equally good job in co-ordinating the field study, then first year graduate students can do field work without impeding their progress in general psychology.

In many large departments the general requirements upon all students have become relatively light. So far has the division of the departmental offerings into subspecialties gone that a student is able to take care of his general requirements by taking two courses each quarter or semester for two years while devoting the rest of his time to "research." Obviously this "research" could just as well be presided over by social psychologists interested in promoting field study of the kind we have described. As a matter of fact, it would be the responsibility of social psychologists as much as of any others to see that graduate students were well grounded in general psychology.

Other arrangements might well be tried. Thus, if a student becomes deeply involved in field studies during his first year, he might very well postpone most of his graduate requirements for completion during his second year. In any case, activist social psychology students could keep pace with their fellows in other areas of specialization as far as meeting general departmental requirements is concerned.

It would seem a good thing if the student had some connection with applied work at all stages of his career as trainee. Probably he would be best off if he worked with professors who themselves were involved in activities that combined research and action, whether in institutes for the study of human problems or elsewhere. Another way in which graduate students might be enabled to get close to the action is through being teaching assistants in undergraduate courses largely devoted to field work. Such courses are becoming common today largely in response to student demands, and the alert graduate student in social psychology might easily find it possible to learn through teaching.

Students studying students

Social psychologists and their students do not need to go beyond their own university or even their own department in order to find opportunity for combining inquiry and action. Consider the phenomenon of student activism, which has major implications for those who study students as well as for those with responsibilities for education. Investigators are a part of the "establishment" that students have been criticizing: for example, much traditional practice in higher education receives support from the testing industry and the assumptions upon which testing is based. It remains to be seen what benefits students will get from researches into student attitudes and values. The trouble comes from wrong conceptions of the person, inadequate research strategies, and misconceptions of the relations of research and practice. The particular functions that are chosen to measure are *not* isolated in the person; a student is *not* merely a passive respondent to the stimuli present, deriving from them only the meanings that the testers have in mind; the student *does* have a stake in the research operations—not only in the ultimate uses of results but in the immediate effects of testing activities upon him. Colleges know far more about students than students know about the determinants of their formal education. Information about students is obtained without their knowing the implications of what they are revealing, and it is fed into a decision-making apparatus that usually does not include students and may or may not have their interest at heart or even know what would help them to develop.

Reforms in higher education research

I have been arguing this viewpoint since I first became involved in studying students in the early 1950's (Sanford, 1958). I have become increasingly unhappy about the way research on students has been conducted, and want now to propose some reforms in higher education research, as an example of the human problems approach.

One spring in the late 1960's I taught a course called "Social Science and Higher Education" at the Graduate Theological Union, a consortium of theological schools which awards Ph.D. and Th.D. degree in cooperation with the University of California at Berkeley. In this course, six students carried out a study of their own institution. By means of rather intensive interviews, they studied half of the GTU's 100 students. They composed a comprehensive interview schedule, after examining various other schedules and after interviewing each other and taking hard looks at themselves. They conducted trial interviews and exchanged notes on how to do it, carried out formal interviews with everybody in the sample, worked out a scheme for quantifying their material (obtaining scores on over a hundred variables), analyzed the results, and prepared a report for the whole GTU community.

They met more than a few times without their teacher, and when the quarter ended they did not stop their work. As I described in chapter 1, they next turned their attention to a sample of faculty, and made comparative studies of other graduate students.

All members of the class thought this was the best learning experience they had ever had, meaning that they had not only acquired some skills and knowledge but also developed personally. What interested observers was the impact of their study upon the interviewees and even upon the other half of the GTU student body. Many interviewees reported great benefit from the self-analysis that was set in motion (one made a life-changing decision in the middle of the interview), and from a sense that, for the first time, they really belonged to the GTU. The inquiry started a process of change in the whole institution. Students saw their goals and what they were doing as students and, discovering that their hopes and dissatisfactions were widely shared, became prepared for group action to improve their education. The GTU students have now organized themselves formally and set up an action group to work with the faculty and administration to make the school what all know it can become.

This modest experiment could easily become a model for social scientific activity in many settings. I am proposing, indeed am urging, a pattern of activity that combines research, teaching, and other actions.

Perhaps I should say nothing about its economy lest the news spread to funding agencies. What was accomplished by these students could easily be dressed up as a $50,000 project, when in fact it can be done with pleasure and profit by lazy teachers of a wide range of graduate courses in social science. Of course a project combining research, teaching, and action is likely to get lost among the departments of funding agencies, which often are no less fragmented than the university itself. Perhaps the applicant had better present the plan as a project in teaching, *or* in research, *or* in development.

Want to learn but not be taught

When students are helped to study themselves, the objections that our research is dehumanizing or irrelevant can be overcome at once. Instead of asking increasingly sophisticated and skeptical students to fill out more questionnaires, which will be used by other people to plan procedures that are not necessarily in those students' interest, the research will help answer *their* questions, with a view to their planning their own education. What was undertaken at the GTU could be done in various graduate departments and schools of a university; or for that matter, a group of college seniors could conduct technically adequate and thoroughly enlightening studies of various samples of their peers.

There is nothing new about the idea that students learn by doing. Note, however, that the students of the GTU class not only acquired some skills, but became more aware of themselves at the same time that they gained understanding of their research subjects. This is like Peter Madison's method of using case histories of students in classes in which students at the same time prepare case studies of each other and of themselves. The procedure discussed here, however, is far less clinical and less demanding of the instructor. It is really a way of reducing the gap between researcher and subject.

The procedure proposed is well adapted for those students of today who are said to want to learn but not to be taught. Problems of authority are overcome at once. The teacher becomes a true resource person who does not have to explain anything except what students want to know about. Within limits, the more the teacher leaves to the students, the better. The procedure cannot be recommended for those teachers who feel they work hard to present in neat packages the latest fragments from the "explosion in knowledge."

Building a sense of community

Research on students should be educational for those studied as well as for those who do the studying. As has been shown, research of the kind under discussion has an *impact* on students. What justification can be offered for kinds of impact that are not favorable to the student's development? One might say that if research on students is not educational in its processes as well as in the uses of its final results, it is based on inadequate theory, probably trivial, and dubious in respect to its ethics.

Research on students affects them not only individually but as a group. Ever since the work at the Harvard Psychological Clinic in the 1930's, it has been known that intensive studies of students, properly conducted, build a sense of community among those studied and bonds of respect and friendship between them and those who do the studying. In the impersonal world of today's university a sense of real community is more likely to be encouraged by projects that allow people to work together and to understand their own lives than by fragmented studies done "from the top," no matter how brilliant a set of recommendations is filed at the end. Where the institution or department studied is relatively small, as in the case of GTU, research "from the bottom" can be a major force toward integration. As suggested above, there is no good reason why faculty, administration, and the researchers themselves should be left out of this liberating activity.

Research can release the constructive activism latent in students. Just as the individual student who is interviewed carefully is almost bound to begin shaping his career in accord with the insights he gains, so a group of students will begin to think about changing their educational environment in the light of their shared awareness of discrepancies between the ways things are and the way things might be; and in the climate of today the thought easily becomes father to the deed.

The way to change a social structure, such as a school or department, is to study its "personnel," especially those in the lower echelons. Anyone who does not believe this has only to propose the inclusion of the GTU course in a graduate department or school. Recently this idea was introduced at a leading university and immediately encountered all the types of opposition available to the average committee on courses. A study of this sort of opposition reveals the underlying social structure of the school or department, showing those interested in change what resistance may be encountered but also revealing where leverage may be had.

The main forces for change are, of course, in the students themselves, and there is no way in which a determined researcher can be prevented from working with them. Someone who is already teaching in the department has only to remind his colleagues of the basic academic dictum that nobody tells a university man what to do or not to do in his classroom. An outsider could become a consultant to the students, keeping in mind that most teachers in a graduate school are about as unhappy as most of the students, and changes that do not consider their interests and help to liberate them will not be sustained.

Process of inquiry as agent of change

Many people nowadays are asking how to implement some of the good ideas for improving higher education. How do we innovate in our colleges and universities? One answer is that a process of inquiry can serve as an agent of change. Instead of continuing to conduct surveys, report the findings, and expect somebody else to apply them, a researcher can recognize that studies of students, properly conducted, are "interventions in the system," and he can guide the process of change thus begun in ways that will benefit all concerned.

Graduate students can combine inquiry and action in projects not only on campus, as in the example just given, but also in the variety of agencies and organizations they encounter in four years of field experience. Projects of this kind will help students and the rest of us to develop models more sophisticated than the conventional one, in which institutional crisis is followed by a study "from the top" with a set of recommendations which is "respectfully received" and filed as the researcher goes home.

It would be a fine thing, of course, if the student's Ph.D. dissertation grew out of his action-oriented research. This might well require, however, that departments accept theses based on clinical research or participant observation as well as those that describe the carrying out of designs for testing hypotheses. This desirable reform might be particularly difficult to bring about, and we would not want our case to rest very heavily on it. Instead, we propose something that would cost the department very little and could not possibly threaten its "standards": let there be a requirement that trainees in social psychology (those who have elected to go the way of clinical-social) complete a year's internship in some agency, office, or institution directly concerned with human problems. We have in mind such examples as a state employment service, a state senator's office, a prison, a labor union, the office of a Public Defender. This internship could come after the student had completed a thesis based in experimental work if that is what the department preferred, but if it came before the thesis, and largely determined content and design of the thesis, so much the better.

Never too late

Finally, they say that it is never too late to learn. There remains the possibility of acquiring more action-orientation *after* the student has completed his professional training. His prospects here are actually quite good. Post-doctoral or post-professional training programs, continuing education, refresher courses and the like pose no threats to the departments of the university, and they have been carried out whenever individuals interested in starting them could find the money or whenever interested funding agencies could find the leadership for them. Fellowships to enable a person with a Ph.D. in one field to obtain advanced training in another were available in the early 1930's. This sort of thing suffered severe reverses during the great trend toward specialization that began after World War II, but it is being revived today, as in programs in community psychiatry and community psychology.

Training for research and action on human problems could be offered not only by university departments but by human problems institutes such as we describe in chapter 15. Unlike the typical department of psychology, an institute could base its training program on the frankly interdisciplinary idea that individuals cannot be understood apart from the social context in which they live and that an understanding of social structures and processes depends in part on knowledge of personality dynamics. An institute could easily help its doctoral students to integrate these lines of inquiry by providing field experience throughout their normal four years of training, experience in taking some responsibility for one or more individuals in a clinical setting or in one of a variety of public organizations or agencies.

If an independent institute of this kind were located near a major university, it could recruit part-time faculty of the highest quality. As long as departments fail to provide the kind of training sketched in this chapter, some of their most respected and lively members will be delighted (as we are discovering in Berkeley) to give some fraction of their time to a PhD. program in human problems which is offered by an independent institute.

Staffed by experienced teachers of clinical, experimental, personality and social psychology, as well as anthropology, education, law and sociology, this sort of graduate program can, I believe, serve as an example to departments and can meanwhile attract first-rate students who will later help to staff similar programs within the university.

Problem-centered Institutes

15

I have been urging universities for some years to set up multidisciplinary, problem-centered institutes that would work on more than one problem at a time, and I have had some experience in such an institute (Sanford, 1964, 1965, 1967). Without taking back anything I have said about the need for university-based institutes, I now want to suggest that what this country needs is a new kind of agency for research and action, one that is independent of (but closely related to) the university and other institutions of our society.

The guiding principles of this new agency should be, in the main, the same as those I have tried to state for the university-based human problems institute:

(1) Action and inquiry must be viewed as mutually related: action must be based in knowledge and we acquire further knowledge by taking action and studying its effects. Only when efforts are made to change a social situation or institution is its underlying structure revealed, making it possible to develop ideas that are useful in practice.

(2) Problems that arise as a result of social changes constitute new ranges of empirical phenomena; they cannot be attacked by conventional research designs but instead call for exploratory or qualitative study—study directed to their proper definition, to the understanding of their connections with other problems, and to the generation of new concepts and methods.

(3) Since knowledge of how things cling together is as important a part of science as knowledge of how things may be isolated, social scientists must be willing (some of the time) to adopt holistic and comprehensive approaches to complex and wide ranging social phenomena. They will be forced to do this if they are practical, and thus required to gauge the various consequences of a particular action. Social scientists who become motivated in action-oriented research come to realize how

intellectually demanding the work is, and they overcome any contempt they might have had for "applied science."

(4) Social scientists who work on social problems must participate in setting the goals of action. Individuals and organizations looking to science for help often have narrow or short-run views of what they desire, and the social scientist cannot avoid acting in accord with his own value-orientation.

(5) The human problems institute must work on several different problems at the same time. This kind of exposure to a variety of problems and the accompanying association with colleagues from different disciplines, serves to educate the staff in a generalist orientation. Little would be gained if a scientist gave up a disciplinary specialty only to become a specialist in some applied area. Work on several problems at the same time also leads the staff to look for underlying affinities among them—a style of thought often leading to advances on the conceptual and theoretical front.

The need for independence

It would be highly desirable if institutes of this kind could be established within universities, but the very circumstances that make it desirable also make it extremely difficult or impossible. Obstacles arise from the position of the university in society, from the university's organizational structure of departments, schools and specialized institutes, and from the attitudes and values of faculty members. The university is a conservative institution, more a reflection of society than an instrument of social change.

While the new institute obviously is not conceived of as a center for social revolution, it must be free to advocate policies and to initiate actions that are called for on the basis of its research programs and findings. Recommendations or actions would not need to be very radical in order to threaten the interests of at least some organized groups in society who would then find it easy to put the university in an embarrassing position.

Work on problems of the kind being discussed here is not excluded from the university; indeed, there are university institutes devoted to the study of one or another of them. The university must be prepared, however, should controversy arise, to take a position of neutrality, which it may do by stressing its role as a center for pure inquiry. It thus loses the benefits to be gained from a combination of inquiry and action without achieving true neutrality either, for in a rapidly changing society neutrality is conservatism.

The university does not avoid involvement in practical affairs. It can and it does work, certainly not inappropriately, to further practical objectives which are understood and approved of by the man in the street, such as the improvement of agriculture, the building of armaments and the advancement of technology generally. Government support for work of this kind constitutes a substantial proportion of the budget of large and prominent universities; and, accordingly, these institutions act in such a way as to protect their sources of funds. Usually, therefore, arrangements are made for funneling proposals originating with individual faculty members through a central university agency. It is a reasonable presumption that the university's central agency will in the long run tend to favor projects that either represent specialized pure science (promising to support or challenge theories in the forefront of professional concern), or in the case of human problems research, are "safe." From the point of view of the university's survival and growth this may be wise policy, but it does mean that not all applications are considered soely on their merits and that fund-granting agencies do not see all the proposals that faculty members might want to direct to them.

Private universities might seem to be free of some of the constraints upon state institutions, but in practice this is not always the case. Prominent private universities, always short of funds, are also heavily dependent upon government funds; and they also have large and diversified constituencies who can be counted on to make trouble when the university engages in controversial activities.

An independent institute would be able to take "far out" or otherwise controversial proposals directly to foundations or private donors without fear that a university's reputation would be damaged. It would also avoid the numerous small frustrations, and the expense, of working within and through a large bureaucracy that contributes nothing to the success of the work itself.

At the same time an independent institute located near a university and having various kinds of relationships with it, and with some of its parts, would have positive advantages.

Universities have sometimes found it wise to encourage and assist the setting up within their environs of independent institutes that worked on problems which, though of interest to the university, did not fit their programs or policies. Most characteristically, perhaps, the problems worked on at such institutes have been brought to them by private organizations or individuals. It seems reasonable to expect that university officials or faculty members might wish to pass along to a nearby independent institute projects bearing on public issues too controversial to be addressed from within the university itself. (Before 1960 very little research on race relations or the effects of segregation was done in prominent universities, nor were government agencies or large foundations supporting research on these controversial subjects, but there was no shortage of concerned university men who would have liked to see such research done.) Should this happen in the case of an institute of the kind proposed here, we should expect that these officials and faculty members would be available for consultation on these projects, and even that some of them might join the institute as staff members on some temporary or part-time basis.

Easier for outsiders

An independent institute might serve a university by studying some of its processes. For technical reasons alone, such studies were best carried out by an agency outside the university. If students were interviewed, for example, they would find it easier to express themselves if they felt sure that what they said could in no way affect their fate as students. If the study were carried out in accord with the general principles set forth above, students would know that the study was itself an intervention in the university's processes, as well as a way of improving their lives. They would also know that the process would by definition include "feeding back" of information, consultation on what innovations in practice might be undertaken, and even assistance in the carrying out of new educational procedures. This would help to lift educational research out of the depths of triviality into which it has been sinking, mainly through an insistence upon a narrow conception of science.

Enormous interest is vested in the maintenance of the university's present structure. Universities expect their professors to define themselves primarily in terms of their discipline, or their speciality within a discipline, and to be loyal to their departments or schools.

As I explained in Chapter 12, the process of specialization

begins early. A graduate student is given so much work within his own department that he has little chance of finding out what other departments might offer. He is rarely able to work on problems that interest him deeply because he must restrict himself to methods that are approved by departmental committees, and this, in the social sciences today, almost always means methods for demonstrating hypotheses rather than methods that could lead to discovery.

Exclusion of generalists

The pressure on a scholar to remain a specialist is continuous, and applied where it is felt most keenly, upon his need to find a relatively secure position. One might suppose that human problem institutes within universities would be natural academic homes for generalist scholars; and so they are as far as various kinds of "psychic income" are concerned; but the hard fact is that tenure appointments in universities can, except in very rare instances, be made only through departments and schools. Such appointments must, of course, be reserved for men who are loyal and who represent specialities that departments and schools must include among their offerings if they are to keep pace with developments in their disciplines. This means that the generalist, if he does not already have academic tenure, must live precariously from grant to grant.

The professional schools of a university would appear at first glance to be natural places for multi-disciplinary, problem-centered work, and, indeed, some of them in recent years have been innovating along these lines. Unfortunately, however, the applied work to which these schools are committed does not usually have status as high as that enjoyed by the sciences and humanities, so that members of these schools are drawn to imitate the established sciences, and instead of addressing themselves directly to the human problems their schools were set up to cope with, they apply themselves to research which in its "purity" often outdoes that of the admired older disciplines. Sadly enough, this does not improve the status of the applied field. The educational psychologist who does work that psychologists generally approve will be called a psychologist, and the fact that he is in a school of education will not be held against him, but psychologists will still disclaim any knowledge of education, lest they be suspected of association with education people. For these same reasons, problem-centered institutes in universities tend to be transformed into centers for specialized inquiry.

In view of all these pressures, is it impossible to establish and to maintain a human problems institute within the university? Probably it could be done with enough money and persuasiveness, particularly if these were applied at a time when graduate students were in open rebellion against "the system" and when there were public demands for greater attention to pressing problems.

However, if established independently a human problems institute is likely to enjoy not only more success in its own pursuits but more influence upon a nearby university. If an independent institute became known as a good place to work, a place where interesting and important things were done, and done well, individuals and groups within the university might be challenged to undertake a similar adventure themselves. Such an outcome would, of course, be highly desirable. But even if many human problems institutes were established within universities, there would probably still be need for independent institutes that were free to become involved in implementation of policies they advocated.

In any case, the proposed institute would cultivate relationships that began with the institute's study of some of a department's students, or with assistance in the training of such students, and that might blossom into collaborations on research projects—perhaps ones in which the institute became the "action arm" of research carried out mainly by the department. Or a university institute might undertake to collect and process data in connection with a project initiated by the independent institute.

Opportunities for professors

The faculty member's outlook is largely determined by the general situation in which he works, but in time his attitudes and values become deeply ingrained, and are not likely to change as soon as he attains academic tenure or moves to a university whose formal organization is different. Typically, his major values are purity, objectivity and ethical neutrality. He becomes a bit nervous if a colleague publishes something that is interesting enough to appear in the newspapers, he takes a dim view of a teacher whose course is popular with students, and he looks askance at a colleague who writes for a general audience. In his professional role, therefore, he could hardly be expected to support a human problems institute of the sort proposed here.

At the same time, however, there are several ways in which

an independent institute and the individual faculty member might develop mutually beneficial relationships. Few university men are fully identified with their roles or totally embraced by them. A man whose professional behavior was tightly governed by standards of purity, objectivity, and ethnical neutrality might, as an individual, be broadly intellectual and generalist, ethically highly sensitive, and deeply concerned about social problems. In this case he would have difficulty finding, within the university structure, opportunities for the expression of these aspects of himself—least of all, opportunities for their concerted or integrated expression.

Various kinds of relationships

The proposed institute, in contrast, could offer the university faculty member just such opportunities; at the least it would be a place where on weekends he could take part in intellectual activities that contrasted with his everyday work, and at the most he might be a part-time staff member who embraced the institute's orientation to problems and assumed a major role in its activities. The institute would seek to develop various kinds of formal and informal relationships with members of the university, making use of their specialized knowledge (they could be lecturers, discussion leaders, consultants and members of research teams) while offering them new patterns of intellectual companionship.

I can think of several ways in which such an institute might be established and made to operate: for example, a foundation could do it at once, using such funds as were necessary to attract generalist social scientists. If people involved in the institute wanted to influence legislation, say on drugs, alcohol, abortion or the behavior of the police) they could set up a taxable corporation in the same building. Or a group of social scientists who knew how to make a lot of money (such as by rendering services to industry) could use their profits to set up the institute as a nonprofit corporation in which they would invite like-minded colleagues to work.

A Model for Action Research

16

A friend in operations research told me about doing a cost-effectiveness study of one of our great universities. In the late 1960's he and his colleagues had been seeking new funding through the U.S. Office of Education and the Committee on Basic Research of the National Science Foundation. Enthusiastic about his work, believing he could show its usefulness to the university, my friend awaited his answer from the Committee. Finally he got the message that the funding agencies were wildly enthusiastic about the proposal but, of course, could not fund it because it was not "basic."

I wondered how far this rigid separation of research and action had gone. Clearly the term "action research" is not exactly on everybody's tongue nowadays. The contrast with the 1940's and the early 1950's seems to me striking. Particularly during the late 1940's there was an outpouring of reports of action research from the Research Center for Group Dynamics and the Commission on Community Interrelations. One, such as myself, who during that hopeful time was taken up with promoting psychoanalysis and personality research, could and did easily form the impression that action research was a dominant trend in social psychology.

Yet in 1957 when I spoke before the Society for the Psychological Study of Social Issues about social science and social reform, basing myself on the work of my colleagues and myself at Vassar College (Sanford, 1956), Brewster Smith said with surprise and, as I thought, with some pleasure: "So you are really following the old Lewin model of action research." I thought, of course, that mine was a new and improved model; but I knew it could not have existed without the work of Lewin, and was surprised to hear the latter spoken of as if it belonged to the past.

What Lewin wrought

What was Lewin's model? I think it was well set forth in his paper, "Group Decision and Social Change" (Lewin, 1947). The example he used had to do with how to change people's food habits. Action research consisted in analysis, fact-finding, conceptualization, planning, execution, more fact-finding or evaluation, a repetition of this whole cycle of activities; indeed, a spiral of such cycles.

Leon Festinger told Alfred Marrow that Lewin's greatest contribution "on the abstract level may have been the idea of studying things through changing them and seeing the effect. This theme—that in order to gain insight into a process one must create a change and then observe its variable effects and new dynamics—runs through all of Lewin's work" (Marrow, 1969). This seems very close to common sense. It is the way to solve any practical problem or to learn any skill. Yet for Lewin this kind of involvement with practical problems was a never-failing source of theoretical ideas and knowledge of fundamental social-psychological relationships.

Action research is still very much alive. It has strong advocates in high places. Martin Deutsch, in his presidential address before the Society for the Psychological Study of Social Issues, said that the need for knowledge of the effect of experiences upon development, as a basis for changes in policies and organizations, "clearly points to an emphasis on action programs and action research as fundamental tools of the social scientist" (Deutsch, 1969).

Recent examples of action research

Programs clearly labelled action research, or which could properly be so labelled, have not been hard to find. As of 1970, for example, four major ones could be found within walking distance of the Wright Institute in Berkeley. There was Soskin and Korchin's "after-school school," a program for offering people of high school age what (on theoretical grounds) they seem to need for their development but do not get in school (Soskin and Korchin, 1967). There was Peter Lenrow's "collaborative problem solving" with teachers and administrators of the Berkeley School System, an action-research program with some distinctive new features (Lenrow, 1970). There was Joan and Douglas Grant's "new careers program" which demonstrated that prison inmates can be an important source of manpower in the human-service fields (Grant and Grant, 1970). And there was the program of Wilbur Hoff and his associates for training poor people for jobs to be defined and instituted in hospitals and clinics (Hoff, 1970). I should mention here too the Wright Institute's doctoral program in social-clinical psychology, based on knowledge of the situation and needs of graduate students and guided by a theory of individual development and organizational processes (Sanford, 1970, and chapter 8 of this book).

My planned systematic survey of action research programs has not yet taken me beyond the Berkeley city limits but, even so, I receive reports from time to time of highly significant programs in less favored parts of the country. I recall, for example, Robert Sinnett and Angela Sachson's impeccable evaluation of their project for demonstrating that severely emotionally disturbed students can be given satisfactory care in a rehabilitation living unit in a regular university dormitory (Sinnett and Sachson, 1970).

Studying the effects

The survey of which I speak should pay particular attention to publications in the fields of public health, social welfare, and criminology. I suspect that more action research on the Lewin model is done by specialists in these fields than by social psychologists. A great deal of work in the spirit of action research also goes under the heading of "community psychology," as shown, for example, in Adelson and Kalis' systematic treatment of this subject (1970). Action research sometimes also occurs under the heading of "evaluation research," as when Donald Campbell (1969), Samuel Messick (1970), and Michael Scriven (1967) carry to a high level of sophistication the essential fact-finding feature of Lewin's model. Scriven, indeed, in distinguishing between "formative evaluation" (which serves program improvement) and "summative evaluation" (appraisal of the final product), goes a long way toward filling in Lewin's cycle with precise operations. Although these three authors assume a division of labor between the evaluators and those responsible for execution, their work shows beyond question that much can be learned from studying the effects of actions.

The fact remains, however, that none of this work—evaluation research, community psychology, or true action research—is in the mainstream of social psychology or social science generally. Although the great bulk of Federal funds for social science do go to applied social science, as academic social scientists never tire of pointing out (Beals, 1970), how many of these projects could qualify as action research? Very few, because nearly all of applied social science emphasizes the application to problems of what is already known, rather than the study of actions as a means for advancing science.

The separation of science from practice is strongly advocated by leaders in academic social science. Thus George Miller in his presidential address before the American Psychological Association used a revealing Biblical image to enforce the separation: "Many psychologists, trained in an empiricist, experimental tradition have tried to serve two masters at once. That is to say, they have tried to solve practical problems and simultaneously to collect data of scientific value on the effects of their interventions. Other fields maintain a more equitable division of labor between scientist and engineer. Scientists are responsible for the validity of the principles; engineers accept them and try to use them to solve practical problems" (Miller, 1969). If the two masters are God and mammon, we do not need to ask which was being claimed for academic psychology.

Similarly, George Albee, in *his* presidential address before the same Association, insisted on the fundamental difference between research and practice and strongly implied that never the twain shall meet (Albee, 1970). Possibly Miller and Albee do not speak for the majority of psychologists, but they certainly speak for what might be called the psychology establishment, whose voice has also been heard from the psychology panel of the Survey of the Behavioral and Social Sciences, under the auspices of the Committee on Science and Public Policy of the National Academy of Sciences, and the Problems and Policy Committee of the Social Science Research Council.

Minor concessions

Among the thirteen recommendations of this panel, one does propose that "psychologists increase their research on problems related to social action programs and field experiments" which "may provide insights into principles of human behavior that are difficult to study in any other way" (Clark and Miller, 1970). But in general the report reflects massive complacency about the achievements of psychology, and suggests no major changes in the present allocation of resources.

At about the same time the broader social science establishment also spoke through the report of another blue ribbon commission: the Special Commission on the Social Sciences of the National Science Board. This Commission showed considerable sensitivity to the present "identity crisis" of social science and awareness of the need for fresh approaches to our social problems. I think Kurt Lewin would have applauded, as I did, the recommendation of Federal funding for multi-disciplinary, problem-oriented institutes. But, like the other authorities just cited, this commission seemed to be stuck with the science-engineering model, in which discoveries are first made (in the lab as it were) and then "applied" (Special Commission, 1969).

A sort of orphan's role

What has happened to action research? I would say now that, contrary to the impression I had in the late 1940's, it never really got off the ground. By the time the Federal funding agencies were set up after World War II, action research was already condemned to a sort of orphan's role in social science, for the separation of science and practice was institutionalized by then, and has been basic to the Federal bureaucracies ever since. This truth was obscured for a time by the fact that old-timers in action research were still able to get their projects funded. Younger researchers soon discovered, however, that action research proposals *per se* received a cool reception from the funding agencies and were, indeed, likely to win for their author the reputation of being "confused."

In this situation the old-timers in action research have not been reproducing themselves, at least not at the usual rate for psychologists. When jobs for action research open up, as occasionally does happen, trained people are nowhere to be found. Lipton and Klein, for example, report the absence of adequate role models in their Boston University program for training psychologists for practice and research in problems of change in the community. They write, "there are few psychologists available to undertake the direct supervision of the student seeking a community-psychology experience. Apparently few psychologists have made their way into fields of application like group relations and community relations" (Lipton and Klein, 1970).

Consequences of the separation

In attempting to summarize what I suspect is a familiar story, I would say that we have separated (and then institutionalized the separation of) everything that from the point of view of action research belongs together. Analysis of the problem, conceptualization, data gathering, planning, execution, evaluation, training—the intimate family of activities that constituted Lewin's model has been pretty well dispersed.

The categorical separation of research from practice has made it very difficult for a social scientist to study phenomena that cannot be experimented upon in the laboratory or social structures that can be understood only through attempts to change them. Likewise, it has laid the social sciences wide open to the charge of irrelevance, not only by students but by men of affairs. It would hardly occur to a college president to look to the social science literature for help with his problems, and as Blum and Funkhauser (1965) have shown, social scientists are among the last people state legislators would consult about the problem of drug-abuse.

Despite the fact that social-scientific work on practical problems poses the greater intellectual challenge, "pure" science was said to have more prestige, so that once these activities were wrested apart, academics gravitated toward the latter. One result has been that efforts by Federal agencies to do something about the problems of society soon became bogged down. When new bureaus or "study sections" are set up to do applied social science, their personnel seek to avoid appearing second-class by being just as hard-nosed or "scientific" as their heroes in the academic social sciences, and end by being just as narrow. When centers for research and development are set up within universities, academic social scientists, who are needed to lend prestige to the enterprise, seize the opportunity to get funding for what they were doing already, and things go on much as before. This same tendency is displayed by the newer professional schools of universities—education, social welfare, criminology, public health—which become distracted from their purposes by putting in Ph.D. programs which ape (but seldom match) those of the older disciplines.

Well-heeled but unhappy

Once science is split off from practice, further splits develop. We have on the one side experts in conceptualization, theoretical model-building, research design, and experimentation; on the other side experts in planning, execution, and evaluation, with each group finding more and more difficulty in talking with the others. Training follows the general trend of events in science: separated bureaucratically from research and from action at the funding level, training is mainly in the hands of segregated experts. For example, sensitivity training, a proceeding of enormous potential with some solid achievements to its credit, has been lifted out of its natural context of social structure and social practice and rendered free-floating, apparently on the assumption that its recipients are also free-floating.

Small wonder that social scientists generally seem to be well-heeled but unhappy. We do not want to be "mere technicians" who carry out other people's purposes, as Sherif (1968) has so eloquently said; yet we have so detached ourselves from practical affairs that we do not know enough to make decisions in important matters ourselves. There should be a large place for idle curiosity in a civilized community, but if we are not doing action research, we find it hard to indulge our curiosity at a time when basic institutions seem about to fall to pieces. As liberal intellectuals we would like to make social science available to people who need it the most, but for this task the model of "science" followed by "engineering" is hopelessly inadequate.

How did we get into this fix? The basic trouble is the fragmentation I have described, which can be understood as an aspect of the general tendency toward specialization in modern science and scholarship. Effective social problem-solving calls for multidisciplinary work, yet departmentalism seems everywhere on the increase. The psychologists' panel mentioned earlier did recommend consideration by universities of the idea of a Graduate School of Applied Behavioral Science, which would offer a place for low-prestige "engineering" work on social problems so long as it would not require any changes in existing departments and schools.

Specialization exists within as well as among the disciplines, in consequence of which we have a fantastic proliferation of bitsy, disconnected, essentially unuseable researches. A natural accompaniment of high levels of development in science, specialization has obviously led to intellectual and practical payoff in the past, but the compartmentalization of social scientific activities and the scarcity of efforts to pull things together calls for explanation.

Like professional practice, social science has been adapting itself to the requirements of an advanced technological society, which demands more and more segregation of functions and the training of experts to perform them. Just as professionals in health, education, and welfare no longer deal with the whole person, but only with particular symptoms or functions, so psychologists in their research and theory-making focus more and more on part-functions without bothering to connect them with central structures in the person. Indeed, as I have argued in chapter 4, the very concept of the person, downgraded and ignored, seems about to disappear from the literature. Not only have we contributed to the dehumanization of our research subjects by reducing them to "respondents" for the sake of enterprises that never yielded any benefit to them, and to the dehumanization of ourselves by encouraging self-definition in terms of narrow specialties: we have also been disseminating a most unfortunate image of man. Where social scientists see only an aggregate of meaningful "behaviors," great masses of our people likewise are reduced to a conception of the self as fragmented and externalized: one *is* what one can present to others in a particular situation.

Another way to work

In contrast to the corrupt and dangerous model of social science prevalent today, I want to sketch a contemporary model for action research (or as I would prefer to say, research-action).

Let us consider some if its main features in turn:

(1) Analysis determines what kinds of questions are to be asked. These should be practical, although somewhat general and open-ended. In one of our studies the questions were how to improve teaching, how to change features of academic culture, and how to promote the development of individual faculty members. Most social science questions, in my view, should be of this general kind: how to arrange the environment, institution or the social setting in such a way as to promote the development of all the individuals concerned.

Analysis with attention to the nature of the basic questions can save the researcher a great deal of trouble. Four or five years ago we sent a government agency a proposal of a longitudinal study of graduate students. We were kept dangling for three years and were never funded. During this waiting period we realized that we were genuinely concerned about graduate students and that we did not need to study them in order to know that many were very unhappy or were not getting what they needed for their development. So instead of undertaking a conventional program of research we started a new program of graduate training in social-clinical psychology (Sanford, 1970). Now we are really finding out what needs to be done and something about how to do it. Had we been funded we would probably still be bogged down in the analysis of data.

If development becomes the criterion

(2) The aim of promoting individual development has several important implications. We must go far beyond the highly abstract formulations of Kurt Lewin, filling in his scheme with particular kinds of needs, dispositions, values, conflicts, and so forth. An approach that is concerned with individual development must be comprehensive. An interest in changing one aspect of the person or of his behavior must take into account the implications of such change for the total person. To understand the person we must see him in his total setting. Research action is properly multidisciplinary—and in my view only a focus on problems, ultimately problems of human development or human welfare, will bring about collaboration among the academic disciplines.

The concern with human development, of which I speak, is a concern with development now rather than in the future. It means that we must behave toward our subjects in a way that is favorable to development: for example, to their autonomy, privacy, and self-esteem. We go contrary to this value if we use our subjects as means to some other end, including the end of their own well-being in the remote future.

The subject is the client; reporting to him is an action. Lewin considered that his action research would favor the purpose of "social management" as well as the self-management of groups. During World War II, and in the years shortly thereafter, it was easier than now to assume that "management" would use social science knowledge in the interest of all concerned. For surely there was much more agreement about large national purposes then than there is now. I am not suggesting that we ought to deprive management of knowledge about the functioning of those it is appointed to manage, but the information ought to go simultaneously, if not first, to those on whose responses the report is based.

Planning by the "subjects"

(3) Planning, or "planning ahead," does not have such an important role in the present model as in the action research of the past. These days many people will upset plans which they have not helped to make. To arrange things in such a way that the "natives" (students, faculty, poor people, ethnic minorities, and so on) can and do take part in the planning, should become a goal that supersedes planning from above by experts. In the

case of the Wright Institute's graduate school, we might well have devoted a year to planning, preferably with the aid of a "planning grant," before beginning any operations. Instead we decided to do it now and plan it later. It seemed to us that our graduate students would have to take part in the planning in any case, and that the experience of helping to plan a graduate program would be of considerable educational value. This, however, puts heavy emphasis upon what Michael Scriven (1967) calls "formulative evaluation." We institute a procedure, see how it works, and make a change if this seems necessary or wise, always in a spirit of continuous experimentation. I hope that after a decent interval there will be some "summative evaluation," but I also hope that this would be "formative" for the next program in graduate education.

Who will lead the way?

Action research as an alternative way to work offers obvious intellectual as well as practical advantages, but seeing the advantages is one thing and being able to enjoy them is another. Who will lead the way in making the advantages widely available? Organized social science, as an elite, is part of a larger system, the political and economic establishment, which it often verbally opposes but upon which it depends for support. Like other industries, social science has been polluting its environment, not only by treating its research subjects as means rather than ends and disseminating a rather monstrous image of researchable man, but also by creating an enormous amount of waste in the form of useless information. Much of what ought to be left to decompose we now make great plans to "retrieve." From the developmental point of view it looks very much as if the system were designed by and for professors still in the stage of achieving a sense of competence.

We have got to make some changes. But how?

We are confronted with the old problem; we can't change the system without changing the individuals in it; and we can't change the individuals without changing the system. Where is a start to be made? One possibility is to bring pressure to bear from outside, in the form of money, of course. The usual procedure is to build new structures on top of or alongside those we already have. The U.S. Congress may take an interest in this matter; and if by some chance they should ask me, I would say the main thing is to restore the independence of social science. If we do not want to be "mere technicians" and if we do not know enough to make major practical decisions, we nonetheless have much to offer people who are interested in changing themselves singly or collectively. Social science needs to be free of national and state political and economic establishments so that it can work out mutually beneficial relationships with people who do not ordinarily benefit from its activities, and the individual social scientist needs to be free of the social science establishment so that he may contribute according to his own lights.

The funding of project research ought to be abandoned. It has spoiled the academic community, damaged undergraduate education almost beyond repair, given status to trivia, created an expensive bureaucracy, and corrupted thousands of investigators. This change will have to come from above, for the funding apparatus has no built-in mechanisms for self-correction. A friend of mine, an anti-establishmentarian from way back who has said publicly many times that most of our published experimental work fails to meet minimum scientific standards, has recently been induced to serve on a study committee for the National Institute of Mental Health. She will inevitably help to perpetuate what she decries, but, as she says, "NIMH has done a lot for me."

Action research on academic culture

I would not, however, put the control of social science research back into the universities if I did not have an idea as to how the academic culture might be changed, in part through action-research studies of departments, colleges, professional schools, universities, state psychological associations, the American Psychological Association. The idea is not exactly new. Some years ago when the psychology department at Berkeley was caught in one of its perennial crises, the Dean of Letters and Science appointed a committee to see what could be done. When a question about the role of institutes came up at one of the meetings of this committee, its chairman said, "what we need is an institute for the study of the psychology department."

There has been much recent discussion of studying the American Psychological Association. How might this be done? Shall a task force of the central office select a national sample to whom questionnaires will be mailed, then make the data available to a committee who will use it to plan our lives? I would say not. This sort of thing might have been all right in past studies of students and other "natives," but surely for ourselves we can arrange something more humanistic. At least we can be clients at the same time that we are subjects.

So let a few professors and students from Hayward State study a department at San Francisco State, and a group from the latter institution study a department at Berkeley, while some professors and students from Berkeley carry out a research-action at Hayward. No master plan would be needed, for those who were studied would in each case take part in the planning, contributing questions they wanted asked of others and of themselves. All that would be needed to begin would be general agreement that all hands would be interviewed. A process of change started in this way could easily continue under its own steam. For the model that has been offered is not only designed to encourage professors to be subjects of action-research, but also to arouse interest in the carrying out of action-research. The particular example that I have offered —that is, of studying academic culture—is in my view the key to acceptance of action-research by professors who need to be rescued from one another.

What happened in particular departments or schools could easily spread and start discussions of our identity crisis on a national scale. The widespread use of the present model would have good effects of a more general nature. By demonstrating our ability and our willingness to study ourselves we would go some way toward restoring trust in our competence to study others singly and collectively.

How better than in microcosm?

The study of a department or even of a profession may seem small and timid compared with consulting for national policy-making bodies or advocating policies before legislative assemblies, but how can social science be better on the national scene than it is in microcosm? If we are to build a better society, a good place to begin is with making our own department, institution, school, or association a truly human community. If it is our purpose to liberate women and other "minorities," let us begin at home. If we are to promote human development generally, let us begin by showing that we know how to promote the development of our students.

Actually, I am not neglecting the impact of our work on the larger community. I agree with those writers such as Miller (1969) and Snoek (1969) who suggest that our influence on the body politic has been less through the dissemination of knowledge than through the presentation of an image of man. Of course, I take a dimmer view than do these writers of the sort of image we have been presenting. But I strongly agree that our major influence is through what we do and are. The good that we may do will derive less from the models we finally build in our own domains, than from the model we present in the building. And this, I hope, will be a model of man trying to understand and to improve himself and his society.

Moral
Character

Education for Enjoyment of Life

17

The central question for education, as I have argued in earlier chapters, is how the settings in which people live and work favor or hamper personal development. Knowledge of this matter opens the way to the further and really crucial question for the scientist and the whole society: how may settings be changed, or created, so as best to sustain the development of the people in them?

The kind of setting, the community or institution, that best favors individual development is also one that embodies values basic to democratic society. Chief among these, I think, are trust, love, justice, freedom and truth. These values are closely interrelated, and they fall into a hierarchy. If truth is the highest value, trust is the most basic. Without trust there can be no community, for each person in an aggregation would regard each of the others as an enemy. Unless the infant can trust someone he cannot grow beyond psychological infancy, and unless the adolescent is trusted, he cannot become an adult.

No one can become fully human unless he is loved, and loves someone else; no one will have any impulse to help others or to contribute to his community unless he is allowed to feel he is worth something, unless he knows he will be the object of concern and care when he is in trouble. Without justice men become aggressive and cynical, and in time, they take up positions outside the system that has denied them.

We need freedom in order to develop ourselves and to be ourselves. The highly developed person is a freely choosing person; his ability to choose depends on his having had opportunities to make choices, and his actual choosing requires an environment that offers genuine alternatives. Truth, of course, is the overriding value, particularly in colleges and universities. It is the basis for our control of ourselves and of our environment.

A natural hierarchy of values

There is ample evidence, as I suggested, that these values are arranged in an order, whether in an individual or in a collectivity. People will not care for one another unless there is trust among them, and without some minimum of caring and being cared for, justice will not become an important value; if people do not have justice, they are unlikely fully to appreciate freedom, and without freedom, they will lack both the capability and the disposition to seek the truth.

This line of thought calls to mind the University of Richmond in the late spring of 1929. Members of the graduating class, of which I was one, were just beginning to ask what they would do with themselves now that June was at hand. With the exception of a few young men who had long since decided to become doctors, lawyers, or Baptist preachers, most of us had given the matter little thought. All we were certain of was that we wanted to live somewhere not very far from Richmond and to maintain relationships with family and friends. They would take care of finding us jobs; if worse came to worse, they would just take care of us. Another thing was important. It was generally assumed at that college, at that time, that in all areas save the professions, preparation for a job would be taken care of by on-the-job training (This was long before the time of what Ivar Berg has properly called "the great training robbery.")

The outlook of the college seniors in "the good old days" was actually based in a philosophy of education, although it was not very well spelled out. We used to debate whether the purpose of education was to teach how to make a living or how to live. Naturally, most of us came out in favor of the second alternative. I now see that this preference reflected a whole cultural pattern, one that accented family relationships, friendships, kindness, community, and individual self-development. It was, in short, aristocratic education, on the model advocated by Thomas Jefferson. It had somehow filtered down to us, mainly small town boys living on the edge of poverty. To me it still makes sense to advocate an aristocratic education for everybody. (Jefferson, of course, wanted it for *nearly* everybody.)

Nothing gayer than wisdom

At this time, fifty years later, when more and more people are tired of, or calling into question, their strivings for success, status, power, money, we do well to look to a different theme in our heritage. Such a theme is expressed in what Montaigne wrote about wisdom: "People are very wrong to paint her to children as inaccessible with a countenance gruff, frowning, and terrible: who, I would ask, has masked her with this false face, pale and hideous? There is nothing gayer than wisdom, nothing jollier, more playful, or I could almost say, more madcap."

Montaigne was telling us that the wise man is one who knows how to enjoy life. It must be added at once, of course, that if one is to enjoy life and find a great deal of meaning in it, he really has to do some work. Until he has gained familiarity with the Bible and Shakespeare he has hardly begun to prepare for a good life.

This is a way of saying that education for the enjoyment of life should begin with subjects that open the way to full participation in our culture—reading, literature, art, math, music, science, drama, history, skills, sports. These subjects give access to the boundless satisfactions to be had from the life of the imagination.

The study of these subjects is vitally important for people whose work is not likely to be very demanding; and for a society that suffers from the over-production of material goods and will need for its economic well-being the employment of more and more people whose activities cannot be duplicated by machines. People educated in this way will want to work. We need not worry about that. They may even *enjoy* their work, as far too few people do today. And if a person falls in love with one of the subjects mentioned, he is assured of much satisfaction in life.

Unhappy, they make trouble

There is another crucially important reason for accenting education for enjoyment. People who cannot or do not enjoy life cause a great deal of trouble in this world. Unable to find satisfaction in ordinary human activities, they resent other people's enjoyment. Unable to permit themselves any small vices, they sooner or later become involved in big ones. They become mean and punitive toward people they perceive as not living up to their own strict and narrow moral standards. They engage in anti-social movements called crusades. Unsure of their control over their vital passions, they strive to control other people, revealing in this respect an insatiable need for power. Their mark is humourlessness, whether they be government officials or youthful revolutionaries. May we be delivered from both.

Human development, becoming highly developed as a person, is the over-arching value; it has been defined as such by great thinkers and great educators from ancient times down to the present. The major goals of development were set by Socrates when he said "know thyself", and by Jesus who said "love thy neighbor as thyself." Social scientists can add little to these statements, beyond helping to state them in terms that will permit us to see their interrelations and to understand the ways in which they depend on educational policies and procedures.

Relations of love and knowledge

Our love of our neighbor, for example, increases with our knowledge of him, but it also depends on our knowledge of ourselves, for if we are blind to our own weaknesses and aggressive impulses, we may easily attribute them to our neighbor and make them grounds for hating him. Our love of our neighbor also depends on our love of ourselves, love in the sense of respect and acceptance, for self-contempt and self-doubt make us selfish and egotistical, and unable to give anything to a neighbor.

But to know ourselves, we must be loved by others; otherwise we would lack the confidence that self-examination requires; and in order to love ourselves with full knowledge of ourselves, we need to be regarded with understanding and compassion. It follows from this that when we love our neighbor, we help him achieve self-knowledge.

Development is progressive; advances occur when challenges are suited to the state of readiness in the personality, when they are great enough to evoke new responses aimed at mastery but not so great as to elicit defensive reactions, and when the person reflects upon the new responses. If a person to whom the interventions of an educator are directed does not understand what is happening and is not encouraged to think about it in relation to the self, this person is in effect being manipulated. Changes in behavior may occur, in response to external control, but the person does not develop.

People develop together. A child will not develop well if its mother is still essentially childish and cannot respond to the child's presence by enlarging and further integrating her personality. A husband can hardly develop himself if his wife can conceive of him only as a child or as a father. She must respond, developmentally, to changes in him; and the same holds for student-teacher relationships. For example, it is difficult for students to develop beyond authoritarianism when their teachers are authoritarian; but if students rebel and, with the help of agencies or social forces outside their school, begin moving toward mature autonomy teachers have to become more autonomous also, or else sink even more deeply into authoritarianism.

Let us look more closely at moral or ethical development because of its particular importance for education. I confess I have approached the subject with some reluctance, and have sought a new way of getting into it, because it seems that everybody is talking about these subjects these days, taking full advantage of such captive audiences as they can find. Yet the subject is important. I have given it considerable thought over the years, and I believe that good and evil are too important to be left to the theologians and politicians.

Genuine or high morality and the enjoyment of life go together; they interact one with the other, and both are features of the highly developed person. This thesis was dramatized, for me, time and again in the summer of the Watergate hearings as I watched the exchanges between Senator Sam Ervin and the men who appeared before his committee. Everybody is, in some sense, moral. Thomas Jefferson thought that man was "endowed with a sense of right and wrong." This sense, he wrote "is as much a part of his nature as the senses of hearing, seeing, and feeling. . . . State a moral case to a ploughman and a professor. The former will decide it as well as, and often better than, the latter because he has not been led astray by artificial rules."

A conscience based on what?

As a psychoanalyst I would agree that conscience, if it is not born within us, is universal and inevitable, at least in the case of people raised in families. Certainly everyone is capable of acting in the name of conscience, or in the name of some external moral authority. But this does not take us very far, for the great atrocities of history have been carried out by people who believed they had some kind of moral sanction for what they did (Sanford and Comstock, 1970). The question is, What are people moral about? What values are being upheld or espoused? And what is the basis for these values—most essentially, how far are they rooted in individual character?

The answers to these questions have much to do with the level of the person's development. (I say the *person's* development because in my view moral development cannot really be separated from the development of the rest of the person, including the intellectual and affective parts.) A value for success, for example, is readily attained by a 10 year old boy, and loyalty to the social group is often said to be characteristic of adolescents, while genuine tolerance—in the sense of appreciation of group differences and respect for individuality—can usually be attained only by mature people. Mature people may also value success and loyalty, but when they do they hold these values in a different way than does the child or the adolescent. These values will be less absolute, less likely to be at the top of a value hierarchy.

The basis for the individual's values lies primarily in his past and present relationships with other people. The child's moral behavior depends on what his parents say and do, while adolescents are heavily influenced by pressure from the peer groups to which they belong. College freshmen commonly look to an external authority for moral guidance—while the grand old seniors, after passing through a phase of relativism, arrive finally at principles and commitments based largely in their best thought and judgment.

Stages of moral development

Unfortunately, most people in our society do not develop beyond the level at which authority and conformity with group pressures form the basis for moral outlook. How can they be assisted to develop further, and how can we assure that they come that far?

We should begin, I believe, with the observation that every person, with the possible exception of the man on a desert island, lives within a social system such as a family, school, college, professional training system, church, business, industrial organization, or retirement community, and that his or her development depends on the workings of the system as a whole.

Character development, for example, depends crucially on the child's parents and his relationships with them, singly and together. He will not develop well unless they, and their relationship, are more or less stable. The young child's failings or distortions in development are not, however, irreversible. He may find a stable relationship later, perhaps at school, that becomes a basis for character formation.

To move beyond conformity with external authority or with the standards of a peer group the individual needs education. And he usually needs education beyond the high school, for adolescents typically are not ready to expose themselves to the challenges and opportunities for self-discovery that colleges have to offer. To be moral, and thus able to enjoy life, the individual must be relatively free of guilt; he must have found means for impulse expression that are safe and gratifying both to himself and others. This requires knowledge of people and of the world; it requires in a given situation the ability to see possibilities and alternatives and the capacity to carry out a chosen course of action. As the individual acquires these attributes, in college and throughout the rest of his life, he gains confidence in his ability to make moral choices. Nothing is more liberating to the mind, the spirit and the emotional life.

The college, particularly the independent college which has not yet been embraced by the national system and thus homogenized, offers great promise as a means for opening up these possibilities. What matters is how subjects are taught, and to what purpose. The professor who teaches his subject with a view to his students attaining mastery of it, and who conveys some sense of what it means to be in love with a subject, is making a contribution to student development. Educators interested in moral development should think about how much character it takes to meet the demands of (say) mathematics or a foreign language, or better, of how the attainment of the required precision of thought and expression *is* character development. At the same time, professors have to recognize that their scientific and scholarly work takes place in a context of value, and that they must let their values show, in a restrained and modest way of course, if they are to reach their students.

Prone to paranoia

But all this knowledge and expertise and humanity will not come to much, indeed it may not even find expression, unless faculty and students trust one another and all have some degree of trust in the administration. Paranoia is the social disease to which institutions of higher learning are particularly prone. When the level of paranoia gets too high, which is anwhere above average on a scale yet to be devised, the best course is to drop everything else in favor of a massive self-study, focused especially on sources of anxiety and blockages in the channels of communication.

Students who have a healthy interest in their own development have to realize that development is, in one respect at least, like happiness: it is not to be attained by focusing too intently upon it. It is more a by-product; a benefit to be had through the attainment of various sub-goals such as mastering a subject, acquiring a skill, understanding an interpersonal relationship, helping another person.

What a student—and everybody else—can focus upon is the development of *other* people. Each of us lives and works professionally or otherwise, in social settings, in which people have a chance to develop. I would like to express the hope that in everything we do, for or with people, we can learn to be guided by a consideration of whether our action will favor or hamper the development of the others.

Higher Learning and Moral Development

18

In the last chapter I discussed the kinds of relationships on which the development of a moral capacity depends. Here I want to summarize some of the ways in which formal education can assist in sustaining this kind of complex growth.

The concept of education as individual development is largely a restatement in contemporary terms of the traditional philosophy of humanistic education. We find it expressed in the Ancients; the British university colleges were strong on it and so were the Founding Fathers; this concept is still set down in the catalogues of our liberal arts colleges as their main objective. The full development of the individual as a person is not only the major aim of institutions of higher learning, but a fundamental aim of the political and social order itself. A good society will come when its members are capable of the highest satisfactions of the mind and spirit.

I am not talking just about excellence in productivity of various kinds, but about a tasteful and fulfilling use of leisure; about a kind of logical rigor which enables people to enjoy taking part in argument; about creative expression for individual fulfillment as well as for the sake of culture or technology. I am talking about the inclination and capacity to contribute something to the community and to social action, about a whole range of interrelated qualities of the person. This is in keeping with the old image of universities as institutions that should enable their students to enjoy life, and to participate fully in the life of their society. This is the kind of education often called aristocratic, often associated with British universities which try to do something for a young person besides enabling him to learn a trade. In our affluent post-industrial societies of today there is call for aristocratic education for everybody, or at least for as many as possible.

For solving the kinds of problem confronting us on our

campuses today, especially in Canada and the U.S., the only thing really workable will be this developmental approach. It is no good for our great metropolitan universities today to stick to the notion of a set curriculum or the idea that higher education is only for those who can benefit from it as it is. More and more people are going to be included.

This kind of developmental education must be guided by a theory of what a person can become and how he can be enabled to become this or that. We must accept the fact that a lot of eighteen-year-olds do not know very much and that many will be unlike the students usually admitted to four-year colleges. We shall, however, find in this new breed of student plenty of talent which, though of kinds not previously rewarded, is well worth rewarding and using. In deciding upon an appropriate education for these young people, we can still learn much from the liberal arts college tradition.

Take any virtue

Further in support of the present ethical position, we may take any virtue of the sort liberal educators have listed among their goals—competence, wisdom, compassion, among others. It is easy to argue about how high such a virtue stands in a hierarchy, but no one will deny that it *is* a virtue. We then think of how it might be developed: for example, educators might say competence is to be developed in schools, compassion in other institutions. But personality functions as a whole; virtues are interrelated; and actions to promote one will have consequences for others. From the point of view of personality theory what we most desire is high development in many virtues, a chance for superlative development in some, and serious neglect of none. This state is one of complexity and wholeness in the person.

The contemporary neglect of the concept of the person is a serious matter. In Chapter 4, I pointed out that professional practice in education as well as in the health and welfare fields is rarely directed to a person but only to particular capacities or needs. This state of affairs is related to the declining popularity of personality theory in social science, in which the person is fragmented by psychologists, merged with collectivities by sociologists. Likewise the university in America today is organized under a whole range of offices each having some particular responsibility directed towards some particular process or function of the person; but no one is appointed to deal with the student as a whole person.

Our first goal must be to reconstruct the idea of the person. Research, scholarship, the development of strong professions are, in the last analysis, for the benefit of man and society, for the service of distinctively human needs, not merely for keeping people alive. Students, like other men, should be regarded as ends, not means; it makes no sense to dehumanize students now, while they are in school, in the hope that their processing will somehow enable them to contribute something to mankind later on.

Education depends heavily, of course, upon culture. It is mainly through the use of culture—shared symbolic experience—that men find meaning, resolve inner conflicts, develop, sustain, and express their individuality. Education for individual development is therefore inconceivable without a curriculum deeply based in a cultural heritage. But such education is a far cry from mere exposure to that heritage, from the mere learning of facts, and from the sort of academic training that prepares a person to become a specialist in a subject. Education occurs when the student truly assimilates, in his own way, some cultural product; when he becomes capable of using that product in expressing his emotional needs or resolving his inner conflicts through imagination or vicarious living. We know that this is happening when a student becomes involved with, gets excited about, or falls in love with a subject. It is almost impossible to predict what will assure such responses in students, so we are wise to offer a wide range of subjects. It does not follow, however, that for purposes of individual development one subject is as good as another. Cultural products (and whole cultures for that matter) have to be evaluated. This is a matter for continuing inquiry, the basis for evaluation being how well these products or culture serve man's distinctively human needs.

As education depends on culture, so culture depends on education. Cultures need to be improved, and institutions of higher learning are directly involved in this work. The key role here must be played by relatively highly developed individuals—people who can appreciate and people who can create.

As if they did not exist

Culture, technology, and education can, in theory, be mutually supporting. The trouble is that technology without deliberate control tends to be the most determining of the three. Our world is increasingly filled with manufactured objects, including buildings, with no symbolic or aesthetic value, and institutions originally designed for human welfare more and more follow the model of industry, with specialization of function, rigid definition of roles, no chance for the expression of personality. Graduate students in many institutions suffer as much as undergraduates from the impersonality of their environment.

Consider an example. Graduate students who were members of a teachers' union at a great American university decided after much debate and searching of consciences to go on strike and set up a picket-line. Professors by and large ignored the strike, but in order for some to get to their offices they had to pass within a few feet of those striking students with whom they had been working very closely—whose dissertations they were supervising, for example. In many instances they did this without speaking to these students or permitting themselves to catch their eyes—acting, in short, as if students with whom they had intense discussion yesterday did not exist today.

To match this behavior, we would have to go back to the Hollywood practice of letting a man know he was fired by removing his nameplate from his door, or even the practice in Hitler's Germany of treating an old friend who had been condemned by the Nazis as if he were already dead. It is painful to think of the psychological state of graduate students treated in the way described. Not only must they realize that what they thought was a personal relationship does not in fact exist and probably never did, but, unless they wish to sacrifice their whole careers, they have no alternative to going back to their professors and acting as if nothing had happened; they have to face the fact that they are effectively enslaved.

Clearly, we must find some way to humanize and to unify—to humanize through unifying—our institutions of higher education. The scientific and artistic goal of finding unity in diversity has its parallel in the practical task of integrating the activities of the university. The student is the only person who interacts in a human way with all the features of a university; nothing except concern for him could possibly bring together all the people who work in universities. What else could they find to talk about? Students have the largest stake in this undertaking; happily, they realize it with increasing clarity and thus furnish a motive force for change.

We must deliberately go about the task of de-bureaucratizing the universities. We ought to be able to use our intelligence and our science to construct an organization really devoted to humanistic ends. This is what social scientists should be studying. They could quickly overcome the hiatus between science and practice if they made the institutions in which they live the object of their own inquiry and their own value judgments.

Unless these values are upheld

We have been discussing moral issues—what man ought to become, what institutions ought to do in order to favour man's becoming all that he can. In post-industrial society, as the church declines in influence the burden on the university increases. Moral principles that used to be taken for granted in the universities now have to be spelled out and their implications made clear.

The hierarchy of values discussed in Chapter 17 is essential to the educational purposes of an institution. Unless the values are upheld there is little point in even discussing conventional educational procedures. It is much easier to see the consequences of their neglect than to describe their positive effects—just as the consequences of breathing impure air are more noticeable than the consequences of breathing pure air. We have to think of ways in which devotion to these values may be developed in students, and other people. Obviously it is no good simply preaching them. Here, probably more than anywhere, teaching has to proceed by example. If we had teachers who really embodied integrity, tolerance, independence, fairness, decency, and faith, we would worry much less about students. Show me a colleague that you and I can trust and I will show you one that students trust.

Trustworthiness in administrators and faculty members ought not to be regarded primarily as a character trait which some have and others lack, nor is the behavior of the American professors toward their striking students to be explained on the basis that the university had somehow been invaded by low types. The inconsistent or impersonal behaviour that students observe is due less to personality than to the various and sometimes conflicting requirements of the roles and statuses of faculty and officials. These men, in other words, are caught in a system—one in which virtues like trust-worthiness apparently are becoming irrelevant.

Most parents are happy if their sons and daughters simply receive the vocational training that will enable them to go up in the world, and the great majority of students come sooner or later to see the advantages of adapting themselves to the system. Most important of all, from the point of view of the educational reformer, is the fact that most university professors are prepared to resist change in a system within which they have become successful. There is no denying that the kinds of changes urged in the United States in the 1960's by black student unions and "third world" students—which had been urged for many years by progressive educators—would cost established professors something.

Not much of what I have said here has been lost upon intelligent students. They (and I) have perhaps exaggereated in order to make a point. The university does not sell its soul every day in order to get money. But we need to understand that it need do so only once in order to disillusion a few thousand students.

The full robust range of life

One way in which students responded to recent conditions in the universities and colleges was by demanding that their education should be "relevant"—often without saying what it should be relevant to or even what was meant by relevance. One kind of relevance which students desperately want and need has been described for them by John Dodds of Stanford: "We have too often failed to make the humanities relevant to the human and cultural needs of our students. If I have a main point, it is this: that to deal with the full robust range of life which is the essence of the humanities and to render that life sterile is the unforgivable academic sin. . . . If, as we pretend, the philosophies and the literatures and the arts distill the wisdom of the centuries, somehow we must make that wisdom viable for our students —or at the very least, we must not desiccate it. If we really believe that the humanities feed the needs of the human spirit, we must lead people to see the relevance of the humanities for those needs today" (Dodds, 1968).

Professor Dodds is polite. The desiccation has already gone far. While there are many professors of humanities who see things as he does, most influential departments are dominated by men who want to apply the simple quantitative methods of science in their scholarship—or else have gone in for a kind of compulsive antiquarianism. Students don't need to limit their criticisms of universities to involvement with the Institute for Defense Analyses—they can criticize professors on the basis that, in their concern for their own careers and their professionalism, they have neglected education. It is as simple as that. Note that Dodd says, "we must lead people," not just students. What people outside universities are doing today in order to "feed the needs of the human spirit" often seems to border on desperation, as witness the flowering in the United States of all kinds of wild "encounter groups" and cults.

By "relevance" most people mean "social relevance." In the 1960's expectations rose that the universities would "do something" about poverty, race relations, and the deterioration of cities. And the universities responded in a characteristic way. Once outside demands were heard for particular kinds of service, or inquiries into particular areas, the universities spoke as if these were the things they had wanted to do all the time. The setting up of institutes for urban studies, however, is not likely to satisfy radical students or those at the bottom of our social heap.

It is unfortunate that universities in the United States, because of their practice of trying to meet all demands that are backed by money, created the impression that they could and would take action to change conditions in ghettos and to improve the lot of the poor, particularly those who are both poor and members of racial or ethnic minorities. It is true, as we shall see, that the university can do a great deal to improve a society, but what it can do by way of direct action to change conditions in urban or rural slums is severely limited. These conditions will yield only to the right social and economic policies, and whereas university scholars and scientists can serve as consultants in these matters, the university itself, acting through its schools, departments, or institutes, cannot make or implement such policies. To do so would be to lose what is left of its unique status as an institution that is beholden to no particular group of constituents and is thus free to pursue the truth, to generate and entertain all kinds of ideas including radical ones, and to serve as an intellectual critic of society.

What the poor can expect

It is true that the university is to a considerable extent "politicized" now in the sense that it serves directly the interests of some segments of society such as agriculture, industry, and the military but not others such as welfare recipients, or unorganized labourers. This, of course, is unfair, but what needs to be understood by poor people and their supporters is that powerful groups with access to the university's services do not owe their power primarily to the university; they have been able to command these services because they are powerful, and the same rule will hold for poor people. In their quest for political power they can form alliances with students and faculty members; they can arrange for increasing members of their young people to have access to the same kind of education the powerful have had; and they can easily obtain expert knowledge and consultation from university people; but they cannot expect the university itself, or parts or sections of it, to lead their fight for political power.

As the poor obtain power a balance will begin to be restored with respect to whom the university serves. Meanwhile the answer to selective politicalization is de-politicalization. Instead of trying to make the university respond to a new set of political interests, and thus threatening it with the loss of such autonomy as it has, students and their allies might rather work to bring about its withdrawal from those arrangements that have been entered into merely to serve the powers-that-be or to get money or status.

The university cannot do everything asked of it today. Above all, it cannot be both a center for free inquiry and an adversary in political struggles, except in defense of values upon which its life depends. A way out may be found in two parallel lines of endeavour: encouraging the development of other institutions and agencies to take pressure off itself, and working for internal reform which, coupled with the education of its publics, will enable it better to serve society on its own terms.

If not the university who?

There are other institutions such as governmental and quasi-governmental institutes for research and development, industrial research organizations, voluntary agencies, professional societies, and independent institutes that can well perform some of the tasks now expected from the university. As I have suggested in chapter 15, especially important services to society can be performed by independent institutes for applied social science, or better, for social action-research. Problems centering about race relations, poverty, and welfare are bound to be controversial and to call for a kind of involvement that is not in keeping with the academic style of work. What is needed both for the amelioration of problems and for the advancement of social science, is an agency that can define a problem, make inquiries into how to attack it, take action affecting it, and evaluate the effects of that action before deciding what to do next (Sanford, 1968).

Resistance to such institutes comes less from external pressures on the university than from interests within it. Academic social scientists tend to have a low opinion of what they call "applied science," higher status being accorded to pure research, which is almost always highly specialized. It is not commonly recognized that the kind of action-research that can come to grips with social problems is far more demanding intellectually than the usual academic exercises of spinning out theoretical models or carrying out conventional research designs. Again, the organization of the university around departments and professional schools is highly resistant to change.

At the same time, however, faults of the present system have been widely recognized, many faculty members have become unhappy about its restrains upon them, and fresh efforts have been made to counter the fragmentation of the university and to render its social scientific activities more socially relevant. In 1961, for example, a group of us started the Institute for the Study of Human Problems at Stanford University, with the idea that a generalist approach to inquiry and action on problems would also provide an ideal atmosphere for undergraduate education. Soon thereafter new colleges were started—for example at the State University of New York at Old Westbury and at the University of California at Santa Cruz, which planned that students would spend a good part of their time at fieldwork in cities while being offered a curriculum integrated with their experience. If such a plan were ever fully carried out, we would be in a position to ask what would happen to the scholarly disciplines once the generalist approach to education, inquiry, and action became dominant. One answer is to build institutes for the scholarly disciplines: let there be institutes for advanced study in economics, sociology, political science, psychology, and so forth, where some scholars can pursue their specialized work in peace, free of the responsibilities for undergraduate education with which they are now burdened—and which is itself burdened by their reluctant presence.

Reaching adults where they are

When we think of the university or college entering the community, as in the original plans for Old Westbury or Santa Cruz, we are led to consider a form of service to society that has been sadly neglected: the education of the general public. Adult education has been regarded by university men with much the same contempt that has been accorded applied science. "Courses for adults have to be watered down," they tell us. "Adults cannot learn." But times are changing. It is increasingly well understood that adults must be further educated if they are to provide a climate in which the university can flourish. Adults also need education more and more in order to keep pace with the changing requirements of their work and in order further to develop themselves and maintain their humanity in an increasingly cold and complex world. There must be programs that reach adults where they are, organized around activities in which they are already engaged, programs that do not require adults to adapt themselves to the usual academic ways of doing things. As universities and colleges reach out into the community in this way, they will discover that there are many adults without advanced degrees who have much to teach as well as to learn.

The university should bring to its work with adults the same spirit that informs its work with students. It must be guided by its own lights. While listening to what people say they want, it must participate in the definition of their needs, not permitting itself to become a mere instrument in the service of their missions and programs. It can best serve society by being a model society itself, one whose primary concern is with the good of students, and which knows that what is good for students is good for humankind.

The Need for Authority

19

In Chapter 18 we examined some of the preconditions for moral development and, in particular, the role to be played by higher education. In this chapter and the next I discuss the consequences of failing to sustain an adequate level of moral development in our young people and in their teachers and other adult models. In looking at consequences, I will give special attention to authoritarianism and will draw most of my examples from the 1960's when issues were sharply drawn.

Authoritarianism is an old concern of mine, and fifteen years after co-authoring *The Authoritarian Personality* I went back to it, partly because some social psychologists had at last discovered the subject and begun giving it, I think, due attention in their courses—I mean people such as Roger Brown—and partly because I was offered support by the Centre for the Study of Collective Psychopathology at the University of Sussex, England, a group that was trying once again to understand the Nazi phenomenon. And of course, I had long felt a continuing concern with what happens to students as they go through college, with the prospect that authoritarianism might still be reduced at that stage. In my view, authoritarianism is at the core of the worst forms of violence, that which is carried out in the name of some kind of authority and in the belief that the enemy or the victim is totally bad or even less than human (Sanford and Comstock, 1970). To reduce authoritarianism is a major aim of education in a democratic society.

In the 1960's, of course, attention was focussed on the (shall we say) anti-authoritarian students, the protestors, those who engaged in demonstrations, closed down universities and the like, but we mustn't forget that the great rank and file of students, in our country at least, were still pretty well sunk in a kind of authoritarianism. In those years I visited a university not far from home that had 14,000 students. During lunch in the women's dormitory, we looked out on the patio and saw probably 100 girls dressed in bikinis sunning themselves, giving rise to the usual imagery of youth. It was explained to me that the building was called the "cow palace." This, I thought, was a dead give-away of what was in fact the case, that a kind of fraternity system dominated the student culture of that university, and with most of the students nothing was happening. Caught up with conformity, striving for status, assuring a comfortable future, the students were absorbed by their sex relations, their relations with each other, the possibility of finding total security in their future lives. They were taking courses and getting their grades and graduating, and nothing much was happening to them.

During that same year I was teaching at the Unitarian seminary (or "school for religious leadership") in Berkeley, a place about as student-centered as you can get. When I first had the thought that it might be interesting to teach in a seminary, I went up to look the place over. I wanted particularly to meet the students and so we had a seminar with about a dozen. Half way through I found that they were in fact looking me over, and it dawned on me that it was quite literally true that the students at this seminary decided who was going to teach there, or at least they had a veto in this matter.

Giving him your stuff

But anyway, having sweated it out while they decided whether or not I could teach there, I was finally admitted and began giving a seminar, in something like "social science in society." And there I found that the usual ways of proceeding wouldn't do at all, that I hardly had a chance to say anything. I had assumed that, as in most university courses, if you suggest that something be read, the students will at least pretend to have read it. In fact the seminarians in my course were apparently reading something else, or at least wanted to discuss something else. In short, I couldn't seem to get a word in edgewise, and we struggled through the term trying to straighten out our relations with each other. The students seemed to be mainly preoccupied with their own development or with their own identity, or with their relationships with each other and with the faculty, and so on, whereas I had the somewhat naive idea that we could discuss purely intellectual matters. I would say that throughout that quarter there was a kind of dubious struggle going on about how we were going to relate to each other. I found, as a matter of fact, that the students were largely preoccupied with their relationship with the power structure of this seminary which consisted of 21 students, a President, and three faculty members. Every week there was a big debate about representation of students in faculty meetings. They won representation in faculty meetings, but we of course began to hold faculty meetings by telephone in order to do our real business.

The thing began to get a little bit clear for me in the winter quarter when a really distinguished theologian came to teach at the school. He had his seminar the first day and almost everybody showed up for it. That evening there was a party at the President's house and I was talking with this old gentleman as he greeted various of the students who came in. Each time he would say, "I appreciated your remarks in seminar this afternoon." Another student would come in and he would greet him and say, "I appreciated your remarks in seminar this afternoon," and so it went. A little later I spoke to a student whom I knew and I said, "It seems to me the old boy wasn't getting a chance to say very much." He said, "You know what they were doing, don't you? They were giving him your stuff." That was enlightening for me. It appeared that they were willing to learn something from me, even though I had been billed as a kind of an authority, but they were not yet ready to let me know that this was indeed the case. So on the one side we have students at the large university who expected everything to be laid out for them by the instructor, and then we have the student-centered places where life for the instructor is very difficult. These students become very good ministers. But half-way through the year I was saying to myself, "This is great but I wish they could do it without being so hard on their teachers."

Difference between power and authority

It seems to me that what is called for today is some discussion of the meaning of authority and the kinds of relations with authority that young people have. Then perhaps we can apply these lessons to problems of education and some of the larger problems in our country, and perhaps from that will emerge suggestions as to directions in which we can go. I think first we have to consider the difference between authority as status or position and authority as relationship. According to most dictionaries, authority is the right to command obedience, respect and confidence, and certain positions in social groups are vested with this right. People such as parents, judges, presidents, professors, and so on are in "positions of authority" and are vested with the right to command some obedience, respect, and confidence. But whether or not they are in fact able to command these responses still depends upon the way in which they occupy those positions; it depends also upon the readiness on the part of the students, young people, or others to accept them in this particular position.

We have to distinguish between power and authority. Power is, I think, the ability to influence behavior, but that influence can be had by means other than authority. When we speak of student power or black power we are speaking, I think, of the ability to influence the behavior of a lot of us, but yet we have not vested these groups with any particular authority. Authority is always constituted or sanctioned by the social group and it always has, I think, an element of concern for those of whom obedience and respect are expected. But any display of these tendencies will in turn depend upon the readiness for obedience, or confidence, or respect, on the part of the people to whom the authority is directed.

Walter Lippmann, speaking at the Center for the Study of Democratic Institutions, once bemoaned the disappearance of authority in the world—he referred to the Middle Ages, to the breaking of established authority, and to the fact that ever since then men have doubted themselves and wondered what in the world to do. As he put it, they had lost the help and discipline, the light and the leading, the guidance and support that they used to have, and since then have been looking everywhere for this kind of authority. He thought perhaps that the university could now supply it: in fact, he thought the university was the *only* institution that could supply it.

Sources of values

What the university could supply is not "power" but a kind of authority to which we could look for guidance and support. There is always some social process by which the right to exercise authority is conferred, be it the divine right of kings, or the right that parents are usually supposed to have, or the way in which we assume that authority in democratic societies is going to be wielded with the consent of the governed. We in the democratic societies are taught to respect the status of a position of authority, but not too much; we are careful about the people who occupy these positions, careful to make arrangements so that they can be removed if difficulties become too great, and so that one authority is a check on others.

It makes all the difference what kinds of values are being furthered by authoritative positions— political, religious, educational, and so on. If the values have to do with the expectation of external life or a stable society above all, the outcomes will most certainly be different than they would when the authority is concerned with the fullest possible development of each individual. It could very well be that if the authorities of the Middle Ages, in which Walter Lippmann was interested, had advocated freedom of inquiry and individual development, those authorities might have persisted until this day.

What has happened in recent times, of course, is that the influence of the church has dwindled, and various other institutions have rushed into this vacuum. Psychiatry, for example, has been widely viewed as a source of the kind of guidance that people used to get from the church, and Walter Lippmann was suggesting that guidance has to come from the university. Perhaps most important for our purposes is the style of authority, the way in which it is actually exercised, and this is where authoritarianism comes in.

The difficulty I had at the seminary sprang from the students' assumption that all authority must be authoritarian. They were unwilling, it seemed to me at first, to make a distinction between legitimate, constituted authority and unhealthy authoritarianism. I want to suggest that we must draw this distinction. In certain circumstances authority is good; it is often necessary; and mature people can sometimes relax and enjoy it. To show something of the difficulty that young people have with this, I would mention a survey in the 1960's of Stanford freshmen about their drinking practices and attitudes towards drinking: although 77% answered "yes" to the statement, "Most young people nowadays drink merely to defy authority," only 33% agreed that, "young people or college students should be allowed to drink when, where and what they please." What this means is that they expect to have authority; 66% think that somebody around should tell them when, where and what to drink, even though most of them are going to defy this authority. This gives us a fresh appreciation, I think, of the problems of deans. They have to be authorities, but they have to expect that their authority is going to be ignored.

When the authoritarian style is manifested by people in positions of authority, we find a kind of rigidity that takes no account of individual differences, or the developmental status of different people, or the requirements of a particular situation. We see this in school teachers who insist that everybody in the class be treated exactly alike, that serious breeches of the rules be treated just like minor ones. She will say, "The next sound I hear from this class, everyone will go to the principal." She has been pushed into a position where total actions are her only recourse. Or we see it in the parent who says, "do it because I say so, don't ask so many questions." Or when other people tell us, "do it for the good of the state." Now this kind of wielding of authority, I think, fundamentally has more to do with the needs of the person in a position of authority than with any consideration of the well-being of the people to whom it is being directed.

Little autocracies

Even good authorities, individuals who are psychologically sound and who mean well, can be driven to authoritarian behavior in situations which for them are desperate. A teacher who treats her class in an authoritarian manner may be afraid of the principal, and the principal is probably running his school in an authoritarian way because of his fear of the superintendent, who in turn is afraid of the school board. When people in authority are so afraid of some kind of irrational outburst in young people, or when they are so afraid that outbursts on the part of young people are going to threaten their own control of impulses, then they swing over into authoritarian types of discipline.

Some colleges are still run as almost total autocracies in the United States. Probably the best examples are some of the small church-related colleges or some of the black colleges in the south. I know one in which the President wields total power, in which the only faculty who have academic tenure are men who have displayed total loyalty to him personally, and where any kind of activism on the part of the students is dealt with by their immediate dismissal or by withdrawal of their scholarship funds. So there's plenty of authoritarianism around in blatant forms in academic institutions, and there's plenty of it around in implicit forms.

One thing that my brief experience at the Unitarian seminary taught me was how much we ordinary people rely upon authoritarianism in students in order to have our way. We just take it for granted that we will say what is to be done, and this will be greeted with deference, if not praise, on the part of young people. So, one thing we must do is to differentiate between legitimate, constituted, everyday authority, and authoritarianism. Then having done this, we have to turn to the ways in which kinds of authority affect the development of our young people.

The help of an external agency

What kind of arrangements are good for people, what kind favors their full development to a point at which they can become their own authorities? As I have stressed throughout this book, the best kind of society to have, is one that favors the full development of the individual. We all need some kind of authority sometimes. Young children need it most and can tolerate it best. Adolescents need a lot but have very little tolerance for it, and the ideally developed person needs relatively little and can tolerate it well. What I want to do here, in the context of moral development, is slightly to extend the "short course in human development" offered in Chapter 2.

The child needs authority because his own impulses lead him to imagine punishments of the most horrible and catastrophic kind, and he is very glad to have some kind of external guides and supports to protect him, as it were, from himself, from his own impulses, and from his own fantasies. He, of course, has no alternatives in any case because of his dependence upon his parents, and he obeys in exchange for having his various needs met. But ideally, the child becomes increasingly able to control himself as he grows older, and the parent recognizing this gradually imposes less and less authority. The child not only internalizes the parental sanctions and prohibitions, but as he grows older develops his own capacity for judgment.

This goes on for a long time, longer even than adolesence, and we still find in college that the need for authority is often acute and yet unrecognized. College students still have the problems of controlling their impulses, they still have painful decisions to make, and would like the help of some external agency. We still find, also, in college students, that internal authorities may be too severe, and students will look for some external agency to help them make decisions. This is why we find so often that college students will use their own peers as a source of knowledge about what to do and what not to do since they can't use their parents any more.

Our research indicates that autonomy or freedom from authoritarianism increases pretty directly during college. We know that college students become increasingly critical of institutions, and at the same time increasingly accepting of people. (Even much later, when they are fully developed, they will still need some kind of external support for their value positions.) But things can certainly go wrong. Unfortunately, too few parents are well qualified for the role they have seized or have had thrust upon them. I should say that the most serious things that happen, happen early in the child's life as a result of parental indifference, or neglect, or ignorance, all of which is experienced as an absence of love by the child, and which gives him the idea of the essential untrustworthiness of the world. This is a source of serious psychotic and psychopathological disturbances.

Harsh, rigid, punitive

More commonly perhaps, the difficulty comes from authoritarian discipline, from discipline that is harsh, rigid, and punitive, just because the parents don't know what to do or are over-eager to see to it that their children adapt themselves strictly to the prevailing standards of society. Given this situation, the child will respond with hostility in turn. But this strikes him as very dangerous; so he suppresses his hostility toward his parents, tells himself that they are not bad, but very, very good, and directs his hostility toward various out-groups. That is the fundamental core, I think, of authoritarianism, and it remains one of the basic problems of our times.

In my view, this pattern is at the bottom of all that paranoid thinking about the nature of the enemy so common today. It is at the basis not only of racism and international conflict, but the generation gap itself. If a person insists that his own family or group are the only good ones, and that hostility can only be directed toward bad people who belong to other groups, we should not be surprised when the pattern is reversed and hostility is directed toward parents and other authority figures.

In America, young men tend to feel they must rebel against father, or else their manhood can easily be called into question. It takes us a long time to get on a good basis with our fathers. I have recently noted two novels, one by Herbert Gold and the other by William Gibson, in which authors in their forties finally undertook to write about their fathers; and both confessed that it was only now that they were able to be sufficiently objective to undertake this writing. So that we have not only authoritarians but we have a kind of irrational anti-authoritarianism which takes the form of a persistent need to rebel against all kinds of authority.

A distinction often lost

On the national scene we find people in the universities and elsewhere who are afraid to exercise authority because they know that they will immediately be accused of authoritarianism. People engaged in attacking leadership or abdicating it, have been heard to cite *The Authoritarian Personality* in support of their actions. As a matter of fact, when our book first appeared, various of my friends and relations were disturbed and said: "You are undermining authority. How are parents going to bring up their children if you suggest as you do that all authority is bad?" I am still trying to make the distinction which I tried to make then between authoritarianism and the legitimate, salutary exercise of authority.

In general, I think, we suffer in our nation from a failure of leadership, and from unwillingness on the part of the people to move into leadership roles, and to take it upon themselves to say how things should be. At the same time, we have failed to come to grips with authoritarianism: our empire-building has been borne on a kind of authoritarian ideology which assumes that we must be missionaries, that we must carry the gospel to all these benighted (and perhaps even slightly less than human) people all over the world. In the United States a kind of pseudo-liberalism says that we will accept everybody if they will become just like us. Now this is very far from being the worst form of ethnocentrism. It does not match German or Italian Fascism of the 1930's and 40's. According to that view, certain people could not possibly become just like us; they were so fundamentally and innately and inherently different that they were condemned to liquidation or at least eternal subjugation.

In higher education, a reduction in authoritarianism is not yet widely accepted as a major goal; and many parts of the system still rely heavily on authoritarian outlooks, and have great difficulty in meeting the changing needs of students. As educators, we must continue to try to find ways to help many students overcome their authoritarianism, while dealing simultaneously with students who are already liberated, or who are already displaying a kind of anti-authoritarianism. I would argue that much can be done in college through educational procedures that are based on knowledge of how students actually develop. This will impose upon student personnel people of all kinds the particular task of making it quite clear to all concerned how students do in fact develop, and how the total educational environment can be arranged in such a way that students will be helped to overcome their authoritarianism.

It seems to me a striking thing, that whereas today we generally recognized that racism, jingoistic nationalism, and imperialism, are at the bottom of so many of our problems, educators have not widely accepted the major task of changing these authoritarian structures in their students. They still go on acting as if it were enough to teach the usual kinds of courses or as if the learning of content in college would somehow bring about all the good things that need to be brought about. I think what we have to do is to deliberately institute procedures that can change authoritarianism. A number of them can briefly be suggested.

Counter-measures

In a general way, anything that develops the decision-making processes of the student counteracts authoritarianism, as does anything that gives him the knowledge to resist dogmatic offerings by his elders, anything that gives him practice in criticism, so that he can bring his own judgment to bear upon issues that are being presented. What we need to do is offer students challenges in measured dosages. We know from George Stearn's work that, if students from conventional homes are brought into a college and given total freedom, they will either leave college, or insist upon some kind of external authority in irrational ways. We must constantly challenge them to think for themselves, but we must bear in mind that the degree of challenge must depend upon the degree of capacity already developed.

Anything that increases the student's self-esteem will give him the confidence to deal with authorities in a realistic way. And yet most of our colleges run things in such a way as to downgrade the student's self-esteem. Anything that increases the student's awareness of himself will likewise help to overcome authoritarian tendencies which, as I suggested earlier, derive from a failure to understand what one is doing with one's aggressiveness. One way to bring about this self-awareness is through a study of literature, which can be taught so as to help students become familiar with the whole range of human feelings and needs, and gradually to become aware of their own. If this occurs in a setting in which the student is not being criticized, then we can get a vast expansion of his self-awareness, and hence a readiness for freedom from this tendency to see all bad things as existing in other people.

A climate of freedom

I would say that authoritarianism can be countered by the general climate of freedom in the university. If professors can be made to bow to external pressure, this will easily unnerve the students, who are already doubtful about whether or not they are going to be able to think for themselves. We ought to give students more and more freedom as they become increasingly capable of managing it. We don't do too badly to have rules, and to maintain them, until the students bring pressure to bear to change them. We should not feel disgraced when we give in to students. We should say instead that these students are winning more rights through the right kinds of procedures. In the 1960's when students agitated for more liberal parietal rules, many adults anticipated dangerous outbreaks but, after the liberalization, life just went on much as it had before.

Obviously, one can use liberalizations in rules as ways of taking off the steam, but I would not be too hasty about this. I would not just hand students freedom that they haven't asked for, because this could easily make them anxious. I would be inclined to let them win it and to assume that the very winning of it through the right kinds of methods is favorable to their development.

At Stanford drinking on the campus was finally instituted in the 1960's after years of agitation on the part of the students. Nothing happened. I mean nothing happened except that people were now more relaxed about the behavior in which they had been indulging anyway. But I know of another college in the middle of our country in which the president had the idea that it was foolish to have these liquor laws, and he immediately allowed drinking on the campus. The result was that his students every day felt bound to give cocktail parties. They staggered around the campus with martini glasses in their hands. Things got completely out of control and the rule had to be changed back. In other words, the culture of that college was not such that this kind of change could be instituted. I think we have to find ways to gauge what kind of readiness exists in the student body, and make judgments about whether they are now able to make good use of a given freedom.

What about the liberated ones?

While we are helping the more authoritarian students by teaching them how to gain freedom and how to use freedom, we still have to deal with the new breed, the more activist student or students who seem to be liberated already when they arrive at college. In the 1950's and early 60's, I always paid most attention to the question of how to liberate students. This, of course, was based on our work at Vassar, where the young women then were not very liberated. But on many campuses today, students arrive already liberated. They are already non-authoritarian or more likely anti-authoritarian, like those at the Unitarian seminary.

Now some of these students can be very tough to deal with. In the 1960's some of them were members of political groups who were actually out to close the universities down. But even these tough students have to be talked with. Somebody in the dean's office or the vice-chancellor's office must constantly be in touch with them. When this is done, as it was belatedly at Berkeley, the result is not agreement with these students, but avoidance of the most troublesome and dangerous kinds of confrontations. In dealing with these students, administrators had to be very careful to avoid being pushed into authoritarian positions, and to avoid stereotyping the students—which is easy to do. It is very easy to withdraw, not to talk with them, to assume that they are all alike and beyond the pale. Somebody must continue talking with them no matter what, and in doing this one must not assume that what they say is determined by irrational emotional factors. Whatever they say has to be treated as a part of the discourse, not as a psychiatric symptom. No matter how irrational it might seem, we have to deal with their arguments on their own terms.

Far more numerous than the students I've just discussed, however, are those bright and idealistic students who want change of the same sort that many of the rest of us want. Concerning educational change, these students have not yet proposed anything more radical than I myself have proposed in various writings. So my approach to them is to work with them when they agree with me, and to try to carry on a dialogue with them when they don't. For the students who really are more or less liberated when they arrive at college, we've got to offer more alternative programs than now exist. I mean not only different kinds of curricula, but different arrangements for living than are now offered in most places. To maximize freedom in that way doesn't do us any harm, and it certainly can do them some good. In general, the movement is bound to be in the direction of more and more student participation in their own education. And though, as I pointed out, it is kind of hard on faculty members to be chosen by students, I think we are certainly heading for a situation in which students will have a great deal to say about this, and it probably will not be bad, and it will have very interesting and far-reaching consequences.

Being listened to

I don't want to suggest that we just give students what they want—far from it. But in almost all cases that I know, if the professor, or those who have responsibility, can somehow show students that he is aware of their needs and concerns, he does not have trouble. If students who have been complaining and saying they've got to have this and that, become convinced that they are being listened to, and that their needs are getting some attention, we're not likely to have serious trouble.

For these kinds of things to be done, will require some radical changes in our colleges and universities, which are most likely to occur, in my view, through alliances between the administration and the students. It's rather poignant to consider that in places where there was a lot of student activism, the students almost always tended to see the administration as an enemy. The things students suffer from are mainly the work of the faculty, and it is the faculty who resist radical educational changes in the university. In the 1960's what I hoped would happen was an increase in the power of the president to match the increase in student power, and then the formation of alliances between students and presidents in the interest of genuine educational reform. Perhaps other ways will yet emerge.

Finally, and I think most important, we must have leaders in this country worthy of their authority. This is what young people in the main are actually asking for, and this is the lesson which I learned from that experience at the seminary. It was not, as some people seem to think, that the students wanted to turn the seminary into one of those so-called "human groups" in which everybody was the equal of everybody else, where there was no role differentiation whatsoever. In my view, what these students really wanted—in fact what they got in the end through an enormous effort on my part—was to make sure that the person from whom they were going to learn something was worth learning something from, that he actually deserved to be in the position of authority that had been assigned. But to know this is one thing, to actually bring it about in colleges and in the larger world of learning after college is another. Somehow or another in the universities and in society, we've got to have people in the positions of authority who really deserve to be there, and who, because of their human qualities, can really be respected by the young people and by adults seeking the conditions for continued development.

Loss and Rediscovery of Moral Character

20

I think it is safe to assume that the university is much like other corporate structures today; and that a given university functions much in the manner of other large organizations such as banks, manufacturing companies, hospitals, government agencies and so on. As I mentioned in chapter 4, work is increasingly differentiated and specialized; roles are rigidly defined; communication among various divisions and departments is difficult; responsibility is diffused; individuals are alienated from their work, themselves, and each other, and feel powerless to change anything.

These processes are effective at the top as well as in the lower eschelons. In many cases corporation or university presidents may be replaced without a ripple of disturbance in the ranks. The incoming president simply does what the outgoing one did and life goes on. Organizations may break the law, commit immoral acts, engage in racist and sexist practices without our being able to find any individual to blame or anyone who feels personally responsible for what happened. And even though most people in the organization are, as individuals, against these practices they make their contribution to them merely by performing their assigned tasks (Sanford and Comstock, 1970).

I would not disagree with those who say that we face in all this an inexorable tendency of technology under capitalism or, perhaps, under any other modern economic system. In any case it is well to remember that corruption in high places, credibility gaps, and the domination of our lives by the military-industrial-educational complex did not begin with Watergate.

Erich Fromm and Michael Maccoby are right, I think, in insisting that systems "shape the energies of people in such a way that their behavior is not left to conscious decisions whether or not to go along with social demands, but people want to act as they have to act to keep the system moving." In the case of the modern organization, as Maccoby says, the "social character" required for success includes such traits as punctuality, accuracy, orderliness, efficiency, detachment, competitiveness, cooperativeness, fairness, and playing by the rules. But the rules, as they function, are rules of survival not of morality.

Let me offer you some examples from my own recent experience and from recent history. After our home was more than half destroyed by fire I had to deal over a period of four months with a wide variety of people out there in the "real" world, such as insurance adjusters, estimators, inspectors, building contractors, wreckers, haulers, carpenters, electricians, plumbers, day-laborers, representatives of various public utilities, occupants of several bureaus in City Hall. If you want to build (or rebuild) your own house, you apply for a permit in the category of "owner-built." "Owner-built" is a deviant status in the Berkeley housing code, meant only for the hardy and the curious.

Trapped in a vast system

It all began with the remains of the fire. You and I might suppose that approximately one half of a unique house built in 1905 ought to be preserved. Not a chance: too many features not "up to code." Well, at a time of dwindling natural resources, how about at least preserving the old boards and timbers? It was univerally assumed by pros in the field that the only reasonable course was to have machines knock down and chew up the remains.

Probably no one will be surprised to hear that few of the people I had to deal with were happy in their work, or that it was almost impossible to get anything done. Having spent almost a lifetime in the academic world, I believe I am familiar with most forms of rascality and skullduggery, but I was still not prepared for the low level of moral conduct commonly encountered in the "real world".

Few of the people I have dealt with seemed to feel any obligation to do what they said they would do. I encountered few remnants of the old idea of "honest work for honest pay." I had to remain constantly on the alert to avoid being cheated. Almost as distressing was the absence from all agencies, bureaus, and small businesses of any aesthetic, ecological, conservationist, or antiquarian values.

I think I understand the situation of the contractor we consulted. He tried to get me to build what would have been essentially a tract home. When I proposed to him that we use old boards for sub-flooring upstairs, so that we could enjoy looking at them from below, he said it would be impossible: we would have to use plywood because it goes on faster. How about a nine-foot ceiling? Not unless you want to throw your money away. Two-by-fours come sawed in eight or sixteen foot lengths; any deviation from the standard would be costly both in material and in labor. Our man was pleasant, if a bit mournful, about all this. It is easy to imagine that he went into the contracting business because he liked to build—indeed he showed signs of having a value for quality—but now he finds himself trapped in a vast system of building regulations, union rules, and unpredictable pricing of materials.

Preserving integrity, curiosity

And, I fear that the situation is not much better within the university. Knowledge of my building effort may be of some comfort—albeit of a somewhat chilly sort—to university students who enter their various schools or departments with high hopes but soon find that it is often extremely difficult or even impossible to do what really interests them. It happened that at about the time of my building problems my colleagues and I at the Wright Institute were considering the results of an essay contest for graduate students. As I have mentioned earlier, we offered prizes for the best autobiographical essays on the experience of graduate education. The dominant theme in the 96 essays submitted had to do with how a student could preserve something of his or her self, some integrity, something of the curiosity and inspiration that had led to graduate work in the first place, while meeting requirements that seemed arbitrary, senseless, and unfair. A student had to spend a great deal of time either trying to figure out a way to "beat the system" or deciding whether or not to remain within it.

Many assumed that their difficulties were due to the whims or special needs of professors and thought that when they got their degrees and became professors themselves they could help to change things. Not likely. Departments and universities really are "systems," as many studnets say. They are corporate structures that go their way more or less regardless of which individuals occupy their diverse roles. While the traditional functions of advancing knowledge and training young people for useful roles in society remain, these have been distorted and down-graded by the need to adapt to the demands of the larger society. As David Breneman has shown, the behavior of university departments can best be explained on the assumption that their primary purpose is self-aggrandizement—to become the strongest department in the university and the most highly rated, by those who know, in the country—and to this end they economically use all available resources including students.

Learning to be on the team

I have been particularly struck by the enormous importance of being a team player for decision-making at high levels in our national life. For example, Adlai Stevenson began going against his principles as our representative in the United Nations because, as he said, he had to go along with the team. Irving Janis has shown the vital role of this value in the decision leading to the Bay of Pigs fiasco (Sanford and Comstock, 1970). In university life I have had a number of colleagues and friends who, once they become deans, began lying to me, apparently without great discomfort.

People who work in large organizations generally accept the required values, at least in their work-related behavior. Indeed, organizations reward conformity with their values and ways, and individuals who remain in organizations vest interest in their roles. Some student leaders of the protest movements of the 1960's used to say that the university, instead of educating its students, merely prepared them for taking the roles necessary to keep the industrial and governmental wheels turning. "Radical historians" of education tell us that this grooming process begins far earlier than this; that the chief function of the schools in our society is to develop the social character desired by the powers that be; hence that the schools won't change until the whole society changes; and that if this seems a remote possibility, perhaps we should try "de-schooling."

We may certainly ask if there is not some alternative to this despairing analysis. I believe that things are far more complicated than the student leaders, radical historians, and building contractors know. A full analysis must make use of the concept of personality, of individual character, as well as the concept of social character because individuals not only have their own inner functioning, but also, in the final analysis, create social structures.

In my house-building episode I did encounter, and came to rely upon, some people who *could* be trusted—who showed up when they said they would, enjoyed their work, held to aesthetic and conservationist values, kept honest time-sheets. They were students of the university, who came through that institution's employment office, and college-educated young men who had either recently found their vocation in a building trade or had changed their vocations after having succeeded in a profession. We had some stunningly beautiful carpentry performed by a young man who graduated in social science from the university four years ago, fooled around for a couple of years before finding his true vocation, that of what he calls "an artist in wood." He accepts a contract when he feels like it or when he needs to and devotes most of his time to reading, studying music, and keeping abreast of the work of his wife, who is a journalist. The bulk of the work is being done by two young men who are meanwhile building their own homes but must hire themselves out to get money for living and for buying materials. They do everything: draw plans, build forms, pull nails, pour concrete, buy and deliver lumber, do the wiring, plumbing, carpentry, and cabinet work. They go about their work with enormous energy and enthusiasm, happily making do with used materials, changing plans when something being done begins to look not quite right.

A house built by strangers

You might want to argue that here is a college professor insisting on doing things his way, in disregard of the real-world costs. It may surprise you to know that this kind of organic building is far less expensive than anything done in the conventional way. I got the basic structure up for approximately half a contractor's estimate (but not, of course, the insurance company's estimate) and was able to splurge on the finishing touches. The house also has character, something almost unattainable in the ordinary way except at astronomical cost. And I have already had the pleasure of telling the people at City Hall, in the words of the old lady being moved off Walton's Mountain, "I couldn't live in a house built by strangers."

In terms of the examples I've introduced, how does an individual personality adapt to organizational requirements? To approach this question we may begin by noting individual differences. Some people take to their jobs as if the two were made for each others. They seem from the start to embody the competencies and the values required. Others come slowly to this kind of fit between person and work role. Still others remain fully aware of the differences between themselves and their role behavior, but do what is necessary with varying degrees of unhappiness, cynicism, resignation or demoralization. A few, a particularly interesting group, try to change the organization. Many of course leave it. (In recent years business organizations have had to abandon various consciousness-raising activities for employees because too many as a result were leaving the company.)

Don't like it but it's policy

Some managers and administrators obviously identify themselves with their roles. I have known academic men who when they became deans began by saying, "I don't like to do this but it is university policy" but soon began neglecting to make the distinction between themselves and their role, becoming in time every inch an administrator. We may suppose that in such cases deeply-based personality needs found expression in the role. Other deans insist on doing some teaching or some research, moving easily from one role to the other while maintaining a strong sense of self.

Again, some men in the business world, in adopting the corresponding social character, order these traits to the system of prohibitions, sanctions, and inspirations that were automatically or unconsciously assimilated when they were children. I know of a cotton planter who genuinely regretted that the mechanization of his business threw 50 men out of work, but having taken it upon himself to make a profit he felt morally bound to fire them. So with our contractor. I think he would feel guilt as well as shame if he did not do what he knows is required to be a success in his business. Both of these men, I think, have fundamentally sound personalities. They have come to terms with an internalized though primitive conscience, but they are not altogether dominated by it. They could adjust to another way of doing things without great difficulty.

They have their life-styles

Men with less responsibility, such as those in middle management positions in organizations are aware of the sacrifices they have to make; they are familiar with conflicts of conscience, but they have made rational decisions to accept the rewards and restraints of middle-class status. They are like the political liberal who, as they say, is a radical with a wife and two children.

Other people find in their work roles, particularly in business, opportunities to gratify primitive personality impulses, for example, a lust for power based on a more or less unconscious fear of weakness or the criminal impulse to get one's own no matter what the cost.

The graduate students who took part in our autobiography contest were, for the most part, aware of the psychological costs of the course they had taken but they were strong enough to push on toward the promised future rewards. In addition, they had their "life styles" which offered ample opportunities to find gratifications outside the academic structure. For that matter, the young bureaucrats at City Hall had their life styles too. I observed what I took to be indications that they intended to preserve some independence and individuality, as in the wide variations in dress and grooming and in the relaxed slowness with which they went about their work. One young man was even tempted to give me a break in connection with a permit but finally decided he had better stick to the rules.

Authoritarianism, for example

Our organizations are not, on the whole, as bad as they might be. They induce conformity by rewards and threats of loss of income or status rather than by inducing hate which would be directed to outgroups. But they are bad enough, and it is appropriate to ask what has been their impact on the American national character.

When I say "character" here, I mean personality. Although each personality is unique it is possible to note many similarities among them, and certain patterns are common (or modal) in a given national, regional, or ethnic group, or social class. I would like to approach the question of change in the American character (or modal personality) by considering what we know, or suspect, about authoritarianism.

As I quickly sketched it in chapter 19, authoritarianism in personality is a deeply-base structure, derived from inner conflicts and personal strivings. It is expressed in such traits as uncritical acceptance of authority, the belief that one's chosen leader can do no wrong, rigid adherence to conventional values and readiness to punish any violation of them, preoccupation with the dominance- submission aspect of human relationships, exaggerated display of strength and toughness, insistence upon the virtues of one's own group and the rightness of one's own course and a disposition to ascribe all manner of evil motives to other people. In the middle 1940's scores on a scale for measuring authoritarianism—the "F scale"—were found to be closely associated with anti-Semitism and generalized ethnocentrism.

I have not been able to find any recent studies of the F scale in relation to presidential choice but there is a very interesting study of psychological differences between supporters of Nixon and supporters of McGovern in the election of 1972.

Shortly before that election Comstock and Duckles administered the Fromm-Maccoby "love of life" scale to 589 Oakland residents, chosen at random, and found extremely significant differences between pro-Nixon and pro-McGovern respondents. I think this scale taps something deep in the personality that has much in common with authoritarianism. At the low end of the scale, "is the person who craves order, certainty, obedience, the past, and the mechanical rather than the organic, who avoids deep feelings, who is fascinated by sickness, dirt, troubles, and finally by death" (Comstock and Duckles, 1972).

When scores on this scale were divided into high and low, 85 p.c. of the Nixon supporters and "only" 51 p.c. of the McGovern supporters had low scores. A set of 13 items pertaining to authority and leadership showed the same kind of sharp differentiation.

Any significant trends?

No doubt there is plenty of authoritarianism around today, but is there more or less than in the middle 1940's when my colleagues and I collected data for our book *The Authoritarian Personality*? More or less than at various times since?

I have a strong impression that the number of "hard core" Nixon supporters was not larger, in proportion to total population, than the number who revered General MacArthur and wanted him to be president. We were very much interested in the support for MacArthur in 1951–52, paid close attention to relevant public opinion polls, and concluded that about a third of our people were significantly authoritarian. I find little reason to believe that the proportion is higher today. It should be possible to get sound evidence on this, since the F scale has been used with various samples of people every year since 1945; but there are great difficulties in the way. Different versions of the scale have been used from time to time, and rarely has the same version been used consistently over the years with adequate samples of people having the same social characteristics.

However, we do know that when Vassar College students took the F scale each year from 1952 to 1959, mean score per item showed no significant trends during these years, nor did the Vassar students as a group differ significantly from the Berkeley studnets of 1945–48. Stanford and Berkeley students in the years 1962–67 produced F scale responses not very different, in respect to mean score per item, from those produced by Berkeley and Vassar students in the 1940's and 1950's respectively.

Based on these and other findings, those of us who thought during the 1960's that students were being widely liberated probably have to take a more sober view. But this is not to say that students who *were* liberated, mainly at the great universities and first-rate liberal arts colleges, did not have some influence on our culture generally.

A psycho-historical concept

I have suggested elsewhere that authoritarianism in personality ought to be regarded as a psycho-historical concept, that we ought not to assume that the authoritarianism we studied in the 1940's was the same as the authoritarianism of today. I may have over-stressed the point, in my insistence that researchers stop relying on the F scale and do some real work: study personality and ideology as we did in the 1940's by means of intensive interviews and various projective techniques. They might come up with some important differences between then and now, if not in the basic structure of the syndrome, then in its content, in the way various attitudes relate to (or are excluded from) the authoritarian pattern. As a matter of fact, Fromm and Maccoby have done the sort of thing I had in mind. Out of their intensive studies of individuals they not only arrived at a somewhat different, and perhaps better, formulation of destructiveness than we did, but they developed a new scale. According to Brewster Smith, their "biophilia-necrophilia" scale is from a psychometric point of view pretty bad. About the only thing it has going for it is the fact that it seems to work.

Actually, there are good reasons why we should not expect major changes in authoritarianism to have taken place during the past 25 years. The basic structure is laid down in childhood, in the setting of the family life, and although it may be altered, for better or worse, in school, college, and the work setting, change (especially change for the better) comes hard. Family life, it seems to me, has not changed all that much during the years in question or if it did, not soon enough to affect in any important way the upbringing of people now old enough to take the F scale. But family life is now changing, at least in the middle and lower-middle classes, in consequence mainly of the liberation of women and other factors making for smaller and more democratic families. A few years hence it will not be at all surprising to find lower levels of authoritarianism in our society.

Down on authority

If authoritarianism has so far changed but little, attitudes toward authority have changed a lot, mainly in the direction of increased dislike of authority. Many of the people I saw every day in the academic world in the 1960's made a point of displaying their "anti-authoritarian" valor. (They say "anti-authoritarian," I say "anti-authority," for having found myself in a position of leadership I complain about their failure to see the distinction between authoritarian and other kinds of leadership.) In California we saw many young professors socialized in the Ivy League who, arriving at their new jobs during the students protests, promptly identified themselves with the students, revealing that their academic "social character" had not gone very deep. I, like many other observers, ascribed the change in attitudes toward authority mainly to the fact that we had been betrayed too many times by people in positions of authority, and to the fact that the leaders we need had long since disappeared into a tangle of occupational roles and social group memberships.

The new attitudes toward authority are not very helpful; they favor neither individual development nor the building of better institutions. They make it more difficult for people in positions of leadership to exercise the authority necessary to maintain an organization and to insure the freedom of the people in it; and they of course do less than nothing to serve the underlying need for structure and for leadership, which the true anti-authoritarian refuses to admit he or she has. During the past ten years we have seen the starting up, and the early falling down, of many new, typically small-scale, educational institutions. Many were started by groups of people who had little in common save their opposition to the establishment. In the absence of a shared vision, and of knowledge of how one might be adopted, nobody would lead and nobody would follow, so nothing happened. Almost always the new schools were to be totally democratic; decisions were to be made in "town meetings" and by consensus. In practice, what looked like decisions were made by the people who could demonstrate that they cared the most, with the result that power was monopolized by a small clique; other members of the group, effectively silenced, soon departed and the end of the experiment was at hand.

Could go either way

Most people, as has often been pointed out, are middle on authoritarianism, and they move toward either extreme, depending on social circumstance. When Eugene McCarthy was campaigning for the Democratic nomination for President in 1968, someone protested that a majority of the American people was in favor of the Viet Nam war. "Yes," said McCarthy, "but if the President of the United States said he was against the Viet Nam war a majority of the American people would be against the war."

Suppose we have a deep economic depression, or suppose we have to begin paying, in ways that involve real hardship, for our exploitation of the world's resources; and then a President of the United States says we must use totalitarian methods to keep order. Which way would those middle on authoritarianism go? Instead of congratulating ourselves on our surviving the Nixon administration, which was really not much of an achievement given Nixon's essential weakness and the incompetence of those around him, we have to consider the real possibility of a major swing toward fascism. The matter is serious enough so that we ought to be planning counter-measures right now.

In the same light, most people are neither charmed nor completely turned off by their organizational lives. Those middle on authoritarianism could tolerate a major rise in organizational rigidity, just as they might adapt readily to a change in the direction of organic management.

I am enough of a social theorist to believe that it is just about as easy to change an organization, in a way that benefits everybody in it, as it is to change in any fundamental way the personality of one of its denizens. For example, if all the assistant professors in a major university were given job security (though not necessarily promises of increases in pay), the functioning of the whole institution would be improved; the level of communication would go up, the level of paranoia down;

teaching would improve, to the satisfaction of professors as well as students, and so would research, in quality if not quantity.

As I see it, the purpose of social science is to build a better society. In keeping with this, the purpose of the Wright Institute is to learn enough about how social settings of various kinds affect the people in them so that we can help bring about social changes that favor human development. This means starting with a conception of man as self-reflecting and, to some degree, self-determining; it means developing theory to explain how experiences in social settings work to favor or hamper his development, and how social settings may be changed or created so that they will be maximally developmental in their effects.

Small alternative structures

This is the context for my concluding remarks about the loss and rediscovery of morality. I have assumed that organizations, like nations, are amoral, and as they become more controlling of our lives they force individuals to be less moral in their behavior than they would otherwise be. Organizations tend to favor authoritarianism in personality.

In discussing the development of moral character let us go back to the young men I mentioned in the beginning—those who could be trusted to do what they said they would. They were in situations that favored moral behavior. They had freedom of the sort enjoyed by students and people over 60. Some did, in fact, have young children. They had circles of friends; were in intimate relationships with people who expected something worthy of them; were spared the anonymity so common among poeple in the "real world." They quickly developed personal relationships with me. All this, I think, is an argument for the development of small social structures outside the major systems.

But these young men had chosen or created their situations. They were able to do this because they had had more or less favorable childhoods, and because they had had good educations, especially at the college level. Education of the right sort works to reduce authoritarianism in personality. It does so mainly through giving individuals the competencies necessary to deal with external authority, and self-insight that enables them to avoid projecting their own forbidden impulses onto other people. Yet the arguments for developmental education have not, so far, swept the country.

Appendix: Freud and American Psychology

Given the centrality of psychoanalysis to this book, readers may find it useful to have the author's account of how that legacy was received by members of his discipline. The following paper was delivered as an address at the University of Minnesota during the celebration of Freud's Centennial, and was originally published in 1958 in a British journal:

American psychology is something like Okinawa, as seen by the native interpreter in *The Teahouse of the August Moon.* We have not had to go out and seek culture; culture has been brought to us by various benevolent invaders from across the seas: Darwin, Pavlov, McDougall; Freud, Jung, Adler; Lewin, Koffka, Kohler; Rank, Horney, Fromm, and many others. In general we have behaved like the Okinawans: we have assimilated the foreign ideas to our own ethic; have chosen among them, modified them, neutralized them, incorporated them in larger wholes; in general have managed them in such a way that we have not had to be deflected from our own course.

Of course we have accepted many of the ideas, and, as we shall see, our psychology has been profoundly enriched; but we are coming up with our own particular version of Freudian psychology. It is less biological, and more social (or other-directed) than the original; in the determination of personality and character it accents later rather than early events in the individual life, higher rather than lower mental processes; and it is more objective, externalized, and differentiated, less systematic and intellectual. In place of classical psychoanalytical treatment, we want something that is quicker, more efficient, less painful; if possible, something more elevating. And it seems that we are well on the road to getting it. In Europe, being psychoanalyzed is valued primarily as a rare and interesting experience; we, in this country want to be healthy, mature, and adjusted; and the quicker the better.

Consider a specific case of this contrast. In Great Britain, Melanie Klein's school of psychoanalytic thought is dominant. She has placed a new accent on instinct, a new stress on the earliest years of life; has refocused attention on the inner life, especially on unconscious fantasy; has proposed a new conception of universal stages of development; has exhibited a marvelous tendency to unchecked speculation; and with respect to therapy, adhered rigidly to the classical role of the analyst. Time is of no consequence: five years is the average length of an analysis. All these things are plainly un-American and, hence, Kleinian psychoanalysis is hardly represented in this country.

But if, by some presently unthinkable catastrophe, psychoanalysis should be banned in Britain, and all the Kleinians should come to this country, we would welcome them, find their ideas interesting if not necessarily true, and speak of finding ways to test some of their hypotheses. The Kleinians would settle down comfortably, if less creatively, with full practices, and let themselves become gradually and pleasantly Americanized.

Gathered in the marketplace

Whereas almost everybody in psychology (certainly everybody in personality and social psychology) has had to come to terms with Freud, different individuals and sub-groups have been differentially affected by different aspects of his work, and at different times.

It seems that the great mass of our people, when the Freudian invasion reached their village, gathered in the marketplace. Having no great stake in the existing psychological regime, they displayed an amiable curiosity, and a spirit of "this too will pass away."

Others stuck closely to their weaving, knowing in their bones that whatever happened there would always be a place for fundamental things like physiological psychology, the design of psychological experiments, and the operation of their 701 adding machines.

Some, like Fred Skinner, came out in bold opposition. But the invading forces shrewdly observed that Skinner, while he was against them, was against almost everybody else as well, and so could be used as a sort of ally.

Some took to the hills. Gordon Allport, for example, dragging some enormous cannon behind him, entrenched himself in the hills of Harvard, where from time to time he fired off great salvos, knocking over nine native behaviorists for every Freudian who was endangered.

Some, of course, perhaps the most discontented, immediately made common cause with the invader; some over-identified with him, becoming more Freudian than the master.

Ernest Jones, writing about the dissemination of psychoanalysis in American, gives a picture of a gradual spreading of the new ideas, a gradual increase in the influence of psychoanalysis (Jones, 1955). This is true, I think, in the case of psychiatry and for American culture generally. But in the case of psychology the picture seems to be rather different.

There was a small flurry of excitement back around 1909, the time of Freud's lecture at Clark University, when men like Stanley Hall and William James expressed interest in psychoanalysis and when Morton Prince accepted articles on it for the *Journal of Abnormal Psychology*. According to Henry Murray, Prince wrote in 1928 that "Freudian psychology has flooded the field like a full rising tide," but Prince was talking about his own field, abnormal psychology and the investigation of "the unconscious." Like Hall and James, Prince was not in the mainstream of American psychology; and as far as that developing discipline was concerned, nothing much happened, respecting psychoanalysis, for a long time.

Most psychologists of my generation, if they were given any introduction to psychoanalysis at all, were taught that three schools of thought existed, those represented by Freud, Jung and Adler, and a student was free to choose among them if he was interested in that sort of thing.

Intellectual immigrants

In the middle 1930's a change occurred. European psychoanalysts, and dynamic psychologists of note, had begun arriving in considerable numbers in this country. Psychologists began being psychoanalyzed. These influences from abroad combined with our slowly developing dynamic psychology to produce enormous advances in the psychology of personality. The field was more or less mapped out and introduced into the major curriculum, thanks in considerable part to distinguished texts by Stagner and Allport. Students were introduced to projective testing, the objective study of psychoanalytic concepts, personality assessment, research on personality and culture. It was the time of Murray's *Explorations in Personality*, the great pioneer effort at integration of academic psychology and various clinically derived conceptions, including Freudian psychoanalytic ones (Murray, 1938).

Then came the war and the spectacular upsurge of clinical psychology. The professionalization of psychology in the years immediately following the war and during the past 15 years has been a major social phenomenon. Its scope is indicated by the growth in membership of the American Psychological Association from 2,739 in 1940 to over 14,000 today.* The great majority of the new members have been clinical psychologists, trained to perform psychotherapy as well as research and diagnosis. Clinical psychology was founded on the theories and methods that were making their way into psychology during the thirties. Ideas which had a kind of fringe existence then are common-place now and make up what is certainly a major trend in psychological thought and research.

I think it is fair to say that an essentially Freudian theoretical orientation to psychotherapy is now the demominant one among psychologists who practice this specialty, despite the fact that psychologists have rarely had the opportunity to receive psychoanalytic training, and that essentially Freudian theories of personality organization lead all others in the work of psychologists who use projective techniques in their diagnostic studies.

As far as research goes, a rough estimate would be that at least half the papers published in personality and clinical psychology today, make some use of Freudian concepts, including deliberate attempts to test some psychoanalytic proposition.

From the point of view of the sociology of knowledge, we may ask why psychoanalytic ideas, available for many years, finally had an effect on organized psychology. One answer, I think, was the shift in power arrangements brought about by a great increase in public demand for psychological services. Another way in which psychoanalysis entered the life space of psychologists apart from their official training, was via the common culture. Like other educated Americans, academic psychologists out of working hours converse quite happily about anxiety, the oedipus complex, infantile sexuality and the like; and when they are faced with some practical problem,

**By 1979 the total had increased to nearly 50,000.*

such as why a colleague cannot seem to get anything published or why a student gets so upset over his oral examination, they come forward readily with psychoanalytic hypotheses.

Perhaps a suitable further approach to the rather large topic before us would be to take up important aspects of Freud's work-method, theory, and findings, and then consider the different kinds of reactions to these aspects in different fields or areas of psychology, at different times.

The method's the thing

I think Freud's greatest contribution, to psychology and to psychiatry, is the psychoanalytic method of investigation and treatment. It was an invention of stunning originality. It could not have been conceived by anyone who did not have absolute integrity of character and a profoundly humanistic spirit.

By the method I mean not just the technique of free association, crucial though this is; I mean the whole contractual arrangement according to which both therapist and patient become investigators, and both objects of careful observation and study; in which the therapist can ask the patient to face the truth because he, the therapist, is willing to face it in himself; in which investigation and treatment are aspects of the same humanistic enterprise; in which the better parts of two people, in alliance, can overcome the forces of resistance and transference.

Although the method is integral with much of the theory, it had a certain priority. Once the technique of free association could be used, by someone who understood himself, the other great discoveries could follow. And they did. And many enormously important discoveries were made by Freud's early followers. Anyone who adheres to the method can make discoveries. I have made some myself. The fact that I later found they had already been discovered by other people did not altogether eliminate the initial joy. Melanie Klein and her followers, by sticking very closely to the classical psychoanalytic method have made discoveries leading to some profound revisions of Freud's fundamental theory (Klein, 1948). Carl Rogers and the other non-directive therapists, following a method that partakes very fully of the spirit of the original, have made discoveries, not all of which had previously been made by psychoanalysts.

As Erikson has pointed out, the psychoanalytic method is "a tool for the detection of that aspect of the total image of man which at a given time is being neglected or exploited, repressed or suppressed by the prevailing technology and ideology"—including hasty "psychoanalytic ideologies" (Erikson, 1964). Thus the content of neurotic conflict may change (as indeed it does); the psychoanalytic theory of personality may be revised (as it has been) or incorporated in a more general theory; but the method remains as valuable as ever.

These considerations make it all the more regrettable that so few psychologists have been able to avail themselves of the method. I suppose it is useless to speculate about what would have happened if we, instead of psychiatry, had had hundreds of analyzed psychotherapists, as early say as 1940. It is certainly useless to bemoan that unkind trick of history by which the great influx of leading European psychoanalysts came only about 10 years before American psychology was ready for psychoanalysis, so that Freud's creation had to find a home in organized medicine rather than, as he had hoped, in the university. One can only express the hope that psychologists will keep up their efforts to avail themselves of all methods for investigating and treating people. And one may remark that the results of this historical trick have not been altogether negative. Psychologists have gone on to invent other interesting and promising methods of treatment, and other methods for investigating personality, methods such as personality assessment, which yield at least some of the kind of material that psychoanalysts have had at their disposal.

Well conceived in the first place

The question is often put as to why Freud's theoretical scheme has persisted (more or less unmodified) for so long. Sixty years is a long time for a theory in science. I was surprised recently to hear a distinguished psychologist, in a public lecture, explain the whole phenomenon of this persistence solely on sociological and psychological grounds, somewhat as follows:

Alone and open to attack as he was, Freud developed a paranoid-like tendency to relate everything to everything, to adhere rigidly to the principles he had laid down, to insist on conformity in his followers. Psychoanalysis developed in the manner of a religious movement, as dogma became increasingly rigid and systematized in response to attack from outside, and dissenters were ejected forthwith.

There may be something to this; and certainly the sociology of the psychoanalytic movement is a fascinating study. But this approach to the question certainly leaves a great deal out of account. For one thing, it does not explain the persistence of the theory among many psychologists, who have certainly been free of the loyalties which membership in a psychoanalytic society might entail. I think it ought to be conceded that the general theory has lasted because it was well conceived in the first place, and because it has been increasingly validated by objective studies and by clinical utility as the years have gone by.

I say with all possible emphasis that the clinical psychologist who prepares to work with patients and who does not have, in his bones and at his finger tips, the observations and formulations of patient behavior contributed by Freud (and by other early masters such as Abraham and Ferenczi) is simply not educated or ready for what he is about to undertake. He does not, of course, have to agree with these pioneers, he may conceptualize things differently, and use techniques other than psychoanalytic ones, but not to know Freud—that would be like presuming to work as a professional philosopher without having read Aristotle.

Apart from the matter of demonstrated validity—which though considerable is very far from being complete—the theory has persisted because of its open texture. Start working with any one of the Freudian concepts (one of the defense mechanisms, say), design some objective studies to define it or to test some proposition embodying it: you will probably wind up quite uncertain as to whether you have done what you set out to do, but the chances are that you will have discovered something interesting, invented a few concepts of your own in the general area of the original and you will have been enormously stimulated.

No one will deny that the things Freud was talking about are things of perpetual, often consuming interest. In conceptualizing them he seems to have made them just hypothetical enough, and just remote enough from anything directly observable, in order to insure the perpetuation of his theory: we cannot ignore his formulations, nor can we disprove them. The concepts can be *defined* operationally, in the modern, sophisticated sense; and so they cannot be dismissed as vagaries of the imagination; yet it is extraordinarily difficult to devise any crucial *tests* of them. And so we keep plugging away, fascinated and frustrated; and surely at this stage of our development as a science, it would be importunate to ask more of a theory of personality.

Areas of influence

Gardner Murphy, in his valuable survey of the impact of Freud's psychoanalysis upon various fields of psychology, shows that the impact has been greatest upon personality psychology and clinical psychology and least in the cases of intelligence and physiological psychology (Murphy, 1956).

What is particularly striking is the relatively small degree to which social psychology has been influenced by Freud. It is striking not only because personality and clinical psychologists and social psychologists are often regarded as kindred spirits, but because psychoanalytic psychology *is* social psychology, in its major part. The therapeutic relationship, which Freud was at such pains to formulate, is a social situation; and the Oedipus complex, perhaps the most Freudian of all Freud's constructions, is a system involving interactions among people. Here is another reason why I think the general theory of the future will resemble that of Freud. He specified the social inputs and incorporated them in the scheme. Modern personality theory is definitely trying to do the same thing.

But Freud never paid much attention to the real aspects of the contemporary social situation, as determinants of behavior, nor did those personality psychologists who were attracted by his views. There developed a kind of polarity, with personality psychologists claiming as much as possible for inner determinants, and social psychology making claims for the contemporary social

It may be noted here that, if the personality and clinical people had Freud, so the social psychologists also had a great man on their side, Karl Marx. A theory of society that could "explain" the invention of psychoanalysis and the whole psychoanalytic movement as aspects of the class struggle was a very potent weapon indeed. Not that many social psychologists were self-consciously Marxist, but they certainly had the benefits of a great tradition of social and economic theory. Happily psychoanalysis and social science, personality psychology and social psychology are beginning to find common ground, and to make common cause.

Having said a word about Freud's method and his general theory, I want to touch upon his concept of libido. Much of what we refer to as the libido theory is in the nature of first-order generalization from a mass of concrete observations. The primary focus, of course, is infantile sexuality.

With respect to the theme of sexuality, Freud's work has helped to change the general cultural climate in which he carried on his activities. If, as seems to be the case, sex is less often a crucial factor in the etiology of neurosis today than it used to be, this is in no small part because of the work of Freud and his early followers. As Erikson has pointed out, "the psychoanalyst is an odd, maybe even a new kind of historian: in committing himself to influencing what he observes, he becomes part of the historical process which he studies" (Erikson, 1950).

Anthropologists have pretty well demonstrated that the Oedipus Complex is not found in all cultures in precisely the form that Freud described. But this, I think, has not been to demonstrate very much. Anyone who is going to carry on psychoanalysis, or make any attempt at cultural reform, in societies where there is family life, would be well-advised to include the Oedipus complex within his theoretical scheme of things. Freud, of course, took a great gamble when he leaped to the conclusion that what was true of himself and of the Viennese ladies was, in some ways, true of everybody. But he had the right instinct. He was calling to our common humanity. He was saying, in a particularly heroic way, "nothing human is alien to me," or conversely, no matter how alien a pattern of behavior may be, it is still human. I am saying that the Oedipus complex as Freud described it *is* pretty general, if we only acknowledge that behind the "mother" and "father" figures lies a more abstract formulation, in terms of love and hate and the figures of the early environment.

Stands by itself

To say that Freud over-estimated the factor of sex, and that psychoanalysts generally have tended to attribute to libidinal functioning things that were more accurately attributed to something else, is not to take much away from the theory. The libido theory stands by itself. There is nothing in all psychology that is quite comparable to it, for showing the fundamental relatedness of such manifold, superficially diverse phenomena. The theory states that the sexual libido may attach itself to (may cathect) now one object (or mode of behavior or zone of the body) and now another; that in special circumstance it may become fixated at one of these points; and that later in difficult circumstances, it may regress to an earlier phase.

When I say that most of Freud's conceptions will eventually be incorporated in a more generaly theory, I mean his libido theory too. This will be a sad day, in a way, for the libido theory as it stands is magnificent. But psychology will find some model other than Freud's hydrostatic one, based upon the flowing and damming up of libido, and will press beyond certain other limitations of the theory. For example, it will not be generally claimed, as psychoanalysis has seemed to do, that all curiosity rests upon a sexual motive. A general theory will recognize various sources of curiosity and put them in their proper place. But I don't think it will ever be possible to deny that sometimes a behavioral phenomenon like curiosity is traceable, through a network of transformations, to an infantile fixation.

Apart from his own curiosity, his genius, courage, nobility of spirit, and enormous capacity for work, Freud was also very fortunate: he appeared on the scene at just the right moment of history, and in just the right type of society, in order to channel together trends which had been in progress for a long time. The suppression and hypocrisy of the Victorian era were bound to yield to the truth sooner or later; the vast amount of humanistic knowledge then existing, based upon insights achieved by poets and philosophers, was bound to be applied by someone whose professional task it was to relieve human suffering; a number of men in psychiatry and psychology were on the point of saying that if hysteria could be cured by verbal means it must be psychological in its origins. It was this cultural readiness for psychoanalysis that made many people say they had known it all the time, and made others feel they could have discovered it themselves (and that they almost did).

Fell to his lot

More than this, it seems that the creator of psychoanalysis had to have been neurotic himself, had to be a member of an ethnic minority, or at least socially marginal. I would even go so far as to say that he had to have sound training in biological science, in order to attain the security necessary to the scientist who would speculate about inner psychological processes.

As Freud, I think, once put it, it "fell to his lot" to discover psychoanalysis. And once the cultural streams were joined, in him, the same thing could not happen again. No one else could be first. This has been a thorn in the side of a number of brilliant men. Some have been goaded by it to discover other things; but these things were not psychoanalysis. Many psychoanalysts have lived out their lives with a gnawing sense of frustration, partly mastered by wry humor, that they could not seem to discover anything that Freud had not already discovered. "The old man was right," they would say.

The revisions of Freud have all been somehow incidental. After the great original conceptions had been put forward—infantile sexuality, repression and the unconscious, resistance and transference—further work in psychoanalysis had an aspect of tidying up on the fringes. One could say that the unconscious was the source of high as well as of low human dispositions, that there were other fundamentally important motives besides sex, that events of importance for personality formation may occur at other times besides childhood. Freud could afford to relax and ask, "what of it?" He himself could not improve his sysem much after *The Interpretation of Dreams*. The great effort to put Freud's psychoanalysis in its place or to "see it in perspective" by presenting it as one of several approaches to psychoanalysis—an effort that has persisted for at least 35 years in this country—has been something of a failure. And so have been the efforts to use telling arguments against one aspect of Freud's work as a basis for rejecting the whole, or to take one aspect and build it into a competing system. The fact is, Freud got hold of some fundamentals.

I must say a tendency to over-estimate Freud is sometimes encountered nowadays. I have noticed it particularly among young clinical psychologists, trained at places where there was a fairly strong psychoanalytic orientation. Perhaps it is not so much a general over-estimation but rather a tendency, appearing as part of a general positive evaluation, to credit Freud with some things that he did not actually do. A common conception is that psychology consisted of introspectionism and classical behaviorism, and then Freud came along, or his ideas won some acceptance, and then we had a dynamic psychology.

McDougall was my man

I feel somewhat sensitive about this, because I came into psychology along a path which I think was quite independent of Freud; and I counted myself a dynamic psychologist before Freud's work entered into my scheme of things. William McDougall was my man. I can still relive the excitement generated by a reading, as an undergraduate, of his *Social Psychology*

(McDougall, 1908). It seemed to me almost unbelievable that anyone could write in a scientific book things which I thought no one but I had experienced. I knew at once that psychology was my dish. My copy of the *Social Psychology* was published in 1908; and I believe that up to that time McDougall had not been influenced by Freud. Rather, he was in a tradition of British psychology that stemmed mainly from Darwin.

I am happy to note that Ernest Jones regarded McDougall as the most distinguished social psychologist of the 20th century (Jones, 1955). McDougall has always suffered a sad neglect at the hands of American psychologists, primarily because he was a dynamic psychologist, out of step with the introspectionism and behaviorism of his day. This neglect has been of such long standing that even Gardner Murphy, one of the few historians that we have, forgot to mention McDougall in his recent careful survey of the situation in psychology before Freud (Murphy, 1956).

Every graduate student in personality psychology has read Gordon Allport's famous "Reply to Mr. Bertocci," a stirring defense of the doctrine of functional autonomy (Allport, 1940). But who was Mr. Bertocci? Not many can tell you. Mr. Bertocci was a philosopher and a McDougall man; and, if you ask me, he had rather the better of the argument.

My point is that we had a dynamic psychology, largely independent of Freud, stemming from Charcot, Janet, Morton Prince on the one hand, and McDougall on the other. This psychology is what was mainly taught at the Harvard Psychological Clinic in 1930. The real impact of psychoanalysis was not felt there until after 1932, when Franz Alexander arrived in Boston. (It may have been earlier elsewhere.) Until now, Freud was one name among many. I think something could have come of this other dynamic psychology, without benefit of psychoanalysis.

Impulse to oppose or contradict

The impact of Freud on American psychology has not been just a matter of including his ideas; the impulse to oppose or to contradict Freud has led to an enormous amount of productive work, both in experimentation and in theory-making.

Revisions of psychoanalysis, in this country, have been in the direction of making it more American, as in the case of the present accent on ego psychology. Psychologists, while supporting many of these revisions, have not actually initiated many themselves, having had relatively little opportunity to practice analysis. They have rather developed their own theoretical systems with their own terms, "translating" Freud when they wanted to use some of his ideas or findings.

The aspects of Freud's work that have found the widest acceptance among American psychologists have been the mechanisms of defense and the general theory of personality structure: Id, Ego, Superego. Least acceptable, or most controversial, has been the libido theory. If Freud were here he would attribute this to resistance.

In psychoanalytic circles it has long been understood that there were essentially two ways to manage the emotional problems created by being a disciple of Freud: one was to be a good son, to adhere loyally to all teachings of the master; and the other was to identify with Freud's father role and to seek disciples oneself. In America, we have never found it difficult to reject the role of obedient son. Our deeper feelings of love and submission toward the father are likely to be suppressed or unconscious. As an external agency of guidance and control we have preferred the social group, the organization, and the profession, rather than the image of any particular man. But I hope that our concern with establishing our independence, and our disposition to look to the future rather than to the past, will not prevent us from finding inspiration in the kind of psychologist Freud was, and in the kind of man he was.

We may best do this, it seems to me, by paying most attention to Freud's approach to human problems; and to the psychoanalytic method that I have called his greatest contribution.

References

ADELSON, D., and KALIS, B. (eds.), *Community Psychology and Mental Health.* Scranton, Pa.: Chandler, 1970.

ADELSON, J., The political imagination of the young adolescent, *Daedalus,* 1971, *100,* 1013–1050.

ALBEE, G. W., The short, unhappy life of clinical psychology, *Psychology Today,* September 1970, *4*:4, 42–43 plus 74.

ALLPORT, G., *Personality, A Psychological Interpretation.* New York: Holt, 1937.

ALLPORT, G., Motivation and personality: a reply to Mr. Bertocci, *Psychological Review,* 1940, *47,* 553–554.

BALDWIN, R., Adult and career development: what are the implications for faculty. In *Current Issues in Higher Education.* Washington, D.C.: American Association for Higher Education, 1979.

BEALS, R. L., Who will rule research? *Psychology Today,* September 1970, *4*:4, 44–47 plus 75.

BERGQUIST, W., and PHILLIPS, S. R., *A Handbook for Faculty Development.* Washington, D.C.: Council for the Advancement of Small Colleges, 1975.

BERTALANFFY, L. VON, Theoretical models in biology and psychology, *Journal of Abnormal and Social Psychology,* 1943, *38,* 417–25.

BESS, J. L., Patterns of satisfaction of organizational prerequisites and personal needs in university departments of high and low quality. Unpublished doctoral dissertation, University of California, Berkeley, 1970.

BLOOM, M., and RALPH, N., unpublished staff papers, The Wright Institute, 1971.

BLUM, R., AND FUNKHAUSER, M., Legislators' views on alcoholism: some dimensions relevant to making new laws, *Quarterly Journal of Studies on Alcohol,* 1965, *26,* 666–669.

BOULDING, K., A general theory of growth. In Bertalanffy, L. von (ed.), *General Systems Theory.* Los Angeles: Society for General Systems Theory, 1956.

BROWN, J. W., AND SHUKRAFT, R. C., *Personal development and professional practice in college and university professors,* Ph.D. dissertation presented jointly to the faculty of the Graduate Theological Union, Berkeley, Calif., 1971. (On microfilm)

BÜHLER, C., The curve of life as studied in biographies, *Journal of Applied Psychology,* 1935, *19,* 405–409.

BÜHLER, C., Maturation and motivation, *Personality: Symposia on Topical Issues,* 1951, *1,* 184–211.

BUSHNELL, J., Student culture at Vassar. In N. Sanford (ed.), *The American College.* New York: Wiley, 1962.

CAMPBELL, D., Reforms as experiments, *American Psychologist*, 1969, *24*, 409–429.

CATTELL, R. B., *Personality*. New York: McGraw-Hill, 1950.

CLARK, K. E., AND MILLER, G. A. (eds.), *Psychology*. Englewood Cliffs, N.J.: Prentice-Hall, 1970.

COMSTOCK, C., In praise of academic abandon, *Harvard Crimson*, commencement issue, June 1961, and registration issue, September 1961.

COMSTOCK, C., AND DUCKLES, R., The assessment of destructiveness in personality (unpublished staff paper), The Wright Institute, 1972.

COMSTOCK, C. (on behalf of the Group for Human Development in Higher Education), *Faculty Development in a Time of Retrenchment*. New Rochelle, N.Y.: Change Magazine Press, 1974.

DEUTSCH, M. Organizational and conceptual barriers to social change, *Journal of Social Issues*, 1969, *25*(4), 5–18.

DEWEY, J., *Experience and Education*. New York: Collier, 1963 (originally published in 1938).

DODDS, J., How human are the humanities, *Stanford Today*, Summer-Autumn 1968.

ERIKSON, E., *Childhood and Society*. New York: Norton, 1950.

ERIKSON, E., The first psychoanalyst. In his *Insight and Responsibility*. New York: Norton, 1964.

FREEDMAN, M., AND OTHERS, *Academic Culture and Faculty Development*. Orinda, Ca.: Montaigne, 1980.

FREEDMAN, M., AND SANFORD, N., The faculty member yesterday and today. In M. Freedman (ed.), *Facilitating Faculty Development*. San Francisco: Jossey-Bass, 1973.

FREEDMAN, M. (ed.), *Facilitating Faculty Development* (*New Directions in Higher Education*). San Francisco: Jossey-Bass, 1973.

FREEDMAN, M., Studies of college alumni. In N. Sanford (ed.), *The American College*. New York: Wiley, 1962.

FROMM, E., AND MACCOBY, M., *Social Character in a Mexican Village*. Englewood Cliffs, N.J.: Prentice-Hall, 1970.

GAGE, N. (ed.), *Handbook of Research on Teaching*. Chicago: Rand-McNally, 1963.

GARDNER, J., *The Flight from Teaching*. New York: Carnegie Foundation for the Advancement of Teaching, 1964.

GOLDSTEIN, K., *The organism*. New York: American Book, 1939.

GRANT, J., AND GRANT, J. D. (eds.), Client participation and community change. In D. Adelson & B. Kalis (eds.), *Community Psychology and Mental Health*. Scranton, Pa.: Chandler, 1970.

HANN, N., A tripartite model of ego functioning values and clinical and research applications, *Journal of Nervous and Mental Disease*, 1969, *148*, 14–30.

HAAN, N., SMITH, M. B., AND BLOCK, J., The moral reasoning of young adults: political social behavior, family background, and personality correlates, *Journal of Personality and Social Psychology*, 1968, *10*, 183–201.

HOFF, W., New health careers demonstration project. Berkeley, Ca.: Institute for Health Research, 1970 (mimeographed).

JACQUES, E., *The Changing Culture of a Factory*. London: Tavistock, 1951.

Jones, E., *The Life and Work of Sigmund Freud.* New York: Basic Books, 1955.

Jung, C. G., *Modern Man in Search of a Soul.* New York: Harcourt, Brace and World, 1933.

Katz, D., and Stotland, E., A preliminary statement to a theory of attitude structure and change. In S. Koch (ed),*Psychology: a Study of a Science*, Vol. 3. New York: McGraw-Hill, 1959.

Katz, J., The student activists: rights, needs, and powers of undergraduates. In E. Hopkins (ed.), *New Dimensions in Higher Education.* Washington, D.C.: U.S. Office of Education, 1967.

Katz, J., and others, *No Time for Youth.* San Francisco: Jossey-Bass, 1968.

Katz, J., and Hartnett, R. (eds.), *Scholars in the Making: The Development of Graduate and Professional Students.* Cambridge, Mass.: Ballinger Publishing, 1976.

Klein, G. S., and Krech, D., The problem of personality and its theory, *Journal of Personality*, 1951, *20*, 2–23.

Klein, M., *Contributions to Psychoanalysis, 1921–1948.* London: Hogarth, 1948.

Kluckhohn, C., and Murray, H., *Personality in Nature, Society and Culture.* New York: Knopf, 1948.

Kohlberg, L., Development of moral character and moral ideology. In M. Hoffman and L. W. Hoffman (eds.), *Review of Child Development Research*, Vol. 1. New York: Russell Sage Foundation, 1964.

Kohlberg, L., Stage and sequence: the cognitive-developmental approach to socialization. In D. Goslin (ed.), *Handbook of socialization theory and research.* New York: Rand McNally, 1969.

Kohlberg, L., and Mayer, R., Development as the aim of education, *Harvard Educational Review*, 1972, *42*, 449–496.

Kubie, L., The forgotten man of education, *Harvard Alumni Bulletin*, February 6, 1954.

Kubie, L., The fundamental nature of the distinction between normality and neurosis, *Psychoanalytic Quarterly*, 1954, 23, 167–204.

Lenrow, P., Strengthening early education: collaboration in problem solving. Berkeley, Ca.: Berkeley Unified School District, 1970 (mimeographed).

Levinson, D., and others, *The Seasons of a Man's Life.* New York: Knopf, 1978.

Lewin, K., *Dynamic Theory of Personality.* New York: McGraw-Hill, 1935.

Lewin, K., Group decision and social change. In T. M. Newcomb & E. L. Hartley (eds.), *Readings in Social Psychology.* New York: Holt, Rinehart, and Winston, 1947.

Lidz, T., *The Person: His Development throughout the Life Cycle.* New York: Basic Books, 1968.

Lipton, H., and Klein, D. C., Training psychologists for practice and research in problems of change in the community. In D. Adelson & B. Kalis (eds.), *Community Psychology and Mental Health.* Scranton, Pa.: Chandler, 1970.

Loevinger, J., and Wessler, R., *Measuring Ego Development; Vol. 1,*

Construction and Use of a Sentence Completion Test. San Francisco: Jossey-Bass, 1970.

MARROW, A. J., *The Practical Theorist: The Life and Work of Kurt Lewin.* New York: Basic Books, 1969.

McDOUGALL, W., *Introduction to Social Psychology.* London: Methuen, 1908.

MESSICK, S., Evaluation of educational programs as research on the educational process. In F. F. Korten, S. W. Cook, & J. I. Lacey (eds.), *Psychology and Problems of Society.* Washington, D.C.: American Psychological Association, 1970.

MILLER, G., Psychology as a means of promoting human welfare, *American Psychologist,* 1969, *24,* 1063–1075.

MURPHY, G., Current impact of Freud on psychology, *American Psychologist,* 1956, *11,* 663–672.

MURRAY, H., AND OTHERS, *Explorations in Personality.* New York: Oxford University Press, 1938.

NEUGARTEN, B. L., *Middle Age and Aging: A Reader in Social Psychology.* Chicago: University of Chicago Press, 1968.

NEWCOMB, T. M., AND HARTLEY, E. (eds.), *Readings in Social Psychology.* New York: Holt, Rinehart, and Winston, 1947.

NEWCOMB, T. M., Attitude development as a function of reference groups: the Bennington study. In E. Maccoby, T. M. Newcomb, & E. J. Hartley (eds.), *Readings in Social Psychology.* New York: Holt, Rinehart & Winston, 1958.

OFFICE OF STRATEGIC SERVICES ASSESSMENT STAFF, *Assessment of Man.* New York: Holt, Rinehart, and Winston, 1948.

PECK, R. C., Psychological developments in the second half of life. In Neugarten, B. L. (ed.), *Middle Age and Aging: A Reading in Social Psychology.* Chicago: University of Chicago Press, 1968.

PERRY, W., *Forms of Intellectual and Ethical Development in the College Years.* New York: Holt, Rinehart, and Winston, 1970.

RALPH, N., Report on the Urban Campus of the Athenian School. Berkeley, Ca.: The Wright Institute, 1971 (mimeographed).

RAUSCHENBUSH, E., *The Student and His Studies.* Middletown, Conn.: Wesleyan University Press, 1964.

ROKEACH, M., *The Open and Closed Mind.* New York: Basic Books, 1960.

SANFORD, N. (with D. Brown, M. Freedman, and H. Webster), Personality development during the college years, *Journal of Social Issues,* 1956, *12*:4, 1–71.

SANFORD, N., What is a normal personality? In J. Katz, P. Nochlin, and R. Stover, (eds.), *Writers on Ethics: Classical and Contemporary.* Princeton, N.J.: Van Nostrand, 1962.

SANFORD, N. (ed.), *The American College.* New York: John Wiley & Sons, 1962.

SANFORD, N., A new approach to liberal education, *Saturday Review,* January 18, 1964, 62–64.

SANFORD, N., The human problems institute and general education, *Daedalus,* 1965, *94*:3, 642–662.

SANFORD, N., Social science and social reform, *Journal of Social Issues,* 1965, *21*:(2), 54–70.

SANFORD, N., *Self and Society.* New York: Atherton, 1966.

SANFORD, N., *Where Colleges Fail.* San Francisco: Jossey-Bass, 1967.

SANFORD, N., I know how it is done but I just can't do it: discussion of Rollo May's paper. In R. B. MacLeod (ed.), *William James: Unfinished Business.* Washington, D.C.: American Psychological Association, 1968.

SANFORD, N., Research with students as action and education, *American Psychologist*, 1969, *24*, 544–546.

SANFORD, N., COMSTOCK, C., AND OTHERS, *Sanctions for Evil.* San Francisco: Jossey-Bass, 1970; and Boston: Beacon Press paperback, 1971.

SANFORD, N., Community actions and the prevention of alcoholism. In D. Adelson and B. Kalis (eds.), *Community Psychology and Mental Health.* San Francisco: Chandler, 1970.

SANFORD, N., The decline of individualism, *Public Health Reports*, 1970, *85*, 213–219.

SANFORD, N., The Wright Institute's program for training in social-clinical psychology (contribution to a symposium, "Mental health training: revolution in professional training," chaired by N. Matulef, annual convention, American Psychological Association, Miami, September, 1970).

SANFORD, N., Academic culture and the teacher's development, *Soundings*, Winter, 1971, *54*, 357–371.

SCRIVEN, M., The methodology of evaluation. In *Perspectives on Curriculum Evaluation* (American Educational Research Association monograph series on curriculum evaluation). Chicago: Rand McNally, 1967.

SHEEHY, G., *Passages: Predictable Crises of Adult Life.* New York: Dutton, 1976.

SHERIF, M. If the social scientist is to be more than a mere technician, *Journal of Social Issues*, 1968, *24*: 1, 41–62.

SINNETT, E. R., AND SACHSON, A. A rehabilitation living unit in a university dormitory setting: final report. Manhattan, Kansas: Kansas State University Counseling Center, 1970 (mimeographed).

SNOEK, J. D. Editor's introduction to selected papers, *Journal of Social Issues*, 1969, *25*: 4, 1–3.

SOSKIN, W., AND KORCHIN, S. Therapeutic explorations with adolescent drug users (unpublished manuscript), Psychology Clinic, University of California, Berkeley, 1967.

SPECIAL COMMISSION ON THE SOCIAL SCIENCES, *Knowledge into Action: Improving the Nation's Use of the Social Sciences.* Washington, D.C.: National Science Foundation, 1969.

SUPER, D. E., AND HALL, D. T., Career development: exploration and planning. In M. R. Rosenzweig and L. W. Porter (eds.), *Annual Review of Psychology*, 1978, *29*, 333–372.

THOMAS, W. I. Social behavior and personality. In Edmund H. Volkart (ed.), *Contributions of W. I. Thomas to Theory and Social Research.* New York: Social Science Research Council, 1951.

VAILLANT, G., *Adaptation to Life.* Boston: Little, Brown, 1977.

WERNER, H., *Comparative Psychology of Mental Development* (revised edition). Chicago: Follett, 1948.

WHITE, R. W., *Lives in Progress.* New York: Holt, Rinehart, and Winston, 1952.

Acknowledgements

My indebtedness to Craig Comstock has been growing apace. Since 1966, when he joined the staff of the Institute for the Study of Human Problems at Stanford, he has been my student, teaching assistant, colleague and friend. In all these overlapping roles he has been increasingly helpful to me in various ways. I discovered his editorial skills early on, and almost everything I have written over the past 14 years has benefitted from them. A broadly interdisciplinary scholar after my own heart, and one who is more familiar with my work than anyone I know, he has been the kind of ideal intellectual companion with whom one could test half-formed ideas. He has been a stern but charitable critic, restraining or encouraging me as the occasion required. It was natural that he and I should collaborate in producing the edited volume *Sanctions for Evil.*

Work on *Learning After College* began when we were discussing uncollected papers I had written since 1968. He came up with the idea that we could make a book about learning after college (a title suggested by him), selected and arranged the papers, edited the manuscript, and shepherded the book through the press. He knows that he has my best thanks.

NEVITT SANFORD

Berkeley, December 1979

This book contains material originally prepared for delivery or publication in the following forms:

Chapter 2: contribution to a symposium, "Dynamic psychology and education: contributions from a modern psychoanalytic perspective," chaired by Harry L. Summerfield, American Educational Research Association, San Francisco, April 20, 1976.

Chapter 3: Education for individual development, *American Journal of Orthopsychiatry*, 1968, *38*, 858–868. (Copyright 1968 by the American Orthopsychiatric Association, Inc. Reprinted with permission.)

Chapter 4: contribution to the 40th Anniversary Symposium, Institute of Human Development, University of California, Berkeley, April 26, 1969.

Chapter 5: contribution to a symposium, "Henry Murray at Eighty," chaired by Edwin S. Shneidman, 81st annual convention, American Psychological Association, Montreal, August 27, 1973.

Chapter 6: Graduate education, then and now, chapter 12 in Joseph Katz and Rodney T. Hartnett (eds.), *Scholars in the Making: The Development of Graduate and Professional Students.* Cambridge, Mass.: Ballinger Publishing Co., 1976. (Copyright 1976, Ballinger Publishing Co. Reprinted with permission.) This paper also appeared in *American Psychologist*, November 1976, *31*:11, 756–764.

Chapter 9: contribution to a symposium, "*Explorations in Personality* forty years later," chaired by Rae Carlson, 86th annual convention, American Psychological Association, Toronto, August 31, 1978; *and* Origins of personality assessment at the Harvard Psychological Clinic, in H. Gough and D. MacKinnon (eds.), *History and Present Status of Personality Assessment.* Berkeley, Ca.: Institute of Personality Assessment and Research, University of California, 1977.

Chapter 10: Academic Culture and the Teacher's Development, *Soundings*, Winter 1971, *54*, 357–371.

Chapter 13: address delivered as part of commencement exercises, Department of Psychology, University of California, Berkeley, June 13, 1971; published as Science and social development, *Education*, November-December 1971, *92*, 1–8.

Chapter 14: The Activists' Corner (a column with David Krech), *Journal of Social Issues*, January 1969, *25*:1, 247–255.

Chapter 15: The Activists' Corner (a column with David Krech), *Journal of Social Issues*, July 1968, *24*:3, 165–172.

Chapter 16: Whatever happened to action research?, *Journal of Social Issues*, 1970, *26*, 3–23.

Chapter 18: part of chapter 2, The contribution of higher education to the life of society, in R. Niblett (ed.), *Higher Education: Demand and Response.* London: Tavistock Publications, Ltd., 1969; San Francisco: Jossey-Bass, 1970.

Chapter 19: A failure of authority, address to the Council of Associations of University Student Personnel Services (Canada), proceedings of the annual conference, 1968, 3–14.

Chapter 20: The loss and rediscovery of moral character, in G. J. DiRenzo (ed.), *We the People: American Character and Social Change.* Westport, Conn.: Greenwood Press, 1977. (Reprinted with the permission of the publisher, Greenwood Press, Westport, Connecticut.)

Appendix: Freud and American Psychology, *Sociological Review*, 1958, ns6, 49–60.

In the case of previously published material, the author gratefully acknowledges the permission of the original publishers listed above.

Published Writings of Nevitt Sanford

The following list includes books, monographs, chapters in books, papers in scholarly and professional journals, articles, presentations that appeared in proceedings, and forewords. For convenience the list is divided into three main areas: (1) personality theory and human problems, (2) authoritarian personality and social destructiveness, and (3) higher education and adult development. Within each part, citations appear in reverse chronological order. Books written wholly or edited by Sanford are preceded by an asterisk.

Users of the list may find it helpful to know at the start that Sanford began to publish on higher education and adult development around 1956. In addition to some ninety papers in this area he has so far edited and co-authored *The American College* (1962) and the condensed version called *College and Character* (1964), and also written *Where Colleges Fail* (1967) and *Learning After College* (1980).

Sanford's writing on personality theory and human problems has been appearing steadily since 1935, including *Self and Society*, a selection of papers (1966), and *Issues in Personality Theory* (1970). In the following list, this category draws together work on such topics as projective techniques, psychological assessment, the process of identification, psychotherapy and mental health, alcohol use, action research, and personality as a field of study.

Within the remaining category, Sanford has published on authoritarianism from 1944 through 1958, centering on *The Authoritarian Personality* (1950). From 1970 through 1973 he expanded this line of research to encompass social destructiveness, starting with *Sanctions for Evil* (1970).

On several important projects Sanford has collaborated with other scholars. During the major studies of authoritarianism his colleagues included T. W. Adorno, Else Frenkel-Brunswik, and Daniel J. Levinson; and during the later work on social destructiveness, Craig Comstock. His co-authors in the field of higher education and adult development have included Joseph Axelrod, Mervin Freedman, Joseph Katz, and Harold Webster.

To make it easier to look up papers that have appeared in volumes of selected essays, certain items are marked at the end of the entry with (*S&S*) or (*LAC*) which refer, respectively, to *Self and Society* and to *Learning After College.*

EDITOR

Personality Theory and Human Problems

The loss and rediscovery of moral character. In G. J. DiRenzo (ed.), *We The People: American Character and Social Change*. Westport, Conn.: Greenwood Press, 1977. (*LAC*, chap. 20)

Origins of personaity assessment at the Harvard Psychological Clinic; *and*, The founding of the Institute of Personality Assessment and Research. Both in H. Gough and D. MacKinnon (eds.), *History and Present Status of Personality Assessment*. Berkeley, Ca.: Institute of Personality Assessment and Research, 1977.

A perspective from outside anthropology. In E. A. Hoebel and R. L. Currier (eds.), *American Social and Cultural Anthropology, Past and Future: Proceedings of the Conference at Spring Hill, 1977*. (In press.)

Foreword. In Earl Koile, *Listening as a Way of Becoming*. Waco, Texas: Regency Books, 1977.

Accountability for planned change: the professional as a change agent. In Ruth Heflin (ed.), *Proceedings of the Sixth Annual Meeting of the Association of Administrators of Home Economics*. Manhattan, Kansas: Kansas State University, 1973.

Is the concept of prevention necessary or useful? In S. Golann and C. Eisdorfer (eds.), *Handbook of Community Psychology*. New York: Appleton-Century-Crofts, 1972.

Foreword. In C. Leuba, *A Road to Creativity*. N. Quincy, Mass.: Christopher, 1971.

**Issues in Personality Theory*. San Francisco: Jossey-Bass, 1970.

Community actions and the prevention of alcoholism. In D. Adelson and B. Kalis (eds.), *Community Psychology and Mental Health*. San Francisco: Chandler Publishing Company, 1970.

Whatever happened to action research? *Journal of Social Issues*, 1970, *26*, 3–23. (*LAC*, chap. 16)

The decline of individualism. *Public Health Reports*, 1970, *85*, 213–219.

The activists' corner (a column with David Krech on the training of clinicians to society and problem-oriented generalists). *Journal of Social Issues*, January 1969, *25*:1, 247–255. (*LAC*, chap. 14)

The activists' corner (a column with David Krech on activism as engagement and experience). *Journal of Social Issues*, Summer 1969, *25*:3, 155–164.

The activists' corner (a column with Rae Carlson on the question of training in social psychology). *Journal of Social Issues*, Autumn 1969, *25*:4, 189–197.

Drinking and personality. In J. Katz and others, *No Time for Youth*. San Francisco: Jossey-Bass, 1968.

I know how it is done but I just can't do it: discussion of Rollo May's paper. In R. B. McLeod (ed.), *William James: Unfinished Business*. Washington, D.C.: American Psychological Association, 1968.

Personality and patterns of alcohol consumption. *Journal of Consulting and Clinical Psychology*, 1968, *32*, 13–17.

The activists' corner (a column with David Krech on human problems and the university). *Journal of Social Issues*, July 1968, *24*:3, 165–172. (*LAC*, chap. 15)

Cognition and personality development. In E. M. Bower and W. Hollister (eds.), *Behavioral Science Frontiers in Education*. New York: McGraw-Hill, 1967.

The influence of social-personality theory on research in smoking behavior: overview. In S. V. Zagona (ed.), *Studies and Issues in Smoking Behavior*. Tucson, Arizona: The University of Arizona Press, 1967.

The development of social responsibility. *American Journal of Orthopsychiatry*, 1967, *37*, 22–29.

The public image of business: up or down? The educator's views. In *Proceedings of the 10th Executives' Symposium*, St. Mary's College, California, 1967.

**Self and Society: Social Change and Individual Development*. New York: Atherton Press, 1966.

Psychological and developmental aspects of the adolescent years as they apply to the use of alcohol. In H. B. Bruyn (ed.), *Alcohol and College Youth*. Berkeley: American College Health Association, 1966. (Also available on film through the University of California Extension Media Center.)

Conceptions of alcoholism. In S. Cahn (ed.), *Treatment Methods and Milieus in Social Work with Alcoholics*. Berkeley: Social Welfare Extension, University of California, 1966.

The study of human problems as an approach to greater knowledge about man. In Joshua Fishman (ed.), *Expanding Horizons of Knowledge about Man: A Symposium*. New York: Ferkauf Graduate School of Humanities and Social Sciences, Yeshiva University, 1966.

Psychiatry viewed from the outside: the challenge of the next ten years. *American Journal of Psychiatry*, 1966, *123*, 519–522. (*S&S*, chap. 19)

The prevention of mental illness. In B. B. Wolman (ed.), *Handbook of Clinical Psychology*. New York: McGraw-Hill, 1965. (Also, in briefer form, in *Bulletin of the Menninger Clinic*, January, 1966; and in A. Z. Guiora and M. A. Brandwin (eds.), *Perspectives in Clinical Psychology*. Princeton, N.J.: Van Nostrand, 1968.)

Will psychologists study human problems? *American Psychologist*, 1965, *20*, 192–202. (Also in A. Z. Guiora and M. A. Brandwin (eds.), *Perspectives in Clinical Psychology*. Princeton, N.J.: Van Nostrand, 1968.)

Changing drinking patterns among American youth. *Bulletin of the Society of Medical Friends of Wine*, 1965, *7*.

Social science and social reform. *Journal of Social Issues*, 1965, *21*, 54–70.

The alcohol problem. *Menninger Quarterly*, 1965, *18*.

Preface. In R. Blum and E. Blum, *The Utopiates: An Epidemiological Study of Drug Use*. New York: Atherton Press, 1964.

Individual conflict and organizational interaction. In R. L. Kahn and Elise Boulding (eds.), *Power and Conflict in Organizations*. New York: Basic Books, 1964.

Ego processes in learning. In N. Lambert, et al., *The Protection and Promotion of Mental Health in Schools*, Public Health Service Publication #1226, Mental Health Monograph #5, U.S. Department of Health, Education, and Welfare, 1964.

Personality: its place in psychology. In S. Koch (ed.), *Psychology: A Study of a Science*, Vol. 5. New York: McGraw-Hill, xoy3.

The freeing and acting out of impulse in late adolescence: evidence from two cases. In R. W. White (ed.), *The Study of Lives: Essays on*

Personality in Honor of Henry A. Murray. New York: Atherton Press, 1963. (*S&S*, chaps. 4 and 11)

Research problems relating to measuring personality change in psychotherapy. In H. Strupp and L. Luborsky (eds.), *Second Conference on Research in Psychotherapy*. Washington, D.C.: American Psychological Association, 1962.

What is a normal personality? In J. Katz, P. Nochlin, and R. Stover (eds.), *Writers on Ethics*. New York: Van Nostrand, 1962. (*S&S*, chap. 2)

Creativity and conformity. In D. W. MacKinnon (ed.), *The Creative Person*. Berkeley: Institute of Personality Assessment and Research, 1961. (*S&S*, chap. 13)

Notes on the recognition of excellence. In A. Yarmolinsky (ed.), *The Recognition of Excellence*. Washington, D.C.: Stern Family Fund, 1960.

Discussion of papers: T. S. Szasz, A critical analysis of some aspects of the libido theory, and E. Pumpian-Mindlin, Propositions concerning energetic-economic aspects of libido theory. In L. Bellak (ed.), *Conceptual and Methodological Problems in Psychoanalysis. Annals of the New York Academy of Science*, 1959, *76*, 990–996.

The development of the healthy personality in the society of today. In *Modern Mental Health Concepts and Their Application in Public Health Education*. Berkeley: University of California, School of Public Health, 1959.

Foreword. In M. Deutsch (ed.), *Role of the Social Sciences in Desegregation*. New York: Anti-Defamation League, 1958.

Foreword. In E. Maccoby, T. Newcomb and E. Hartley (eds.), *Readings in Social Psychology*. New York: Holt, 1958.

Report on trip to Russia. New York: Institute of International Education, 1958 (mimeograph).

The new social science and its critics. *The Humanist*, 1957, *2*, 83–93. (*S&S*, chap. 20)

Mental illness and health: the point of view of child development. *Proceedings 1957 Mental Health Forum*. New York: Mental Health Council, 1957. (Also published by Joint Commission on Mental Illness and Health, Cambridge, Mass., 1957.)

Freud and American psychology. *Sociological Review* (British), 1957, *6*, 49–66. (*LAC*, Appendix)

The development of personality. New York: American Telephone and Telegraph, 1957 (mimeograph).

Psychotherapy and the American public. In M. E. Krout (ed.), *Psychology, Psychiatry, and the Public Interest*. Minneapolis: University of Minnesota Press, 1956.

What should one tell? *Newsletter of the Society for the Psychological Study of Social Issues*, May, 1956.

Surface and depth in the individual personality. *Psychological Review*, 1956, *63*, 349–359.

Clinical and actuarial prediction in a setting of action research. *Proceedings of the 1955 Invitational Conference on Testing Problems*. Educational Testing Service, Princeton, N.J., 1956.

The findings of the commission in psychology. *Annals of the New York Academy of Sciences*, 1955, *63*, 341–364.

The dynamics of identification. *Psychological Review*, 1955, *62*, 106–118. (Also in T. Adorno and W. Berks (eds.), *Sociologica*, Frankfort-on-Main, Europaische Verlagsanstalt, 1956; and in the Reprint Series in the Social Sciences, Bobbs-Merrill, College Division.) (*S&S*, chap. 7)

Family impact on personality: the point of view of a psychoanalyst. In J. E. Hulett and R. Stagner (eds.), *Problems in Social Psychology*. University of Illinois Press, 1954. (*S&S*, chap. 9)

Introduction by the chairman, symposium on social variables in personality determination. *Proceedings of the International Congress of Psychology*. Montreal, 1954.

Clinical methods: psychotherapy. *Annual Review of Psychology*. Stanford, Ca.: Annual Reviews, Inc., 1953, *4*, 317–342.

The interview in personality appraisal. *Proceedings of the Invitational Conference on Testing Problems*. Educational Testing Service, Princeton, N.J., 1953. (Also in A. Anastasi (ed.), *Testing Problems in Perspective*. Washington, D.C.: American Council on Education, 1966.)

Masculinity-femininity in the structure of personality. *Proceedings, International Congress of Psychology*, Stockholm, 1951. (*S&S*, chap. 12)

Preface. In B. Aron, *Manual for Scoring the Thematic Apperception Test*. Berkeley, Ca.: Willis Berg, 1950.

The interview. (with others) In OSS Assessment Staff, *The Assessment of Men*. New York: Rinehart, 1948.

Physical and physiological correlates of personality structure. In C. Kluckholn and H. A. Murray (eds.), *Personality in Nature, Society and Culture*. New York: Knopf, 1948.

Relapse into old habits. In G. Murphy (ed.), *Human Nature and Enduring Peace* (Yearbook of the Society for the Psychological Study of Social Issues). New York: Holt, 1948.

Clinical training facilitities. Report of the Committee on Training in Clinical Psychology. (with E. Hilgard, L. Kelly, B. Luckey, L. Shaffer and D. Shakov) *American Psychologist*, 1948, *3*, 315–318.

What are the conditions of self-defensive forgetting? (with J. J. Risser) *Journal of Personality*, 1948, *17*, 244–260.

Psychotherapy and counseling: a symposium: introduction by the Chairman, *Journal of Consulting Psychology*, 1948, *12*, 65–67.

Recommended graduate training programs in clinical psychology. (with E. Hilgard, L. Kelly, B. Luckey, T. Shaffer and D. Shakow) *American Psychologist*, 1947, *2*, 539–558.

Optimism and religion. *American Psychologist*, 1946, *1*, 451 (abstract).

Psychological determinants of optimism regarding consequences of the war. (with H. S. Conrad and K. Franck) *Journal of Psychology*, 1946, *22*, 207–235.

Age as a factor in the recall of interrupted tasks. *Psychological Review*, 1946, *53*, 234–240.

On being a father. A part of the chapter on this subject in Irwin Child (ed.), *Psychology for the Returning Service Men. The Infantry Journal*. Penguin, 1945.

Some specific war attitudes of the college students. (with H. S. Conrad) *Journal of Psychology*, 1944, *17*, 153–185.

Physique, Personality and Scholarship. (with M. Adkins, D. Miller, and E. Cobb) *Monograph of the Society for Research in Child Development*, 1943, *8*, No. 1.

Personality patterns in school children. In R. Barker, J. Kounin & E. Wright (eds.), *Child Behavior and Development*. New York: McGraw-Hill, 1943.

Some personality correlates of morale. (with H. S. Conrad) *Journal of Abnormal and Social Psychology*, 1943, *38*, 3–20.

American conscience and the coming peace. *Journal of Abnormal and Social Psychology*, 1943, *38*, 158–165.

Psychological approaches to the young delinquent. *Journal of Consulting Psychology*, 1943, *7*, 223–229.

A psychoanalytic study of three types of criminals. *Journal of Criminal Psychopathology*, 1943, *5*, 57–59. (*S&S*, chap. 8)

Personality correlates of morale: evidence from individual cases. *Journal of Personality*, 1943.

Scales for the measurement of war optimism: I. military optimism; II. optimism on consequences of the war. (with H. S. Conrad) *Journal of Psychology*, 1943, *16*, 285–316.

Some correlates of the Harding Morale Scale. *Psychological Bulletin*, 1942, *39*, 614 (abstract).

The Thematic Apperception Test: A Manual of Directions for Scoring and Interpretation. (with R. W. White) Cambridge: Harvard Psychological Clinic, 1941.

Some quantitative results from the analysis of children's stories. *Psychological Bulletin*, 1941, *8*, 749 (abstract).

The analysis of qualitative records in longitudinal studies of child development. *Proceedings, Biennial Meeting, Society for Research on Child Development*. Washington, D.C.: Society for Research in Child Development, 1940.

An experiment to test the validity of the Rorschach Test. (with M. Adkins and E. Cobb) *Psychological Bulletin*, 1939, *36*, 662 (abstract).

Observation of experiments and post-experimental interviews. In H. A. Murray, *et al.*, *Explorations in Personality*. New York: Oxford University Press, 1938.

The effects of abstinence from food upon imaginal processes: a further experiment. *Journal of Psychology*, 1937, *3*, 145–159.

The effects of abstinence from food upon imaginal processes: a preliminary experiment. *Journal of Psychology*, 1936, *2*, 129–136.

Some leads for research in adolescent development. *Proceedings, Biennial Meeting, Society for Research on Child Development*. Washington, D.C.: Society for Research in Child Development, 1936.

Psychological work at the Norfolk Prison Colony. *Psychological Exchange*, 1935.

Authoritarian Personality and Social Destructiveness

The authoritarian personality in contemporary perspective. In Jeanne Knutson (ed.), *Handbook of Political Psychology*. San Francisco: Jossey-Bass, Inc., 1973.

Collective destructiveness: sources and remedies. In G. Usdin (ed.), *Perspectives on Violence.* New York: Brunner/Mazel, 1972.

Nevitt Sanford on authoritarianism. *Psychology Today*, Nov., 1972.

The dynamics of prejudice. In P. Watson (ed.), *The Psychology of Racism.* London: Penguin, 1971.

Collective destructiveness and dehumanization. *International Journal of Group Tensions*, 1971, *1*, 26–41.

**Sanctions for Evil: Sources of Social Destructiveness.* (edited with C. Comstock) San Francisco: Jossey-Bass, 1971; and Boston: Beacon Press, 1972.

Toward a critical social science (a "comment" on the My Lai massacre, with E. Opton, Jr.), *Transaction*, March 1970, *7*:5, 4–7.

The approach of the authoritarian personality. In J. S. McCary (ed.), *The Psychology of Personality.* New York: Logos Press, 1956; and Grove Press (paperback), 1958.

A study of authoritarianism and psychopathology. (with M. Freedman and H. Webster) *Journal of Psychology*, 1956, *41*, 315–322.

Some psychodynamic correlates of authoritarianism in women (with M. Freedman and H. Webster) *American Psychologist*, 1955 (abstract).

A new instrument for studying authoritarianism in personality (with M. Freedman and H. Webster). *Journal of Psychology*, 1955, *40*, 73–84.

Recent developments in connection with the investigation of the authoritarian personality. *Sociological Review* (British), 1954, *1*, 11–33.

Individual and social change in a community under pressure: the oath controversy. *Journal of Social Issues*, 1953, *9*, 25–42. (Also in the (British) *Sociological Review* (new series), 1953, *1*, 9–28; and in Read, Alexander and Tomkins (eds.), *Psychopathology.* Cambridge, Mass.: Harvard University Press, 1958.) (*S&S*, chap. 15)

Recent research into the causes of inter-group tension. *Common Ground* (British), October, 1951.

**The Authoritarian Personality.* (with T. W. Adorno, E. Frenkel-Brunswik, and D. Levinson) New York: Harper, 1950. (Also New York: Wiley Interscience paperback, 1964; New York: W. W. Norton paperback, 1969; and Milano: Edizione Di Communita, 1973.)

Ethnocentrism in relation to some religious attitudes and practices (with D. Levinson) *American Psychologist*, 1948, *3*, 350–351 (abstract).

The anti-democratic individual (with E. Frenkel-Brunswik and D. Levinson) In T. Newcomb and E. Harley (eds.), *Readings in Social Psychology* (Yearbook of the Society for the Psychological Study of Social Issues). New York: Holt, 1947.

The measurement of implicit anti-democratic trends. *American Psychologist*, 1947, *2*, 412 (abstract).

Should there be a quota system for minority groups? (with D. Levinson) *Educational Forum*, January, 1946, 217–235.

Dominance versus autocracy and the democratic character. *Childhood Education*, 1946, *23*, 109–115.

Identification with the enemy: a case study of an American quisling.

Journal of Personality, 1946, *15*, 53–58.
Some personality factors in anti-semitism. (with E. Frenkel-Brunswik) *Journal of Psychology*, 1945, *20*, 271–291.
A scale for the measurement of anti-Semitism. (with D. Levinson) *Journal of Psychology*, 1944, 17, 339–370.

Higher Education and Adult Development

**Learning After College*. (edited by Craig Comstock) Orinda, Ca.: Montaigne, Inc., 1980.
College and Character, revised edition. (co-edited with J. Axelrod) Orinda, Ca.: Montaigne, Inc., 1979.
The college student in a turbulent society. In R. L. Simmons (ed.), *Proceedings of Annual Meeting of the Association of College Unions International*, Spring, 1977.
Graduate education, then and now. In J. Katz and R. Hartnett (eds.), *Scholars in the Making: the Development of Graduate and Professional Students*. Cambridge, Mass.: Ballinger Press, 1976. Also in *American Psychologist*, November 1976, *31*:11, 756–764. (*LAC*, chap. 6)
Epilogue: Psychological stress in the campus community. In B. Bloom (ed.), *Psychological Stress in the Campus Community*. (Community Psychology Series, Vol. 3). New York: Behavioral Publications, 1975.
The faculty member yesterday and today. (with M. Freedman) In M. Freedman (ed.), *Facilitating Faculty Development*, Vol. I, No. 1 of *New Directions in Higher Education*. San Francisco: Jossey-Bass, 1973.
The role of athletics in student development (with Karl Borgstrom and Marjorie Lozoff). In J. Katz (ed.), *Services for Students*, Vol. I, No. 2 of *New Directions in Higher Education*. San Francisco: Jossey-Bass, 1973.
And a time to integrate. Delivered on February 10, 1973, as a Charter Day address at, and printed as a booklet by, Texas Tech University Complex, Lubbock, Texas.
The new values and faculty response. In E. McGrath and R. Stine (eds.), *Prospects for Renewal*. San Francisco: Jossey-Bass, 1972.
Humanizing education beyond the high school. In K. C. Edson (ed.), *New Directions in Higher Education: Proceedings of the Northern California Educational Conference*. Iowa City, Iowa: ACT publications, 1971.
Science and social development. *Education*, 1971, *92*, 1–8. (*LAC*, chap. 13)
Academic culture and the teacher's development. *Soundings*, Winter, 1971–72, 357–371. (*LAC*, chap. 10)
Foreword. In A. Cohen and F. Brawner, *Confronting Identity: The Community College Instructor*. Englewood Cliffs, N.J.: Prentice-Hall, 1971.
Loss of talent. In F. F. Harcleroad (ed.), *Issues of the Seventies: Student*

Needs, Society's Concerns and Institutional Responses. San Francisco: Jossey-Bass, 1970.

The campus crisis in authority. *Educational Record*, Spring, 1970, 112–115.

The concept of regional centers for ethnic studies. *Journal of the Association of Governing Boards of Colleges and Universities*, 1970.

Search for Relevance (with J. Axelrod, M. Freedman, W. Hatch and J. Katz). San Francisco: Jossey-Bass, 1969.

The contribution of higher education to the life of society. In R. Niblett (ed.), *Higher Education: Demand and Response*. London: Tavistock, 1969; San Francisco: Jossey-Bass, 1970. (*LAC*, chap. 18)

Research with students as action and education. *American Psychologist*, 1969, *24*, 544–546.

Students in university government. In *The De Young Lectures, 1969*. Normal, Illinois: Illinois State University, 1969.

Making college more educational and less custodial. *Proceedings of the 1st Annual Meeting of the American Association of Presidents of Independent Colleges*, Denver, Colorado, 1969.

Education for Individual Development. (in series called *New Dimensions in Higher Education*) Washington, D.C.: U.S. Office of Education, 1968.

The college student of 1980. In A. C. Eurich (ed.), *Campus 1980: The Shape of the Future of American Higher Education*. New York: Dell, 1968.

Counseling: emerging role in higher education. In E. Garduk (ed.), *New Dimensions of Student Personnel Work*. Washington, D.C.: Howard University Press, 1968.

The aims of college education. In C. W. Havice (ed.), *Campus Values*. New York: Charles Scribner's Sons, 1968.

Personality development and creativity in the Soviet Union. In P. Heist (ed.), *The Creative College Student*. San Francisco: Jossey-Bass, 1968.

What is an excellent liberal arts college? In S. S. Letter (ed.), *New Prospects for the Small Liberal Arts College*. New York: Teachers College Press, 1968.

Education in 1968. In E. Underwood and J. D. Jordon (eds.), *Crisis: Addresses Delivered at the Spring Symposium*. Mars Hill, N.C.: Mars Hill College, 1968.

The university and the life of the student: the next 100 years. In J. Walsh (ed.), *The University in a Developing World Society*. Notre Dame: University of Notre Dame Press, 1968.

Education for individual development. *American Journal of Orthopsychiatry*, 1968, *38*, 858–868. (*LAC*, chap. 3)

A failure of authority. *Journal of the Canadian Council of Associations of University Student Personnel Services* (Proceedings of the 1968 Conference), 1968, 3–15. (*LAC*, chap. 19)

College seniors and social responsibility. *NEA Journal*, 1968, *57*, 52–54.

Preface. In R. Evans, *Resistance to Innovation in Higher Education*. San Francisco: Jossey-Bass, 1968.

Foreword. In W. B. Martin, *Alternative to Irrelevance*. Nashville, Tennessee: Abington Press, 1968.

***Where Colleges Fail: A Study of the Student as a Person.* San Francisco: Jossey-Bass, 1967.

The students we teach today. In E. J. Gleazer, Jr. (ed.), *Selected Papers: 47th Annual Convention of American Association of Junior Colleges.* Washington, D.C.: American Association of Junior Colleges, 1967.

Innovation in higher education: attacking the issues. In W. Hamlin (ed.), *Dimensions of Change in Higher Education.* Yellow Springs, Ohio: Union for Research and Experimentation in Higher Education, Antioch College, 1967 (mimeograph).

New directions in educating for creativity. In P. Heist (ed.), *Education for Creativity.* Berkeley, Ca.: Center for Research and Development in Higher Education, 1967.

On filling a role and being a man. In K. Smith (ed.), *In Search of Leaders.* (in series called *Current Issues in Higher Education*) Washington, D.C.: National Education Association, 1967.

The generation gap. *California Monthly*, 1967, *57*, 28–37.

The college student of today and tomorrow. *Journal of the Association of Deans and Administrators of Student Affairs*, 1967, *5*, 221–228.

The students we teach today. *The Journal of the Canadian Association of Student Personnel Services*, 1967, *1*, 8–16.

Social change and the college student; *and*, The size of the university and its implications. Both in W. A. Geier (ed.), *Today's Student and His University.* Nashville, Tenn.: Board of Education, The Methodist Church, 1966.

The development of social responsibility through the college experience. In E. J. McGrath (ed.), *The Liberal Arts College's Responsibility for the Individual Student.* New York: Institute for Higher Education, Teachers College, Columbia, 1966.

Universal higher education: implications for education and for adjustment of curricula to individual students. In E. J. McGrath (ed.), *Universal Higher Education.* New York: McGraw-Hill, 1966.

Freedom and authority in higher education. (with Joseph Katz) *Comparative Education* (British), March, 1966.

Sex and drinking among college students: prospects for a new ethic. *Old Oregon*, 1966.

The new student power and needed reforms. (with Joseph Katz) *Phi Delta Kappan*, 1966, *47*, 397–401.

The turbulent years. (with Joseph Katz) *Stanford Today*, Winter, 1966, 7–11.

Needed: a clearer definition of sex roles. *Women's Education*, 1966, *5*, 2.

The great univeristy in the great society. *Proceedings of New York State Teachers Association Higher Education Conference.* Albany, New York: New York State Teachers Association, 1966 (mimeograph).

The human problems institute and general education. *Daedalus*, summer 1965, *94*:3, 642–662. (Reprinted in J. Kagan (ed.), *Creativity and Learning*. Boston: Houghton-Miflin, 1967.)

Morals on the campus. *NEA Journal*, 1965, *54*, 20.

Causes of the student revolution. (with Joseph Katz) *Saturday Review*, December 18, 1965.

General education and personality theory. *Teachers' College Record*, 1965, *66*, 721–732.

Students and the university's purpose. *President's Bulletin Board*, (Division of Higher Education, Board of Education, The Methodist Church, Nashville, Tennessee), September, 1965.

**College and Character: A Briefer Version of "The American College."* New York: John Wiley, 1964.

A new approach to liberal education. *Saturday Review*, January 18, 1964, 62–64.

College students and public concern. *Vassar Alumnae Magazine*, Summer, 1964. (Also in *Stanford Review*, Jan.-Feb., 1964, and in *Alma Mater*, Journal of the American Alumni Council, 1964, *31*.

The college our times require. *Proceedings of Asilomar Conference of San Francisco State College*. San Francisco, 1964 (mimeograph).

Measuring the success of a college. In K. Wilson (ed.), *Research Related to College Admissions*. Atlanta, Georgia: Southern Regional Education Board, 1963.

Higher education as a social problem. *American Review*, 1963, *3*, 92.

Discussion–chaos in college admissions. *Changing Times*, August, 1963.

One cheer for excellence. *The Intellectual Climate of the Liberal Arts College*, Proceedings of Claremont Conference of Western College Association, Claremont, Ca.: Western College Association, 1963.

Factors related to the effectiveness of student interaction with the college social system. *Proceedings of Conference on Higher Education and Mental Health*. Gainesville, Florida: Student Health Service, University of Florida, 1963. (*S&S*, chap. 3)

Education and the preservation of freedom. In *Proceedings of 20th Annual Utah Conference on Higher Education*. Cedar City, Utah: College of Southern Utah, 1963.

**The American College: A Psychological and Social Interpretation of the Higher Learning*. (editor and co-author) New York: John Wiley, 1962. (Also Wiley Science Editions paperback, 1967.)

Ends and means in higher education. In K. Smith (ed.), *Current Issues in Higher Education*, 1962. Washington, D.C.: National Education Association, 1962.

Implications of personality studies for curriculum and personnel planning. In R. Sutherland (ed.), *Personality Development on the College Campus*. Austin, Texas: the Hogg Foundation, University of Texas, 1962.

The successful college. *NEA Journal*, November, 1962.

Education for individual development. *Conference of Directors of College and University Counseling Services*. Lincoln, Nebraksa: Counseling Center, University of Nebraska, 1962.

General education and the theory of personality development. *Proceedings of the Symposium on Undergraduate Development*. Brunswick, Maine: Bowdoin College, 1962.

Today's students look at themselves, their society, and their profession. *Professional Imperatives: Report of 17th Annual TEPS Conference*. New York: National Education Association, 1962.

Recent research on the American college student. In N. Brown (ed.),

Orientation to College Learning. Washington, D.C.: American Council on Education, 1961.

Theories of higher education and the experimental college. In S. Harris (ed.), *Higher Education in the United States*. Cambridge: Harvard University Press, 1960. (Also in *Review of Economics and Statistics*, 1960, *42*, 152–156.)

The development of maturity of personality in college. In T. R. McConnell (ed.), *Selection and Educational Differentiation*. Berkeley: Field Service Center and Center for the Study of Higher Education, University of California, 1960.

A psychologist speculates about new perspectives in education for citizenship. In F. Patterson (ed.), *The Adolescent Citizen*. Glencoe, Illinois: The Free Press, 1960.

Childhood experience and the adult personality. In *Berkeley Conference on Personality Development in Childhood*. Berkeley: Institute of Human Development, 1960 (mimeograph).

Discussion of a paper by W. C. Prentice: contribution to APA symposium on recent social change and its impact on higher education. *Educational Record*, 1960, *41*, 335–338.

Knowledge of students through the social studies. In N. Brown (ed.), *Spotlight on the College Student*. Washington, D.C.: American Council on Education, 1959.

Motivation of high achievers. In O. D. David (ed.), *The Education of Women: Signs for the Future*. Washington, D.C.: American Council on Education, 1959.

Social Science and Higher Education: A Comprehensive Bibliography. Boston: Researchers' Technical Bureau, 1958.

The professor looks at the student. In R. Cooper (ed.), *The Two Ends of the Log*. Minneapolis: University of Minnesota Press, 1958.

Changing sex roles, socialization and education. *Human Development Bulletin*, Committee on Human Development, University of Chicago, 1958.

The Mellon Research Program today. *Vassar Alumnae Magazine*, October, 1958.

Impulse-expression as a variable in personality. (with D. Brown, M. Freedman, and H. Webster) *Psychological Monographs*, 1957, *71*, 1–21.

Impact of a woman's college upon its students. In A. Traxler (ed.), *Long-Range Planning for Education*. Washington, D.C.: American Council on Education, 1957.

The uncertain senior. *Journal of National Association of Women's Deans and Counselors*, 1957, *21*, 9–15.

Is college education wasted on women? *Ladies' Home Journal*, May, 1957.

Report on the Vassar research. In *The American College Student*, Proceedings of 1957 Meeting of Policies and Program Committee. Washington, D.C.: American Council on Education, 1957 (mimeograph).

Our students today: individualists or conformers? Albany, New York: New York State Association of Deans and Guidance Personnel, 1957 (mimeograph).

Personality development during the college years. (with D. Brown, M. Freedman, and H. Webster) *Journal of Social Issues*, 1956, *12*, 1–71.

Personality development during the college years. *Personnel-o-Gram*, Proceedings of 1956 Annual Convention of American College Personnel Association, Washington, D.C., 1956. (Also a briefer version in *Personnel and Guidance Journal*, 1956, *35*, 74–80.) (*S&S*, chap. 17)

The students we teach today. *Biennial Record of the National Association for Physical Education of College Women*, 1956 (mimeograph).

Research programs in college health, report of the chairman of Committee 15. *Proceedings of the Fourth National Conference on Health in Colleges*. New York: American College Health Association, 1955.

We study the alumnae. *Vassar Alumnae Magazine*, December, 1954.

Index of Names